D1528384

REBELS WITHOUT BORDERS

Transnational Insurgencies in World Politics

Idean Salehyan

Cornell University Press *Ithaca and London*

First published 2009 by Cornell University Press

Printed in the United States of America

Library of Congress Cataloging-in-Publication Data

Salehyan, Idean.
    Rebels without borders : transnational insurgencies in world politics / Idean Salehyan.
      p. cm.
    Includes bibliographical references and index.
    ISBN 978-0-8014-4744-0 (cloth : alk. paper)
  1. Insurgency. 2. Civil war. 3. Non-state actors (International relations)
4. Transnational sanctuaries (Military science) 5. Ethnic conflict. 6. Transborder ethnic groups. 7. World politics—1989– I. Title.
    JC328.5.S32 2009
    303.6'4—dc22
2008039223

Cloth printing   10 9 8 7 6 5 4 3 2 1

To my family,
everywhere.

Contents

Acknowledgments

This is a book about transnationalism, diaspora politics, and war. It is difficult to say for certain why a person becomes interested in a given topic, but my early childhood experiences have undoubtedly played a role. My family immigrated to the United States from Iran in the 1970s. In our home, news of conflict and violence—first the Islamic Revolution, then the Iran-Iraq War—were not distant abstractions but affected the daily lives of loved ones back "home." Although my family is "typically American" in many ways, bonds of homeland, family, and culture remain strong. The dual processes of migration and war have shaped my life history, and they come together in the pages that follow. Unfortunately, our experience was not unique; indeed, we were among the lucky ones. Despite huge advances in science and technology and countless volumes on the origins of war, humankind has still not learned how to live together in peace. Although this book will not change that sad fact, I remain optimistic that progress is achievable, and I hope to play some small role in advancing that cause.

My education helped me to channel a long-standing passion for issues of peace and social justice, and develop the skills needed to think deeply and critically about world events (even if I am not always right!). Perpetually a student, I continue to learn from the brilliant minds around me. From the beginning of this project through to its end, several people provided invaluable support and guidance. As is fitting for a book on transnational ties, the ideas developed here and the actual writing took place at the University of California, San Diego (UCSD); the International Peace Research Institute, Oslo; the University of North Texas; the University of Essex, UK; and the Swiss Federal Institute of Technology, Zürich. In each of these places, I encountered mentors, friends, and sometimes harsh critics who left their mark on this work. I am grateful to them all.

The seeds of this book were planted several years ago at the University of California, San Diego. I am especially indebted to Kristian Skrede Gleditsch, who opened many doors for me, and Barbara Walter, for the impetus to always question my assumptions. Wayne Cornelius, David Lake, and Gordon Hanson labored through many early drafts, and each offered his unique perspective on politics and research. Nathaniel Beck, Peter Gourevitch, Stephan Haggard, Miles Kahler, and Samuel Popkin deserve mention for their comments and assistance along the way. Sometimes the little things that were said made a huge impact—perhaps more than they know. While at UCSD, I was also blessed to study with many talented graduate students who were wonderfully generous with their advice and friendship. Kyle Beardsley, Robert Brown, Mark Culyba, David Cunningham, Kathleen Gallagher Cunningham, Lindsay Heger, Cullen Hendrix, Ethan Hollander, Susan Hyde, Heather Smith, Laura Wimberly, and Wendy Wong provided valuable input on this project at various stages.

I had the fantastic opportunity to work at the International Peace Research Institute, Oslo in 2005. While in Norway, I was surrounded by stunning natural beauty and incredibly smart people. Scott Gates, Nils Petter Gleditsch, Kristian Berg Harpviken, Håvard Hegre, Ragnhild Nordås, Håvard Strand, and Henrik Urdal, were especially important colleagues and hiking partners during my stay. These and many other Scandinavians continue to form my close network of collaborators. I always look forward to our conversations and hiking trips.

My colleagues at the University of North Texas have been especially important in my professional and intellectual development. I am very fortunate to work with such outstanding scholars and sincere people. John Booth, Andrew Enterline, Michael Greig, David Mason, and James Meernik were instrumental to development of this book. Natalie Elliot and Madhav Joshi were fantastic research assistants whose help was critical during several rounds of revisions. I will always value Chelsea Brown's support and encouragement. Sadly, my colleague and friend at North Texas, Steven Poe, passed away while I was writing this manuscript—he served as a role model for me in many ways and was a person I frequently turned to for advice. I miss Steve.

With the generous support of the British Academy, I had the opportunity to visit and work at the University of Essex in 2007. It was an especially rainy summer during my stay, which forced me to remain indoors and devote many long hours to writing. I am grateful for the warm welcome I received in Essex and for the rain. Han Dorussen, Ismene Gizelis, Kristian

Skrede Gleditsch, Thomas Plümper, Andrea Ruggeri, David Sanders, Vera Troeger, and Hugh Ward made this visit possible and provided useful comments as this book was nearing completion. Many others offered their encouragement, friendship, and memorable excursions to the English coast when the weather permitted.

Lars-Erik Cederman was kind enough to invite me to visit the Swiss Federal Institute of Technology in Zürich as I was making the final round of revisions for Cornell University Press (CUP). The months I spent in Zürich in 2008 were tremendously productive. I owe a special debt of gratitude to the many people at the Center for Comparative and International Studies for their generous hospitality and vibrant intellectual exchanges. Finally, this book would not be possible without the seasoned guidance of Roger Haydon at CUP, the editorial board, and the comments of the reviewers. Their suggestions on substance and style honed my thinking and improved my prose tremendously.

Most important, I will always be grateful to my family for their ceaseless love and support. I dedicate this book to them. My parents, Farzad and Nasrin, as well as my brother, Shauhin, helped me to mature into the person that I am today and gave me the emotional support I needed to complete this book. Knowing that they are behind me gives me great courage. Members of my "diasporic" family—grandparents, aunts, uncles, and cousins spread out over three continents—have always cheered me on. It saddens me that circumstances have determined that we cannot spend more time with one another. Nonetheless, I draw inspiration from each and every one of them. No matter how far away you may be physically, you are always close to me in spirit. I love you all, this book is for you.

IDEAN SALEHYAN

Denton, Texas

REBELS WITHOUT BORDERS

Introduction: The Global Context of Civil War

> This is the generation of the great Leviathan. . . . He hath the use of so much power and strength conferred upon him that by terror thereof he is enabled to conform the wills of them all to peace at home.
>
> THOMAS HOBBES, *Leviathan* (1668)

> The state is a human community that (successfully) claims the monopoly of the legitimate use of force within a given territory.
>
> MAX WEBER, *Politics as a Vocation* (1919)

The Kurdish Workers' Party, or PKK, was formed in the 1970s and has been fighting the Turkish government for several decades in its quest to secure an independent Kurdish state. In addition to attacks within Turkey itself, the PKK has bombed Turkish interests in other countries and has mobilized supporters and resources from the Kurdish diaspora in Europe and elsewhere. Importantly, this rebel organization has benefited from bases and training camps in the remote mountainous regions of northern Iraq and Iran. Sanctuaries in Iraq became particularly important following the first Gulf War in 1991, when U.S. and coalition forces created a no-fly zone in the north and Iraqi Kurdistan won a degree of autonomy from the central government. Turkey has crossed international boundaries on several occasions to attack PKK facilities, leading to diplomatic tensions with its neighbor. For instance, in May of 1997, Turkey launched a limited cross-border offensive against PKK strongholds in northern Iraq, prompting a diplomatic outcry by the Iraqi government.[1]

Despite a number of cross-border counterinsurgency raids into Iraqi territory, Turkey has not, as of yet, been able to defeat the PKK—a truly

---

1. "Turkish Forces Cross Border Into Iraq to Attack Kurdish Guerillas," *New York Times*,. May 14, 1997, A4.

transnational organization. Following the U.S. invasion of Iraq in 2003 and a resurgence of Kurdish nationalism, PKK sanctuaries have become a major source of tension in the region, and Turkey has repeatedly threatened robust military action to root out the insurgents. In March of 2007 Turkish foreign minister Abdullah Gul estimated that up to 3,800 PKK fighters were in northern Iraq and threatened to use military force to eliminate their bases.[2] Throughout the spring and summer, several thousand Turkish troops were deployed near the border in order to prevent rebel incursions and prepare for counterinsurgency operations. Then, on October 17, 2007, following a series of attacks by the PKK, the Turkish Parliament authorized military strikes against rebel sanctuaries in Iraq, provoking strong reactions by Iraqi and U.S. officials. Iraqi foreign minister Hoshyar Zebari—a Kurd—urged restraint, stating, "The PKK should leave Iraq . . . [but] the Iraqi government is uncomfortable with the decision of the Turkish government to send troops to northern Iraq."[3] U.S. president George Bush, hoping to preserve relative stability in northern Iraq, echoed these concerns, "We are making it very clear to Turkey that we don't think it is in their interests to send troops into Iraq."[4]

The feeble Iraqi state, and even Kurdish representatives within the government, sought to placate Turkey by promising to limit PKK activities. Yet owing to state weakness, unwillingness to act, or both, Iraq has done little to dismantle PKK bases. Taking matters into its own hands, Turkey decided to launch a number of air and artillery strikes against rebel positions. In late December 2007, Turkey admitted to air raids in northern Iraq and claims to have killed over 150 militants and hit over 200 targets.[5] Responding to this violation of Iraqi sovereignty, an Iraqi government official stated, "We deplore this interference in our territory."[6] Nonetheless, another spate of air raids occurred on January 18, 2008, that hit approximately 60 targets.[7] Then, in February 2008, Turkey conducted an eight-day invasion of Iraqi territory with ground forces, leaving over 200 dead

---

2. "US Struggles to Avert Turkish Intervention in Northern Iraq," *Financial Times*, March 22, 2007. Guardian Unlimited Source: Financial Times Information Limited.

3. Alissa Rubin, "Turkish Bid to Pursue Kurds Poses Quandary for Iraq," *New York Times*, October 19, 2007, A12.

4. Sebnem Arsu and Sabrina Tevernise, "Turkey Resolves to Give Go-Ahead for Raids in Iraq," *New York Times*, October 18, 2007, A1.

5. Sebnem Arsu and Stephen Farrell, "Turkey Says Its Airstrikes in Northern Iraq Have Killed More than 150 Kurdish Rebels," *New York Times*, December 26, 2007, A8.

6. Sebnem Arsu and Stephen Farrell, "Turkey Bombs Kurds in Iraq; 2 Sides Differ on Casualties," *New York Times*, December 23, 2007, A27.

7. Reuters, "Turkish Army Says Destroyed 60 PKK Targets in Raid," January 18, 2008.

and creating further bitterness with the Iraqi government.[8] As of this writing, tensions remain high on the Iraq-Turkey border, and the conflict threatens to escalate further.

This regional conflict involving Turkey, the PKK, and Iraq, among others, is not unique. A similar dynamic was apparent in central Africa as well. The Rwandan genocide of 1994 shocked the world's conscience for its level of brutality and the rate at which over 800,000 Tutsis and moderate Hutus were slaughtered by their government and their fellow Rwandans. Following the successful overthrow of the Hutu-dominated state by the Tutsi-led Rwandan Patriotic Front, the genocide came to an end, and over one million Hutu refugees fled into eastern Zaire fearing reprisal attacks. Although the genocide itself and the lack of international response horrified the world, the massive emigration out of Rwanda received far less international attention. Yet this exodus fueled more than a decade of instability in Central Africa. Almost immediately following their flight, former Rwandan government officials and military commanders began to mobilize a Hutu insurgent force among the refugee camps in Zaire and prepared for a reinvasion. This prompted two interventions by Rwanda against its neighbor: first to unseat Mobutu Sese Seko, who was harboring Rwandan militants, and then against Laurent Kabila, who had turned on his former Rwandan allies and backed the Hutu insurgents instead. This intervention against Kabila sparked a wider, regional war, which drew in several African governments and cost hundreds of thousands of additional lives.

In another region of the world, the Karen National Union—an ethnonationalist group seeking greater autonomy for the Karen people—and the government of Myanmar have been engaged in a bloody, protracted conflict for many years. Fighting has at times spilled over into Thailand, where Karen rebels have established bases and rely on support from refugee communities. The Karen are not alone; several smaller ethnic rebel groups fighting the government of Myanmar—such as the Shan and the Kachin—are also based across the border in Thailand. The issue of border insecurity is frequently raised in diplomatic meetings, with Myanmar accusing Thailand of sheltering rebels and Thailand objecting to cross-border "hot pursuit" raids that violate its sovereignty. Blaming bilateral frictions on transnational crime and militancy, the Myanmar regime stated, "It is quite natural that any country that harbors criminals, armed terrorists and anti-government

---

8. Sabrina Tavernise and Richard Oppel, Jr., "After 8 Days, Turkey Pulls Its Troops out of Iraq," *New York Times*, March 1, 2008, Section A.

organizations on its border will continue to have unnecessary problems with its neighbors."[9]

The common thread that runs through these conflicts is that the rebel organizations involved in them are not confined to the geographic area of any one state but span national boundaries. In addition, these civil wars became the subject of intense international disputes, and even war, between neighbors. In common parlance, however, the terms "civil" war, "internal" conflict, and "domestic" strife imply contests between governments and armed opposition groups fought within the borders of a given country. International wars, by contrast, typically refer to violent conflicts between the armed forces of nation-states. On the contrary, as the examples above suggest, there is frequently nothing "domestic" about a civil war, and conflicts within countries often give rise to tensions between them.

Governments dealing with rebel groups have often been frustrated by their inability to implement effective counterinsurgency measures against typically far weaker organizations that straddle national boundaries. For instance, the Afghan government and U.S./NATO coalition forces have been unable to defeat Taliban and Al-Qaeda militants despite several years of counterinsurgency operations and clearly superior firepower—their efforts have been hampered by the ability of these groups to slip into Pakistani territory. The Taliban and Al-Qaeda enjoy access to sanctuaries in tribal areas along the border in Pakistan, where the central government exercises only nominal control. Allegations have also been made that elements within the Pakistani government and armed forces have been covertly colluding with the Taliban. This issue has led to significant tensions between the government of Afghanistan, led by President Hamid Karzai, and his Pakistani counterpart, General Pervez Musharraf. In a December 2006 speech, Karzai remarked, "The state of Pakistan was supporting the Taliban, so we presume that if there is still any Taliban, that they are still being supported by a state element. . . . We can't prevent the terrorists from coming from Pakistan."[10] The United States has also been frustrated by Pakistan's inability or unwillingness to evict militants operating in the tribal areas, and the issue has been repeatedly raised in meetings between U.S. officials and the Pakistani government.[11] Instability in

9. Peter Alford, "Thai-Burma Dispute Borders on Intractable," *The Weekend Australian*, March 3, 2001, 11.

10. Carlotta Gall, "Karzai says Pakistani Collusion Threatens Region," *New York Times*, December 12, 2006.

11. David Sanger and Mark Mazzetti, "Cheney Warns Pakistan to Act on Terror," *New York Times*, February 26, 2007.

Pakistan following the assassination of a popular opposition leader, Benazir Bhutto, has further weakened the state, generated concern about the coherence and capacity of the Pakistani government, and emboldened the militants.

Similar transborder dynamics have been evident in another conflict that has captured the world's attention: the conflict in the Sudanese region of Darfur. Violence has not been contained by national boundaries, as Darfurese rebels operate in eastern Chad, where they share ethnic ties with locals and have gathered supplies and recruits within refugee camps. Militias backed by the Sudanese government have sometimes slipped across porous borders to attack rebels and vulnerable refugees. Sudan has frequently accused Chad of harboring and aiding the rebels; similar accusations against Sudan were made after new Chadian rebel groups emerged that demanded the removal of President Deby (see Human Rights Watch 2007). After the Chadian government beat back a rebel assault in early 2007, Foreign Minister Ahmat Allami remarked, "These subversive forces . . . are being manipulated by Khartoum to further its expansionist and racist policy in Darfur and eastern Chad."[12]

These conflicts in Rwanda, Turkey, Myanmar, Afghanistan, and Sudan highlight the role of transnational actors in civil wars. More generally, extensive data collection on rebel organizations reveals that over half (55 percent) of all rebel groups active since 1945 have undertaken extraterritorial operations in countries beyond their target state (Cunningham, Gleditsch, and Salehyan 2007). Transnational insurgent groups are not exceptional but are common to several so-called "internal" wars. The Contra rebels from Nicaragua, Black Nationalist insurgents fighting the Rhodesian government, the Palestine Liberation Organization, and the Tamil Tigers from Sri Lanka, among many others, have conducted a significant share of their operations outside of their target states' sovereign territory.

Despite the pervasiveness of transnational actors in civil conflict, many traditional approaches to the study of insurgency, revolution, and secessionist violence fail to fully appreciate the importance of transnational opposition groups and have taken the "internal" nature of civil war as a given. Studies of international conflict, moreover, often neglect the role of transnational militant organizations in world politics, instead focusing on relations between states. This has been slowly changing, as several recent

---

12. Ali Abba Kaya, "Chadian Forces Repel Rebel Offensive," *Agence France-Presse*, February 1, 2007.

studies underscore the importance of transnational actors and regional conflict dynamics that blur the boundaries between civil and international violence (e.g., Kaldor 1999; Lake and Rothchild 1998; Lischer 2005; Saideman 2001; Scherrer 2002). Transnational rebels (TNR) call into question conventional analyses of civil conflict that focus almost exclusively on domestic factors such as the nature of the economy, the distribution of wealth, difficult terrain that facilitates insurgency, ethnic cleavages, and poor state capacity. External support for insurgents also forces us to rethink the factors underpinning war between states and the means that governments use to undermine their international opponents. Despite progress in this field, we have only begun to grasp the transnational dimensions of political violence. This issue has become even more pressing as militant groups such as Al-Qaeda, who are capable of spectacular acts of violence, are empowered by global communications and technology, which reduce the importance of distance in managing their organizations.

TNRs underscore the difficulty that modern, territorial nation-states face when dealing with transnational social actors that are not constrained by geography. Rebel groups that have access to external territory significantly raise the costs of counterinsurgency while reducing its effectiveness, because state power and authority are territorially defined. In addition, when rebels operate in other countries, analyses that focus on two-actor, rebel-government strategic interactions and bargaining processes are not sufficient. In addition to the possibility that conflicts could become internationalized and draw in other states, the preferences and behaviors of the rebel host country (or countries) must be examined. Thus, this book moves beyond a state-centric view of war by taking into account the regional dynamics of conflict and linkages between civil and international war. I advance a layered, multilevel approach to the study of political violence where transnational social processes and "triangular" bargains between rebel host countries, home countries, and opposition groups connect conflicts within and between states.

Caging the Leviathan: Understanding Transnational Insurgency

As the quotes from Hobbes and Weber at the beginning of this chapter indicate, social thinkers throughout the centuries have argued that *the* defining feature of the state is its command of overwhelming power relative to other groups in society, which it uses to maintain internal order and prevent challenges to its rule. Although states may differ from one another in terms of their political institutions and policies, they all claim the exclusive right to exercise coercive force domestically and use their power against armed threats to their authority. Therefore, the costs of organizing and undertaking a rebellion are extremely high—insurgents risk death—and the probability of success does not appear to be great. Nevertheless, numerous instances of civil conflict—for example in Rwanda, Iraq, Kashmir, and Northern Ireland—indicate that rebellion is not as uncommon as this asymmetry of force would lead one to believe. This presents a puzzle for social scientists and a main research question in this book: Given the expected costs, why do people ever rebel against the state? Related to this, we may also ask: Why does the state fail to maintain order over its territory and among its citizenry?

Although chapter 1 will develop a more detailed answer to these questions, it is useful to offer a thumbnail sketch of the theoretical framework here. The state has an advantage in the *domestic* use of force, but its power is largely constrained by its internationally recognized borders. While states work to monitor and repress dissent at home (Bates, Greif, and Singh 2002; Hardin 1995; Olson 2001), they are limited in their ability to exercise force in territories where they are not sovereign. Understanding this limitation on state power, rebel groups often evade repression by strategically positioning themselves outside of the state's reach. Thus, territorially unbridled, transnational actors—although apparently weak—have a significant advantage against geographically constrained states, whose power and authority are defined by a particular sovereign space. Conditions in neighboring states and the ability to organize in external sanctuaries, therefore, critically affect the bargain between states and challengers by altering the apparent *internal* asymmetry of force (on asymmetric warfare see Arreguin-Toft 2001 and Mack 1975).

The case of Liberia highlights the diminished importance of power asymmetry between states and rebels when opposition groups operate across borders. On December 24, 1989, Charles Taylor and his rebel organization, the National Patriotic Front of Liberia (NPFL), launched an insurgency against the government of Samuel Doe. Taylor's forces, which received training in Libya, consisted of a few dozen fighters armed with light weapons; clearly, this group was vastly outnumbered by Doe's superior military and police forces. The NPFL launched its initial strikes from neighboring Cote d'Ivoire and concentrated its early efforts on targets in Nimba County, which is located along the Liberian/Ivoirian border. Soon, backing for Taylor materialized as members of the Gio and Mano ethnic groups, who felt alienated by Doe's support of his Krahn coethnics, joined the rebellion.

After a period of intense fighting and thousands of deaths, the Liberian army crumbled, and Doe was deposed and later executed by a different rebel faction that had split from the NPFL. Following infighting among various rebel groups, Taylor and the NPFL took control of the capital.

Thus, the Doe government, which had thousands of troops and armaments, was unable to stop a few dozen rebels from sparking a bloody civil war that would eventually lead to the regime's collapse. The weakness of Doe's army was certainly important, yet even this poorly equipped and trained fighting force surely should have been able to defeat a small handful of NPFL fighters. Critically, Taylor's ability to mobilize supporters outside of Liberia and slip back and forth across the border allowed him to evade government forces long enough to be able to reenter the country and lead the NPFL to victory.

One of the most striking findings presented in this book is that a majority of rebel groups have utilized territory outside of their target state's borders in mobilizing and sustaining their activities. Yet a large share of research on civil conflict treats nation-states as hermetically sealed, independent units. Country-level attributes and processes—such as income inequality, ethnic tensions, dependence on primary commodities, and the responsiveness of political institutions—dominate theories of civil war. This is especially true of statistical analyses that, by assumption and for mathematical ease, treat observations as independent of one another.

Transnational rebels complicate this neat picture by bridging the internal/external divide. The bulk of the early work on transnational organizations focused on international economic exchanges and the activities of multinational corporations (see, e.g., Huntington 1973; Keohane and Nye 1971). Political scientists are only beginning to understand the importance of transnational forms of social organization outside of the economic realm (see, e.g., Arquilla and Ronfeldt 2001; Beissinger 2002; Keck and Sikkink 1998; Lake and Rothchild 1998; Risse-Kappen 1995; Rudolph and Piscatori 1997; Saideman 2001). More often than not, territorially bounded nation-states are not perfectly congruent with the polity, or group of people who make claims upon the state. The Leviathan is "caged" by international borders, whereas rebel organizations can and often do organize transnationally, evading state coercive power.

Rebels are more likely to have access to external territory if neighboring states are too weak to prevent access. Failed states, or states with limited control over their territory, pose international security risks, as militant groups often use their soil as a base of operations. In addition to weak states, rival neighbors often deliberately host and support rebel organizations, including by offering territorial access. Rather than fight their international opponents directly, some states choose to delegate conflict to rebel proxies as a substitute to international war. Finally, rebel organizations often use refugee camps as a source of supplies and willing recruits. Rather than mere victims of violence, refugees often become active participants in conflicts back home. Weak neighbors, rival neighbors, and refugee communities in which to mobilize are central to the theoretical framework in this book, as they facilitate extraterritorial rebel bases, which in turn make fighting insurgents more difficult.

Difficulties in counterinsurgency are only part of the story. Importantly, bargaining between TNRs and the state, as well as regional conflict processes and negotiations involving external actors, add another layer of complexity. Violence is simply bargaining by unconventional means, and states could, in principle, offer concessions to opposition groups in order to prevent or put an end to armed insurrection. When TNRs mobilize abroad in relative safety, thus increasing their bargaining strength and ability to extract a better deal, such a strategy hampers negotiations. The external operations of rebel groups are more difficult to collect intelligence on, creating informational asymmetries that hinder bargaining; credible commitments to demobilize rebels and abide by the terms of a peace treaty are more difficult to make; and host states become additional actors in the negotiating environment and can use their influence to block a deal.

This book is not merely about conflicts between insurgents and the state, however. No theory of transnational rebellion would be complete without also considering relations between states and the potential for international violence. A major theme of this book is that civil wars and international disputes are not easily separable, and one must fully consider endogenous and mutually reinforcing relationships between these modes of conflict. Civil wars are frequently both cause and consequence of conflicts between states. Foreign enemies often support rebel organizations in order to undermine a state, and such support further fuels international rivalries. States that are perhaps too weak to evict TNRs may be dragged unwillingly into international disputes as they are accused of harboring militants and face cross-border strikes and retaliatory actions by their neighbors. Thus, on one hand, rebel sanctuaries may become a source of international war, but on the other hand, rebel patronage may be used by enemies as an alternative to war. Rather than treating civil and international conflict as separate research topics, this book—through quantitative and qualitative research—examines this regional conflict nexus in depth and considers multiple layers of interaction between states and nonstate actors.

Why Go Transnational?

Certainly not all rebel groups organize transnationally. As indicated above, slightly more than half of the rebel organizations active since 1945 have utilized external sanctuaries to some degree. Yet this leaves a large number of rebel groups that do not do so. Clearly, these groups are able to circumvent state repression efforts without the benefit of an external base. They may use alternative strategies such as hiding in remote rural areas, in hard to reach mountainous regions, or among the urban underground. The main purpose of this book is not to analyze the strategic decision to "go transnational"— this would merit an entire study of its own. Rather, my analysis begins after this choice has been made by rebel leaders. Although I largely focus on the groups that do organize across borders, it is important to consider, at least briefly, the reasons why a rebel organization would choose such a strategy over a purely internal one.

Mobilizing a rebellion, training forces, and gathering supplies in external territories offers the obvious advantage of evading state security forces; it significantly reduces the costs of organizing violence. Resources provided by other states can also substantially augment the insurgents' ability to procure arms and finances. Yet, this strategy is not without costs. When mobilizing in other countries, rebel organizations may lose touch with their constituents and reduce their ability to monitor rapidly changing conditions on the ground. Local populations in the host state may not welcome their new "guests," who may be blamed for security problems. Rebels may also be positioned far from government targets and be at some distance from the capital or major cities. Most important, accepting support from foreign patrons often comes with strings attached, as rebel organizations are forced to graft the agendas of their backers onto their own. During the Cold War, for instance, many rebel organizations fashioned themselves into a pseudo "Marxist vanguard" and leaders had to accept Soviet training in order to secure funds from the Soviet Union. Many Islamist insurgencies today may be playing up their religious credentials in order to win external funding. External sanctuaries can also be subject to the whims of the host country and vacillations in its foreign policy priorities. Although resources and sanctuary may be valuable, by accepting outside aid rebel groups lose some of their organizational autonomy.

For these reasons, rebels may indeed prefer a wholly domestic strategy. However, this approach may not be feasible, as domestic opportunities to mobilize violence may be lacking. A useful framework for thinking about the decision to organize transnationally comes from work on transnational advocacy networks (TAN). Keck and Sikkink (1998) developed a "boomerang" model to explain transnational networks in human rights, environmental activism, and other protest movements. They argue that when domestic action is blocked by a capable, repressive state, such organizations form social networks with like-minded groups in other countries—typically in liberal democracies where their activities are protected—that can gather information, coordinate activism, and place pressure on the regime from the outside. TANs are able to continue their campaigns even when domestic voices are silenced because they are not subject to the same regulatory framework. Transnational rebel organizations follow a similar logic, although for different ends. However, rather than forming ties with external organizations in an activist network formed of multiple nodes, TNR groups physically transplant part of their activities elsewhere. Still, the boomerang logic is a useful one: if a straight, direct path to challenging the state is not available, rebel organizations can circumvent state power and control by seeking transnational opportunities. Some groups will find that they are not able to do so, or perhaps do not need to, and will focus on domestic mobilization efforts instead. But once a transnational strategy has been adopted, the processes of conflict and the nature of the bargain take an alternative trajectory. This is the focus of this book.

Trends and Definitions

It is useful to specify the nature and scope of the analysis and to define key terms. This book addresses full-blown civil war in which the state lacks authority over significant portions of its territory. It also examines less severe conflicts, such as rebellions and insurgencies, under a common theoretical framework. In this book, civil wars, rebellions, and insurgencies all refer to organized violence against the state by nongovernmental actors for political ends. Terrorism can also be included under this definition, but because of the normative connotations of the term, it is one I prefer to avoid. This definition of organized violence does not include events such as mob violence, in which there is little formal organization; nonviolent protest; internal coups, in which one faction of the government fights against another faction; communal conflict between rival groups that do not involve the state; and criminal acts, in which actors do not have political motivations. Transnational protest movements and organized crime may follow similar patterns, but are not addressed at length here.

Some scholars have adopted the convention of reserving the term "civil war" for conflicts that exceed 1,000 battle deaths or reach some other death threshold. This terminology is unfortunate, however, as it has been adopted for reasons of methodological convenience rather than any theoretical criterion. There are few theoretical reasons to believe that conflicts above an arbitrary threshold are conceptually distinct from and not comparable to conflicts below that threshold. In addition, data sets using the 1,000 deaths criteria undercount the extent of violent incidents, which has methodological drawbacks, as will be discussed in subsequent chapters. For these reasons, a minimum death count is not an integral part of the conflict definition in this work, but conflicts certainly must be violent.

International conflicts are defined broadly in this book. According to a broad definition, "conflict" implies any incompatibility of interests; yet for tractability, I specifically look at threats and actual uses of military force in the empirical analyses to follow. Figure I.1 displays the frequency of conflict by type in the post-World War II period as listed by the Uppsala University/Peace Research Institute of Oslo armed conflict dataset (hereafter, U/PACD). Intrastate wars and internationalized intrastate wars (in which foreign governments have contributed troops) are by far the most common type of conflict, and the number of such wars had been rising until a steep drop in the 1990s. This rise in the number of civil wars occurred because in any given year more civil wars began than were resolved, which over time led to an increase in absolute numbers. The end of the Cold War, however, dried up funding for many combatant groups and broke the deadlock in the United Nations Security Council over where to deploy peacekeepers, so several conflicts came to an end. By contrast, the number of international wars per year has remained fairly constant over the period and hovers between one and ten wars underway each year.[13] Extrasystemic, or colonial wars, are now a thing of the past, with the final colonial conflicts having been fought in the 1970s.[14]

It would be misleading to characterize these conflicts as independent events, however. Conflicts tend to be geographically clustered in certain regions, and the geographic distribution of wars, in addition to their temporal distribution, is interesting to note. As figure I.2 reveals, in several

13. The graph depicted by the Uppsala University/Peace Research Institute of Oslo study only shows international conflicts that generated at least 25 battle deaths. In the empirical analysis in chapter 4, I do not use such a restriction.

14. Colonial wars are difficult to categorize conceptually, however. In some sense, all wars of succession may be termed anticolonial. For example, if one considers the Soviet Union a colonial empire, violent succession in Armenia and Azerbaijan may be considered colonial wars of independence. Similarly, the East Timorese fight for liberation may be considered an anticolonial war against Indonesia.

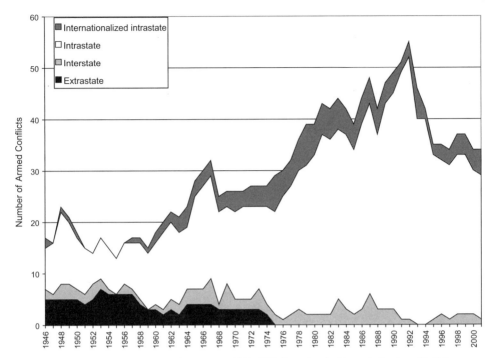

Figure I.1. Number of armed conflicts by type, 1946–2000. Reproduced, with permission, from Nils Petter Gleditsch, Peter Wallensteen, Mikael Eriksson, Margareta Sollenberg, and Haavard Strand, "Armed Conflicts, 1946–2001: A New Dataset," *Journal of Peace Research* 39, no. 5 (2002): 615–37.

regions such as Western Africa, the African Great Lakes region, South Asia, and the Middle East, numerous countries were involved in conflicts in recent years. Even a casual reading of several cases reveals considerable interdependence between conflicts in neighboring countries, as similar issues and actors span national boundaries. In addition, spatial statistics have revealed that this clustering is too regular to be completely random, suggesting that conflicts may be shaped by factors common to the region or the diffusion of conflict across space (see, e.g., Lake and Rothchild 1998; K. S. Gleditsch 2007; Salehyan and Gleditsch 2006; Sambanis 2002). If we were to superimpose a map of zones of *international* conflict over a map of civil wars, there would be considerable overlap as well. This coincidence of civil and international conflicts across regions suggests that there may be considerable interplay between these forms of violence and common mechanisms driving both.

In some cases, common ethnic cleavages may explain the regional clustering of violence. For example, Hutus and Tutsis have come into conflict

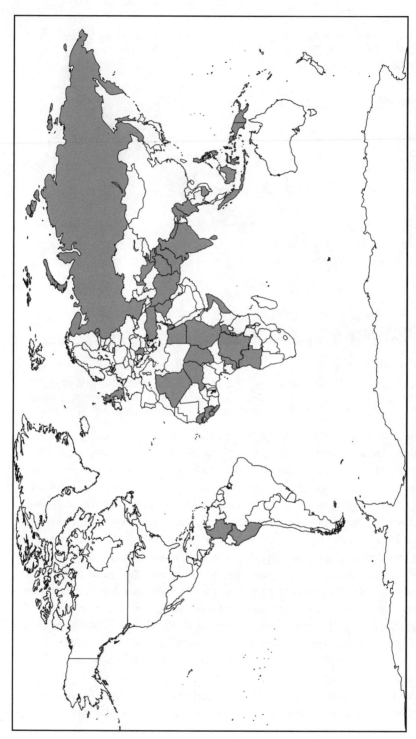

Figure I.2. Location of civil conflicts, 1996–2000 (dark areas indicate countries with conflict). List of conflicts based on data from Nils Petter Gleditsch, Peter Wallensteen, Mikael Eriksson, Margareta Sollenberg, and Haavard Strand, "Armed Conflicts 1946–2001: A New Dataset," *Journal of Peace Research* 39, no. 5 (2002): 615–37.

with one another in Burundi, Rwanda, and the Democratic Republic of Congo; additionally, Kurds have fought for independence from Turkey, Iran, and Iraq. Refugees may also contribute to the regional spread of civil war through conflict externalities and the expansion of rebel social networks (Salehyan and Gleditsch 2006). Refugees from Kosovo in Macedonia, for example, contributed to instability there and were one factor that fueled a short-lived insurrection in 2001. Civil wars may also entail negative economic and social effects for other states in the region, which contributes to local unrest (Ghobarah, Huth, and Russett 2003; Sandler and Murdoch 2004). Thus, civil wars are interdependent phenomena with significant external linkages.

More fundamentally, many conflicts are linked through either transnational ties among separate rebel organizations (e.g., Albanian insurgencies in Kosovo and Macedonia) or rebel groups that span national boundaries. Rather than independent origins, militant groups may influence conflict events in multiple countries. Transnational rebels are defined as armed opposition groups whose operations are not confined to the geographic territory of the nation-state(s) that they challenge. TNRs gather funding and resources among the diaspora, recruit fighters abroad, and secure bases in neighboring countries from which to attack their home state. Although global Islamic militancy will not be addressed in any great detail in this book, TNRs also include organizations such as Al-Qaeda, which targets multiple states across Europe, North America, and the Middle East and seeks to establish an Islamic Caliphate in Muslim lands.

TNRs are fueled by regional antagonisms and, in turn, exacerbate conflicts among target and host countries. Therefore, it is important to analyze regional conflict clusters involving multiple state and nonstate actors rather than treat civil wars in various countries as separate events or make arbitrary distinctions between civil and international conflict. Table I.1 illustrates three such regional conflict clusters: West Africa, the Middle East (prior to the 2003 U.S. invasion of Iraq), and Southeast Asia. Although each of these cases has important local roots, the linkages among rebel organizations, interstate rivalries, and TNR groups across borders make it clear that these conflicts cannot be treated in isolation.

In the West African cluster, the NPFL began a successful insurgency against the government of Liberia using sanctuaries in the Ivory Coast. Liberia under Charles Taylor then backed Revolutionary United Front (RUF) insurgents against the government of Sierra Leone; later, Liberia became a staging ground for Ivoirian rebels pressing for greater rights for minority groups in the north. Instability in Sierra Leone allowed the Guinean rebel group, the Rally of Democratic Forces of Guinea (RFDG), to find sanctuary there; the RFDG was also supported by Taylor's government. In turn, Guinea backed and harbored the Liberians United for Reconciliation and Democracy (LURD) rebels against the regime in Liberia. All the while, a regional peacekeeping initiative led by the Economic Community of West African States sought to contain Taylor and control instability in West Africa. The United Kingdom, France, and other external powers have also intervened in these various wars.

In the Middle East cluster (or at least one such cluster), conflicts in Iran, Iraq, and Turkey have overlapped considerably. After the Iranian Revolution, Iran and Iraq fought one another in a bloody international war while at the same time supporting one another's rebel organizations. International war and rebel support were strategies used in tandem. Iran harbored the Supreme Council for the Islamic Revolution in Iraq, while Iraq supported the Iranian Mujahedin-e Khalq (see chapter 3 for a detailed analysis). These states tried to activate "fifth columns" in the other, as the Iranian government called on Iraqi Shias to oppose Saddam Hussein's regime, and Iraq attempted to rally Arabs in Iran's Khuzistan Province. Both countries funded and supported one another's Kurdish militias, and the PKK from Turkey found sanctuary in the mountainous regions of these neighbors. After the U.S. invasion in 2003, cross-border conflicts have not subsided, as Iran is accused of aiding Shia factions in Iraq and Turkey has attacked PKK rebels based in Iraqi Kurdistan.

The Southeast Asia cluster consists of several ethnic autonomy movements from India—particularly in Assam, Manipur, Tripura, and Nagaland States—finding sanctuary in neighboring countries. India and Bhutan have made efforts to improve security cooperation to evict Assamese rebels hiding on Bhutanese soil, but rebel sanctuaries continue to be a contentious issue in relations between neighbors. In turn, Indian territory was used by Nepalese communist insurgents, which had links to the Naxalite insurgency within India itself (not transnational). Ethnic rebels from Myanmar have utilized Chinese, Indian, Thai, and Bangladeshi territory, often provoking clashes between neighboring governments. Bangladeshi insurgents from the Chittagong region were based in India and operated within refugee camps.

There are many other examples of such clusters: the Caucasus, the Balkans, Central America, Central Africa, and South Asia, among others. These regions also display strong linkages among various conflicts at multiple levels. This book develops a theoretical understanding of these regional nexuses and, through quantitative analysis as well as in-depth case studies, sheds light on this dynamic through empirical research.

Table I.1 Selected transnational rebels

Target Government	Rebel Name(s)	Host Government(s)
West Africa cluster		
Guinea	Rally of Democratic Forces of Guinea	Sierra Leone
Sierra Leone	Revolutionary United Front	Liberia
Liberia	National Patriotic Front of Liberia	Cote d'Ivoire
	Liberians United for Reconciliation and Democracy	Guinea
	Ulimo	Sierra Leone
Cote d'Ivoire	Patriotic Movement of Cote d'Ivoire	Burkina Faso
	Movement for Justice and Peace	Liberia
	Ivorian Popular Movement of the Great West	Liberia
Middle East cluster (pre-2003)		
Iran	Kurdish Democratic Party of Iran	Iraq, Turkey
	Mujahedin-e-Khalq	Iraq
Iraq	Supreme Council for the Islamic Revolution in Iraq	Iran
	Kurdistan Democratic Party	Iran, Turkey
	Patriotic Union of Kurdistan	Iran, Turkey
Turkey	Kurdish Workers' Party	Iran, Iraq
Southeast Asia cluster		
India (eastern)	United Front for the Liberation of Assam	Bangladesh, Bhutan, Myanmar
	People's Liberation Army (Manipur)	Bangladesh, Myanmar
	National Socialist Council of Nagaland	Bangladesh, Myanmar
	All Tripura Tribal Front	Bangladesh
	National Liberation Front of Tripura	Bangladesh
Bangladesh	Shanti Bahini	India
Myanmar	Karen National Union	Thailand
	Rohingya Solidarity Organization	Bangladesh
	Arakan Rohingya Islamic Front	Bangladesh
	Shan State Army	Thailand
	All Burma Students Democratic Front	Thailand
	Kachin Independence Organization	China, India

Plan of the Book

Contests between territorially organized states and transnational insurgents—"rebels without borders"—are a dominant mode of civil conflict, and they necessarily extend to engulf rebel host states in a complex tapestry of interaction woven across the internal-external divide. Chapter 1 develops the theory of transnational rebellion, which sheds new light on civil wars, international disputes, and the dynamics of negotiating settlements, and examines how transnational rebellions touch upon theories of state sovereignty and territoriality, the nature of international borders, the organization of opposition groups, and the prospects for accommodating insurgents. It will also discuss the interrelationship between conflict within states and conflict among them and how triangular negotiations between rebels, target governments, and host governments shape the bargaining environment.

Chapter 2 derives empirical predictions about transnational rebellions and civil wars and then tests several observable implications of the theory. New data on rebel access to external bases indicates that conflicts involving rebels with foreign sanctuaries are much more likely to persist. Moreover, ethnic groups concentrated near international boundaries are more likely to engage in violent dissent.

Chapter 3 develops empirical tests of the relationship between transnational rebel organizations and international conflict. Quantitative evidence indicates that rebel bases in neighboring countries significantly increase the likelihood of an international dispute between host and home countries. Moreover, rival host states sometimes substitute the direct use of force with the provision of rebel sanctuary and support. In addition to the quantitative results, several case studies are used to illustrate the key findings. Chapters 4 and 5 explore two additional cases in depth—the Contra War in Nicaragua and the Rwandan insurgency following the 1994 takeover by the Rwandan Patriotic Front. The case studies explore additional implications of the theory that are difficult to tease out in a quantitative analysis. In particular, they highlight bargaining dynamics between rebels, target governments, and host governments and show how negotiations brought about an end to these wars.

The final chapter recaps the main findings of the book; explores their theoretical implications, and examines the policy implications, with a particular focus on the current conflicts in Iraq, Afghanistan, and Sudan. Unilateral responses to transnational rebellions are not likely to be sufficient. Instead, states must develop robust cooperative relationships and strengthen international institutions to prevent and contain transnational violence.

1 A Theory of Transnational Rebellion

Rebellion is risky. Even when grievances against the state run deep, people who are unsatisfied with their lot will face difficulties in organizing collectively when political opposition activities are likely to be met with violence. Poverty and political powerlessness may be bad, but torture, imprisonment, and death are worse. Thus, many analysts have rightly emphasized the importance of constraints on the use of government coercion. If dissidents can evade the power of the state, organizing a rebellion becomes feasible. Of course, some rebel groups may be able to find safe areas within the state—in remote mountains or amid the urban underground, for example—as the state's strength is never evenly distributed across its territory. Nevertheless, for modern nation-states, power, authority, and coercive capabilities are fundamentally limited by national boundaries, and so in a large share of civil conflicts, rebels seek resources and mobilization opportunities outside of the territory of the state—and rebellion becomes transnational.

Rebellion is a strategy for winning concessions from the government. It is used when conventional politics fails. At the extreme, rebels will demand—and sometimes win—complete removal of the regime in power or an independent state to call their own. In other cases, rebels ask for significant political, economic, or social reforms, power-sharing with the incumbent regime, or some form of regional autonomy. Whatever the demand, disputes between rebels and the state are part of a bargaining process in which actors threaten one another with violence. Insurgents threaten to use force and impose costs on the government if their demands are not met. States can accommodate the opposition's demands or choose to use violent means of silencing dissent. Negotiating is commonly conceived of as antithetical to fighting, yet while bullets are flying and bombs are going off, actors are at least tacitly making demands and counterdemands. They are bargaining. Yet prior to mobilizing an army, rebels lack a credible threat to use force. External mobilization opportunities give rebel groups bargaining power through the ability to impose costs on the state, and they open a bargaining space. At the same time, external mobilization makes finding an acceptable settlement more difficult by creating ambiguity about the rebel's relative strength and the appropriate level of concessions that must be offered; by making it more difficult for the rebels to commit to demobilization agreements; and by introducing new actors into the bargain.

This chapter examines how the norms of state sovereignty and territoriality impose significant limitations on government capacity to repress rebels. After exploring the role of TNRs in civil conflicts, the chapter looks at the implications of transnational rebellion for international relations. Finally, it develops preliminary arguments about the prospects for conflict termination and resolution. Although transnational rebels create tensions between neighbors, they also point to the need for regional security cooperation to limit TNR operations. Regional cooperation and improved diplomatic relations between states will be critical to bringing such conflicts to an end and securing a lasting peace.

Intellectual Heritage

This book builds on earlier studies of civil and international conflict; particularly the literatures on political opportunity structures, conflict bargaining, and the international dimensions of civil war. It expands these intellectual traditions by highlighting how external opportunities for mobilizing rebellion shape bargaining dynamics and how civil wars feed into international conflicts. Emphasis is placed on the political environment in which conflicts take place rather than on group motivations. Although the importance of the particular motivations of rebel leaders and rank-and-file soldiers—such as group grievances, personal enrichment, or ethnic discrimination—cannot be discounted, these motivations are not sufficient explanations for violence.

Ted Robert Gurr (1970) offered one of the best-articulated theories of how group grievances provide a motive for people to launch an insurgency. According to Gurr, when some social groups are disadvantaged relative to others, or when there is a disjunction between group aspirations and their current opportunities, people feel aggrieved and are psychologically predisposed to violence. Similarly, other scholars have argued that income inequality and a hierarchical class structure—especially when coupled with ethnic cleavages—lead to mass discontent and, in turn, political instability and violence (see, e.g., Alesina and Perotti 1996; Cederman and Girardin 2007; Gurr and Moore 1997; Horowitz 1985; Huntington 1968; MacCulloch 2004; Marx, Lenin, and Eastman 1932; B. Moore 1967; Muller and Seligson 1987; Murshed and Gates 2005; Rabushka and Shepsle 1972). Another, more recent line of thought argues that "greed" rather than grievance is a significant motive for several insurgencies. The desire for profit provides fuels some rebel organizations, and scholars have argued that many rebels are not so much concerned with righting wrongs but with enriching themselves through looting natural resources, although rebel leaders may not admit to such motives (Bannon and Collier 2003; Collier and Hoeffler 1999, 2004; Ross 2004; Weinstein 2005).[1]

Although grievance, greed, or other motivating factors can be important, such motivations alone cannot explain insurgent violence, as opposition groups must overcome collective action problems in the shadow of government repression (Fearon and Laitin 2003; Lichbach 1995; Tilly 1978). Arguably, *all* countries contain *some* group that is disadvantaged relative to others, but very few experience rebellion. Instead, most aggrieved groups choose alternative opposition tactics or remain quiescent. In addition, resources for plunder are frequently available: nearly all countries have *some* resource that can be looted. Even if a country is not richly endowed with natural resources, rebel organizations can enrich themselves through extortion or other criminal activities. This is not to say that motivations are unimportant. Without a sense of collective disadvantage or the prospect of economic or political advancement, it is hard to imagine why people would take up arms. Nevertheless, motivation is not enough for individuals to undertake the costly act of mobilizing a rebellion and fighting against the state: motivation must be coupled with the opportunity for action.

Opportunity

Opportunity theories of civil violence do not deny that rebel motivations are important, but they add the probability of success, the costs of collective action, and the costs of fighting to the equation. To be persuaded to fight, aggrieved people must believe that there is a reasonable chance of obtaining their objectives, or else they will not be willing to bear the costs and risks of joining a rebel movement. There must be limitations on the Leviathan's

1. Collier and Hoeffler in their 2004 article modify their earlier 1999 paper. In the earlier paper, they argue that "loot" provides a motive for fighting. In the 2004 piece, they modify this stance somewhat and argue that easily captured resources provide rebels with financing with which to sustain rebellion and that easy plunder lowers the opportunity cost for fighting.

nearly absolute control over the means of coercion for people to believe that challenging the government will be worthwhile.

Charles Tilly (1978) makes political opportunity a central factor in his theory of group mobilization and contentious political action. In his view, the decision to rebel involves a strategic calculation of how the incumbent government is likely to respond, taking into account its capacity for repression. According to Tilly (1978, 101), "Governmental repression is uniquely important because governments specialize in the control of mobilization and collective action . . . to keep potential actors visible and tame." People fear the power of the state to imprison, harass, intimidate, torture, and kill, and they will not turn their dissatisfaction into visible forms of resistance so long as these costs are high. Therefore, the cost of repression is a critical variable for explaining insurgency and other forms of political dissent (see, e.g., Fearon and Laitin 2003; Kuran 1989; Lohmann 1994; Lichbach 1995; McAdam, Tarrow, and Tilly 2001; Muller and Weede 1990; Tarrow 1994; Tilly 1978). This notion stems back farther to Thomas Hobbes, who noted the importance of a strong central authority in maintaining domestic order. Civil wars are more likely when the Leviathan is relatively weak and incapable of maintaining order: when the state loses its control over society, the domestic arena resembles the anarchic international environment (Posen 1993).

Most scholars focus on domestic institutions and constraints on government repression. Some have argued that states that do not allow peaceful reforms through democratic processes, nor have robust repressive capabilities—so-called "weak authoritarian" regimes or "anocracies"—are most prone to civil war (Muller and Weede 1990; Hegre et al. 2001). In addition, rough terrain, such as a mountainous landscape or densely forested regions, inhibits the state's ability to pursue rebels into remote areas and provides insurgents the opportunity to escape coercion (Fearon and Laitin 2003; Hendrix 2008). In some of the poorest states where extensive infrastructure is lacking, government control does not extend very far beyond the capital because the state cannot project power into the periphery (Herbst 2000). Jeffrey Herbst (2004) focuses on the military as an institution and argues that ill-disciplined, corrupt, and incompetent military forces in Africa have been unable to thwart much smaller rebel organizations.

Political opportunities provide the means through which groups translate amorphous sentiment into organized violence. Most studies of civil violence focus on domestic politics and structural attributes of the state such as political institutions or physical geography but ignore forces outside of the state which may be equally, if not more, important. Moreover, the opportunity literature focuses on the political environment without paying much attention to bargains and negotiations between actors, which may obviate the resort to violence. Although environmental conditions shape the *range* of possible behaviors available to actors (Lake and Powell 1999), conflict is not inevitable, and understanding tacit or explicit bargaining processes is important in explaining final outcomes.

Bargaining

Increasingly, scholars of civil war are taking cues from bargaining perspectives on international war, which argue that since conflict is costly and burns resources, states should be willing to resolve their differences through negotiations (see, e.g., Fearon 1995; Powell 1999; Wagner 2000). In the absence of a central authority to bind actors—as when state authority breaks down in a civil war—these agreements must be self-enforcing. Bargaining may break down for several reasons. First, a poor informational environment may lead actors to miscalculate their relative capabilities and resolve to use force. Actors may be overconfident about their ability to prevail in a war, so proposed settlements are unsatisfactory. Second, credible commitment problems complicate negotiations if actors fear that the other side will not live up to the terms of an agreement. Finally, issue indivisibility may be an obstacle to negotiations if the issues at stake do not lend themselves to an easy compromise in which benefits can be neatly divided (see Fearon 1995). Importantly, as Wagner (2000) and Filson and Werner (2002) point out, war does not denote the end of the bargaining processes, but rather bargaining continues even as force is being used. During a war, combatants can opt to end fighting and find a suitable compromise that would be preferable to continuing a costly conflict.

This bargaining perspective has been usefully applied to civil conflict, as scholars have been looking for common ways of understanding violence regardless of whether the conflict is between states or between states and rebels (Lake 2003; Lake and Rothchild 1996; Toft 2003; Walter 2002). War is not the inevitable product of conflicts of interest but results from the inability of actors to find nonviolent solutions prior to violence or to make the necessary concessions to end a war. This perspective, while originally applied to international conflict, must be adapted somewhat to explain civil violence. In an international dispute, states typically have standing armies that they use as bargaining leverage against the other side. In a civil conflict, nascent rebel organizations do not have well-equipped and well-trained units at their disposal; rebellion entails a process of recruitment and mobilization (see Weinstein

2007). Potential rebels must raise forces with which to threaten the government in order to increase their bargaining leverage.

Owing to this key difference between civil and international conflict, bargaining and political opportunity theories can be usefully integrated. Political opportunities and state weakness allow rebel forces to mobilize and pose a credible threat to the government. Thus, a permissive political opportunity structure opens up the negotiating space and grants rebels the bargaining leverage that it lacked before.

As bargaining theories argue, states may accommodate opposition groups and offer reforms in order to prevent the outbreak of violence or to put an end to ongoing rebellions. But states are often unwilling to bargain with rebel organizations while the rebel groups are still weak because they hope for a swift military victory and because it is costly to recognize rebels as legitimate actors (Bapat 2005). Weak insurgents are often dismissed as "criminals," "bandits," or "terrorists." As rebels gain in strength and a decisive government victory becomes less likely, states become more amenable to offering concessions in exchange for peace. Still, as Walter (2002) argues, fears of vulnerability and credible commitment problems following postconflict disarmament pose additional obstacles to peace because disarmed rebels fear reneging and victimization by the state. Thus, state weakness and political opportunity may explain why rebels are able to mobilize a viable threat, but the bargaining perspective adds the failure to find and commit to a compromise to the picture. Sanctuaries in neighboring countries provide the political opportunities needed to mobilize a rebellion; yet at the same time, as explained below, when rebels pursue a strategy of *external* mobilization, bargaining failure becomes more likely that it would otherwise.

The Global Politics of Civil Conflict

Over twenty-five years ago, Theda Skocpol (1979, 19) remarked: "Transnational relations have contributed to the emergence of all social-revolutionary crises and have invariably helped to shape revolutionary struggles and outcomes." Despite this observation, for years most theories and empirical studies of civil war and insurgency focused on domestic conditions.[2] Scholars of international conflict, moreover, ignored nonstate actors, instead privileging states as the dominant players in world politics. A growing tendency in the field of international relations has attributed international-level outcomes to domestic-level factors such as political institutions, domestic instability, and the incentives of national leaders (see e.g. Bueno de Mesquita et al. 1999;

---

2. For noteworthy early exceptions, see Leites and Wolf 1970 and Mitchell 1970.

Chiozza and Goemans 2004; Cowhey 1993; Doyle 1986; Milner 1997; Putnam 1988). Scholars also have shown burgeoning interest in the international sources of domestic politics (Peter Gourevitch 1978), but relatively few studies have used international factors to explain domestic political violence.

This has been changing, as an increasing number of scholars note the importance of interstate relations and transnational politics for civil war. One of the longest-standing theories in this regard is that several local conflicts may be characterized as proxy wars between rival governments (Midlarsky 1992; Rosenau 1964). For instance, during the Cold War, the United States and the Soviet Union were greatly concerned with how civil wars in developing countries could tip the global balance of power, and they actively intervened in numerous conflicts in Central America, Southeast Asia, and the Horn of Africa, among other regions. Rather than fight directly, the superpowers sought to undermine one another through fomenting conflicts in the developing world.

Others have suggested that signals of support for opposition groups by external actors—particularly by ethnic kin—enhance their bargaining strength (Cetinyan 2002) and perhaps encourage risky behavior by dissidents, making conflict more likely (Jenne 2006; Thyne 2006). Additionally, previous research on intervention has shown that external interventions by foreign governments prolong civil wars (Balch-Lindsay and Enterline 2000; Elbadawi and Sambanis 2002; Regan 2002); that foreign governments often intervene in domestic conflicts in order to protect their ethnic kin (Davis and Moore 1997; Saideman 2001; Woodwell 2004); and that third-party security guarantees are needed for combatants to make credible commitments to one another during peace negotiations (Walter 2002). Another group of scholars has noted that civil wars tend to cluster geographically and that conflicts and other social problems often diffuse across national boundaries (K. S. Gleditsch 2002a, 2007; Ghobarah, Huth, and Russett 2003; Sandler and Murdoch 2004; Lake and Rothchild 1998; Salehyan and Gleditsch 2006; Sambanis 2001). More generally, Balch-Lindsay and Enterline (2000, 618) advocate a multidimensional approach to conflict in which inter- and intrastate war reinforce one another, "with cause and effect swirling across the domestic and interstate arenas, as the policy agendas pursued by state and non-state actors alike intermingle in a dynamic, process-oriented environment."

Finally, a few scholars have noted the importance of transnational social actors such as migrant diasporas, "terrorist" networks, and criminal organizations in directly or indirectly contributing to violence (Arquilla and Ronfeldt 2001; Bell 1971; Collier and Hoeffler 2004; Sandler 2003; Sandler, Tschirhart, and Cauley 1983; Shelley 1995). As opposed to "global civil society" groups, these actors represent the dark side of transnationalism. Mary Kaldor (1999) and John Arquilla and David Ronfeldt (2001) argue that in the contemporary period conflicts are more likely to involve loosely organized, nonhierarchical, transnational groups.[3] These organizations are aided by advances in technology, which lower transaction costs within the organization as well as raise the destructive capacity of small groups. Such organizations frequently form links with transnational criminal networks in order to tap into global black markets for illicit goods such as narcotics and conflict diamonds (Bannon and Collier 2003; Collier and Hoeffler 2001). Migrant diasporas, furthermore, may contribute to conflict by providing resources and support to opposition groups in their home countries (Adamson 2006; Byman et al. 2001; Collier and Hoeffler 2004; Lyons 2006; Shain 1989; Tatla 1999).

This literature shares the view that "civil" conflicts are not purely domestic phenomena. To understand the causal mechanisms behind civil violence, we must understand how actors such as foreign governments and transnational organizations influence local conflicts. But as of yet, this literature lacks a coherent framework for analyzing the international and transnational dimensions of conflict. Scholars have focused on particular pieces of the puzzle—such as support from ethnic kin or the organization of terrorist networks—without developing a unified theory of transnational violence. Moreover, scholars have not paid attention to the mutually constitutive relationship linking conflicts within and between states. We know little about how transnational militant organizations influence, and are influenced by, interactions and antagonisms between countries. By placing the study of transnational violence squarely within the literature on political opportunities, emphasizing bargaining difficulties arising from external mobilization, and considering regional negotiation dynamics, this book unifies disparate approaches to the study of civil and international war and provides a common framework for analysis.

State Boundaries as International Institutions

To properly understand the limits of state power and authority, we must appreciate the importance of borders in structuring international politics. State boundaries are perhaps the most fundamental international institutions in

---

3. However, Kalyvas (2001) argues—and I agree—that the new war/old war distinction made by Kaldor ignores historical precedent. Similar issues and tactics were also at play in earlier periods. And as I show in this book, transnational conflicts are not new.

the modern state system (Ansell and Di Palma 2004; Kahler and Walter 2006; Kratochwil 1986; Ruggie 1993; Starr 2006; Starr and Most 1976). Borders define where the authority of one state ends and that of another begins. Borders often determine the units of analysis in contemporary international relations scholarship: states are the primary actors in international politics (Bull 1977; Keohane 1984; Waltz 1979; Wendt 1992). Whereas studies of international institutions frequently focus on multilateral agreements and organizations such as the International Monetary Fund, the European Union, and the North American Free Trade Agreement, state boundaries have received much less attention as international institutions despite their fundamental role in structuring world politics. They have frequently been taken for granted.

Borders are politico-military institutions that define the geographical jurisdiction of the state: they are agreed-upon or de facto lines of control beyond which others have no authority. According to the classic Weberian definition of the state (Weber 1958, 212), the state is an entity that "claims the monopoly of the legitimate use of force *within a given territory*" (emphasis added). Territoriality is therefore an integral part of what it means to be a state. Internally, states have the power to regulate economic activity, establish procedures for the selection and removal of leaders, regulate the media, punish criminals, and suppress armed challenges to their rule. This last point is particularly important, because although states vary greatly in their economic policies and political institutions, all states work to monitor and limit internal threats to their supremacy.

States also work to regulate flows across their borders. As international institutions, borders are the gateways between the state, its citizens, and the outside world. At one extreme, autarchic states seek to prevent the entry of people, goods, and ideas from the outside. The insular policies of North Korea seem to best fit this ideal type. At the other end of the spectrum, some states embrace globalization and have worked to lift barriers to the free movement of goods, capital, information, and so forth. In actuality, most countries maintain some balance between complete globalization and full insulation; for example, the industrialized countries of North America and Western Europe, although relatively open, still preserve barriers to agricultural imports and immigrant labor. In addition, whereas well-equipped and capable states are better able to monitor their borders to prevent unwanted entry, weak governments are less able to patrol their borders. Thus, government *policies* regarding global flows and government *capacity* to control borders may vary.

There has been a considerable amount of debate in recent years over how effective the state has been in managing its borders and to what extent state sovereignty is still a useful concept. Much of the literature on state sovereignty and territoriality argues that the state is being rendered irrelevant by global markets (Camilleri and Falk 1992; Elkins 1995; Herz 1957; Ohmae 1990; Strange 1996) and universal human rights discourses (Jacobson 1996; Sassen 1996; Soysal 1994). Some scholars claim that borders serve a diminished function or are no longer important in regulating international affairs. For example, some have noted that in an area as fundamental as managing immigration—or who is allowed access to the state's territory—government policies to restrict entry are regularly undermined by the forces of supply-and-demand for immigrant labor (Cornelius et al. 2004). Anticipating a radical change from the Westphalian nation-state model, Ruggie (1993, 172) writes, "conventional distinctions between internal and external once again are exceedingly problematic." In short, this view finds that the state has been weakened and the world is becoming increasingly "borderless."

Critics argue that the sovereignty norm has been quite effective in preventing external meddling in internal affairs (Bull 1977). The very existence of exceptionally inept states and respect for their borders in a competitive global environment is cited as evidence that sovereignty matters (Herbst 2000; Jackson 1987). Others doubt that there is a diminished role for national governments in the international economy and have pointed to the importance of the state in managing markets and directing the flow of capital, migrants, and commodities (Cohen 2001; Evans 1997; Guiraudon and Lahav 2000; Helliwell 1998). Still others have pointed to the primacy of the state in defining global human rights regimes and the ability of states to circumvent their international legal obligations in this regard (Hathaway 2002; Joppke 1999). These authors claim that although globalization presents new challenges, the territorial nation-state is still a fundamental actor in world politics.[4] In addition to these approaches, Stephen Krasner (1995–1996; 1999) doubts that the world is now being transformed by globalization and argues that the view that there was once a "golden age" of Westphalian sovereignty is misguided.[5] Sovereignty is not

4. See Rudolph (2005) for a critical discussion of the literature on sovereignty.

5. Krasner (1999, 4) defines four types of sovereignty: legal, Westphalian, domestic, and interdependence. Domestic sovereignty, or the strength of the state to regulate internal activity, and interdependence sovereignty, or the ability to control flows across borders, is not examined in his work. Similarly, Janice Thomson (1995) argues that states have never been able to regulate flows across their borders adequately and that this definition of sovereignty is not particularly relevant. As will be argued below, however, when seen as military institutions, state boundaries have been more effective in preventing infiltration by the security forces of other states.

being weakened in a globalizing world; rather, the concept was never entirely robust to begin with (see also Thomson 1995).

The Military Function of Borders

The literature on sovereignty and state control over borders focuses overwhelmingly on global economic flows while ignoring the politico-military function of borders. As international institutions, *the primary function of international boundaries is to demarcate legal or de facto lines of military control and political jurisdiction.* The military and police forces of one state have no authority in another state, and crossing borders with such forces is seen as an act of aggression. States employ police forces to detect, apprehend, and punish domestic criminals on a daily basis. Furthermore, security agents regularly monitor subversive groups to prevent and defeat insurrections. Although goods and capital may move relatively freely, state agents cannot easily cross borders into regions where they lack authority. A popular, and quite telling, Hollywood cliché involves criminals escaping across the border where they are beyond the jurisdiction of police forces. Thus, the ability of the state to respond to criminals and dissidents is largely restricted by national boundaries.

States jealously guard their exclusive right to exercise political authority within their own territory. Although they do not rule by force alone, states have a comparative advantage in the domestic use of coercion (Hardin 1995). Sovereignty means that states command a preponderance (though often not a monopoly) of military force relative to other domestic actors and that other *state* actors do not have authority on their soil.

Since the Treaty of the Pyrenees between France and Spain in 1659—the first border demarcation agreement—states have insisted upon clearly defined borders and have taken measures to fortify their frontiers against foreign incursion onto their territory (Sahlins 1989). With the intensification of warfare and rising nationalist sentiment in Europe during the late eighteenth and nineteenth centuries (Anderson 1983; Gellner 1983; Tilly 1990), the process of border demarcation accelerated, and nearly all of the continent was geographically compartmentalized into exclusive political jurisdictions. It is important to note that although boundaries were being defined with great care during this period, global flows of goods and capital followed a relatively laissez-faire pattern. In fact, it was not until roughly the turn of the twentieth century that states began to restrict the movement of people across their borders by establishing immigration control laws and issuing passports (Castles and Miller 1993; Torpey 2000). Thus, the establishment of national boundaries was principally for military purposes;

states worked to prevent the intrusion of foreign *state* agents while being less interested in the entry of nongovernmental actors. Currently, except for a few desolate and sparsely inhabited areas of the world, contiguous countries are separated by some form of boundary-line. Most of these borders are agreed upon by treaty, but others—for example, Israel-Syria, India-Pakistan—are simply de facto, but no less real, lines of control (see Herbst 1989).

Several observers have noted that especially since World War II, international borders have constrained the use of force between governments—military lines of control are now more respected than ever (Andreas 2003; Zacher 2001). Mark Zacher (2001) documents a rise in this respect for the "territorial integrity norm," which is partly a function of the postwar international order established by the major Western powers. Thus, although the process of globalization has led to a more economically integrated world, in terms of their security functions, borders are quite robust. Although states may vary in their ability to prevent incursions, no state welcomes military violations of its sovereignty, and border violations are likely to spark an international conflict. Moreover, the international community, as expressed in the UN Charter and several subsequent legal provisions, widely views border violations with disapproval. Acts of aggression across national boundaries elicit censure by the international community; international opprobrium is not costless, especially if coupled with more concrete sanctions.

Figure 1.1 depicts a stylized view of the openness/restrictiveness of borders with respect to particular types of flows in the contemporary period. This presents an ideal type of modern boundaries and global flows in the aggregate; although particular countries may deviate from this pattern, it generally holds for most present-day borders. Global flows of information lie at the open end of the continuum: radio broadcasts, satellite television, and the internet penetrate even the most isolationist countries. Global flows of capital—particularly portfolio investments—are also relatively open in the contemporary period, with millions of transactions taking place across the world each day. Next up the spectrum, international trade

Figure 1.1. The relative openness of borders

in goods and services has expanded dramatically since World War II. Countries still impose significant tariff and nontariff barriers to trade, particularly in politically sensitive areas such as agriculture and defense technology.

Toward the more restrictive end, whereas the global mobility of economic factors of production pertains mostly to capital, most countries still impose limits on labor migration. In order to protect domestic labor and to prevent the entry of culturally "unwelcome" foreigners, barriers to immigration and the mobility of people across borders has not kept pace with other global movements.[6] Nevertheless, flows of legal and undocumented migrants are still substantial (Cornelius et al. 2004; Joppke 1998; Cornelius and Salehyan 2007). According to the International Organization for Migration, over 192 million people—about 3 percent of the world's population—live outside of their country of birth.[7]

Finally, even the most globally integrated states condemn the movement of security forces across national boundaries—here, borders are quite effective in restricting flows. This is not to say that state security forces are not mobile at all. Through bilateral treaties, several governments have allowed the establishment of foreign military bases on their soil (e.g., U.S. bases in Germany and South Korea); by agreement, foreign police and intelligence agents are sometimes allowed access to a state's territory; and forceful occupations of other countries, although relatively rare, still occur. As Krasner (1999) indicates, through contract or imposition, violations of strict sovereignty—even by military forces—do occur.

Nonetheless, for the great majority of states most of the time, security forces are limited to territorial boundaries. Military violations of sovereignty, especially by force, are certainly costly for the initiator as well as for the target, and are thus rare events. We see them happening most often when power asymmetries between states are great (e.g., the United States in Afghanistan and Iraq), but for most dyads, countries cannot easily penetrate national boundaries against the other's will.

In sum, the state is limited by its boundaries—the capacity to wield force, particularly in crushing insurgencies, is largely constrained by sovereign borders. State security forces specialize in maintaining control internally and defending against external aggression. To maintain control and prevent subversion, state agents use prosecution, harassment, imprisonment, torture,

---

6. The lifting of internal migration controls in the European Union is an important exception, however.

7. http://www.iom.int/jahia/page3.html (accessed April 18, 2007).

and purges of political opponents, among other means. Quite importantly, state agents also gather information on dissident activities through surveillance, intelligence gathering, and networks of informants. A state's capacity may not be spread evenly across its territory—the state may be relatively weaker in peripheral regions—but its power and authority drops off dramatically, if not to nil, at its border. This implies that transnationally organized groups, including rebels, are less vulnerable to state efforts to limit their activities.

Transnational Opposition

Not all politically relevant actors, or those who make demands on the state, are physically present within that state's territory. In recognition of this, a remarkable growth has occurred in the study of transnational organizations, including firms, religious institutions, and advocacy networks (e.g. Della Porta and Tarrow 2005; Huntington 1973; Keck and Sikkink 1998; Keohane and Nye 1971; Pauly and Reich 1997; Rudolph and Piscatori 1997; Tarrow 1994, chap. 11). Much of this work focuses on multinational corporations and global "civil society" groups such as human rights and environmental organizations.

Research on civil and international conflict has also noted the importance of transnational actors, particularly ethnic groups that reside in more than one state. In an important body of work, several authors have demonstrated a relationship between bisected ethnic groups and conflict, either within or between states (Cetinyan 2002; Davis and Moore 1997; Saideman 2001; Woodwell 2004). This literature has shown that during periods of domestic unrest, ethnic groups often come to the aid of kin in other countries when they face a threat from their government. Ethnic irredentism to capture territory populated by kin groups is also responsible for several international disputes (Ambrosio 2001; Carment and James 1995; Chazan 1991). These studies suggest that political actors are not necessarily defined by extant national boundaries, but that many groups share common aims with people in another country.

International migration also creates transnational social actors, as migrants form a bridge between their country of birth and their country of residence. Nationals of the country in question—who have a more direct stake in politics—may reside abroad and remain politically active while maintaining social ties to their country of origin. Although state agents are geographically constrained by territorial borders, the citizens of a state are relatively freer to cross national boundaries (see figure 1.1), and in doing so place themselves outside of the reach of the state. Migrants exit the state for a variety of reasons, including better economic prospects, political persecution, and family reunification. While living abroad, these diaspora communities[8] often continue to identify strongly with their homelands and participate in home-country affairs (on diasporas, see Albert, Jacobson, and Lapid 2001; Fox 2005; Shain 1989; Shain and Barth 2003; Sheffer 2003; Van Hear 1998). Political participation and identification with a distant homeland, or what has been termed "long-distance nationalism," creates a disjuncture between the physical boundaries of the state and the social boundaries of the nation (Anderson 1998).

Frequently, the relationship between the state and diaspora communities is mutually supportive. Migrants often send remittances to their home countries, work with governments to facilitate business investment, and support legitimate political parties (Brand 2006; Chakravartty 2001; Fitzgerald 2000; Guarnizo, Portes, and Haller 2003; Levitt and Dehesa 2003; Saxenian 2001). On the other side of the ledger, the home country's foreign policies sometimes work to protect the interests of its diaspora in their host countries (Brand 2006; King and Melvin 1999).[9] Some scholars have gone so far as to call expatriate political participation in home-country affairs "transnational citizenship," implying that states can offer, and emigrants can demand, political rights to those not physically present on their territory (see Faist 2000; Fox 2005; Waldinger and Fitzgerald 2004).

The literature on transnational migrant politics often overlooks politically contentious activities while focusing on legitimate civic participation. As Sidney Tarrow (2005) indicates, however, transnational actors, including migrant groups, can also engage in politically contentious activities. Figure 1.2 illustrates the different modes of immigrant participation in home-country

8. The term "diaspora" has several different meanings in the literature. In the original usage of the term, it applied to the displacement of Jews from the biblical land of Israel. Authors differ in their use of the term based on several criteria, including forced versus nonforced dispersal, the number of host countries, assimilation into host societies, multigenerational ties to the homeland, and the political relationship with the home government. Here, I use the term much more broadly, while focusing on the political identities of diaspora members. In particular, I define a diaspora as a community of people who have left a given homeland, either recently or historically, and who continue to identify politically with that homeland. Political identification is important in this study because, although people may identify with the culture of their ancestral homeland, they may or may not make political claims on the state(s) who control this territory.

9. To avoid confusion, "home," "sending," and "origin" country are used to refer to the state that people have left. This home country will also be referred to as the "target" country when referring to the opposition politics of dissident groups. "Host" and "receiving" countries are those states where these actors reside.

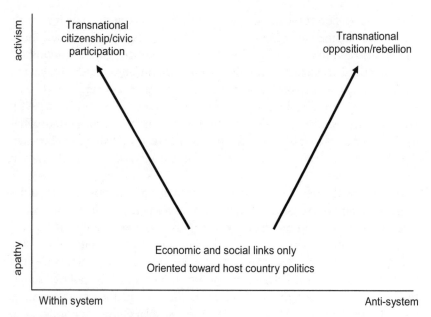

Figure 1.2. Immigrant participation in home country politics

politics. Certain diaspora groups, or individuals in the diaspora, may pay little attention to political affairs in their home countries. Such migrants may maintain family or economic links back home but remain apathetic about politics. These people may also demonstrate greater attention to, and participation in, the politics of their host countries, although host and home-country political participation need not be mutually exclusive affairs. Those migrants that do engage in home-country politics may contribute to what may broadly be termed "civic" activities or legal/legitimate political behavior that are within the constitutional system. Empirical work on transnational citizenship, such as expatriate voting or campaigning, has attempted to model the left-leaning arrow in figure 1.2 (see, e.g., Guarnizo, Portes, and Haller 2003). However, some members of the diaspora engage in unlawful or contentious political activities in opposition to the regime, such as supporting banned dissident parties (see, e.g., Adamson 2006; Lyons 2006; Tatla 1999).

What is important to appreciate about migrant diasporas, and indeed all transnational social groups and networks, is that these actors are beyond any one state's legal, political, and coercive reach. This gives such actors a strategic advantage over state agents who are not as mobile. Tacitly, most political science research assumes a perfect congruence between states and societies; social actors that make demands on the state are believed to lie within the boundaries of the state. All forms of transnational organization call this assumption into question. But even more starkly, the mobility of people across national boundaries implies that *not even all citizens* of the state—namely, persons over whom the state claims authority over and who have an interest in the nature of the regime in power—reside in the sovereign territory of the state, where they are subject to the state's laws.

Rebellion

While transnational firms, advocacy groups, and migrant associations often have relatively benign or positive effects, other transnational actors may be involved in disruptive acts.[10] Many migrant diasporas—particularly those who flee for political reasons—play an active role in opposing their home governments. Some ethnic groups, such as the Sikhs and the Kurds,[11] aspire to establish a national homeland separated from the territory of the state that exercises control over them, and have mobilized support for their cause among diaspora communities. Other migrant opposition groups—for example, Iranians and Cubans—work toward changing the central regime in power in their home countries. Albert Hirschman's (1970; 1978) classic work argues that people who are dissatisfied with the status quo can either exercise "voice," by expressing their discontent, or they can "exit" and leave the state. However, rather than mutually exclusive options, people who are dissatisfied with the state may exit the country but continue to be vocal in their opposition to the regime in their home country.

Perhaps most significantly, political opposition groups abroad may engage in the types of activities that the target government would never tolerate on its own soil (Salehyan 2007a). Because they cannot exercise authority outside of their political jurisdiction, the police and military forces of the home state cannot easily suppress these activities; thus, actors located abroad may engage in several forms of opposition politics that would normally be proscribed within the target state. In addition, although states devote considerable resources to the surveillance of domestic dissent, they are less able to monitor transnational groups. The limited extent to which state agents are able to gather intelligence abroad creates informational asymmetries between states

10. There is a related literature on transnational terrorism: see Arquilla and Ronfeldt (2001), Dorff (2005), and Enders and Sandler (1999). See also Bapat (2006), Byman et al. (2001), and Byman (2005) for a discussion of outside support for insurgencies and terrorist groups.

11. For a discussion of the Sikh diaspora and its political activism toward an independent Khalistan, see Axel (2001) and Tatla (1999). The political activities of the Kurdish diaspora in Europe are documented in Lyon and Ucarer (2001) and Wahlbeck (1999).

and challengers. Often, governments acquire only minimal knowledge of extraterritorial opposition activities and organizational structures. This has important implications for both counterinsurgency operations and bargaining outcomes, as will be discussed below.

Many forms of subversive acts occur abroad. First, opposition groups in foreign countries may create media outlets such as newspapers, radio broadcasts, satellite television stations, and internet websites to voice their views and mobilize discontent. These messages are directed at members of the diaspora as well as people inside the country. Cubans in the United States broadcast Radio Martí, an anti-Castro radio station, to the island; and Iranians in exile have created no fewer than eight opposition satellite channels.

Second, diaspora communities often provide funding and resources to opposition parties *within* their origin state. Sikhs, Tamils, and Kurds living in Europe have provided substantial resources to secessionist groups back home, and Irish-American groups in the United States have provided material support to Sinn Fein and the Irish Republican Army. Third, migrants living abroad may lobby their host government to make policy demands and impose negative sanctions on their home government in order to promote change. Both indigenous and migrant Tamils in India have pressured the government in New Delhi to take a more active role in the Sri Lankan conflict; similar Tamil lobbying has occurred across Europe. Cuban-American groups in the United States have sought to influence U.S. policies toward the Castro regime (Haney and Vanderbush 1999).

Finally, rebel organizations often find it useful to relocate themselves outside of the territorial borders of their target state. Rebel groups, particularly in their formative stages, must evade the state's capacity to repress dissent or else risk an early defeat. The initial process of rebel mobilization is extremely precarious because the opposition cannot survive a decisive attack. As noted above, the literature on political opportunity structures argues that state repression works to deter and eliminate insurgencies; limitations on the state's ability to repress dissidents is a necessary precondition for violence. Rational actors will not rebel if they believe that the probability of victory is low and repression will impose high costs for participation (Lichbach 1995; Tilly 1978). Using this framework, a substantial body of empirical research confirms the expectation that opposition violence is reduced when state coercion is robust (Fearon and Laitin 2003; Hegre et al. 2001; W. Moore 1998; Muller and Weede 1990). Therefore, conditions such as rough terrain, regime transitions, and poor infrastructure, which reduce the state's ability to repress challengers effectively, provide strategic opportunities for insurgent groups to emerge.

At times, domestic opportunities to mobilize supporters and resources will be sufficient; rebels may in fact prefer to remain within the state in order to stay close to their support base and to government targets. Yet there is no reason to expect that in the strategic calculations of rebel groups, opportunities to mobilize, launch, and sustain a rebellion are limited to the geographic area of the state. Instead, rebels recognize that state power is constrained by international borders and will shift some, or even most, activities abroad in order to evade repression, especially when domestic opportunities are blocked.[12] The establishment of extraterritorial bases allows rebels to recruit and train fighters, gather supplies during the mobilization phase, and flee to safe ground during the combat phase.[13]

Neighboring territory will be especially important for rebel operations. Insurgent groups do not have the ability to project force across long distances, and so proximity to the target country will be especially important for military purposes. TNRs may find recruits and support from diaspora communities and state patrons further abroad, but the ability to launch and sustain combat operations will critically depend on nearness to the target state.

Unlike the state, which already commands coercive power, rebel organizations must mobilize an army in order to issue and carry out threats if their demands are not met. Opportunities for rebel mobilization—either internal or external—thus raise the bargaining power of the opposition. As many scholars have argued (e.g., Bapat 2005; Fearon 2004; Lake 2003), rebels and governments engage in tacit or explicit bargaining over the distribution of benefits. Yet prior to mobilizing forces, rebel groups cannot credibly threaten to impose costs on the state; they have little bargaining power. Mobilization opportunities therefore raise rebel bargaining power and open up a bargaining space where force can be issued if concessions are not made. However, as argued below, transnational rebellion poses special challenges for the bargaining process because extraterritorial activities create an information-poor bargaining environment, make rebel demobilization promises less credible, and introduce new actors to the bargaining table.

---

12. We must be careful not to conflate migrants with transnational rebels. Only very few international migrants or refugees participate in violent activities. However, transnational rebels *are* migrants in the sense that they leave the territory of the state, even if it is to organize violence and return to attack the state. Thus, although TNRs are migrants, very few migrants are TNRs.

13. Empirically, Buhaug and Gates (2004) demonstrate that during periods of civil war, conflicts often are fought near international boundaries, providing at least preliminary evidence that border effects are important.

Before turning to conditions under which extraterritorial bases may emerge and their implications for the bargaining process, it is important to fully understand why they are tactically desirable. To begin with, when rebels have access to sanctuaries on external territory, governments cannot easily pursue them across the border, because doing so would violate the sovereignty of, and would risk a confrontation with, the neighboring state. Cross-border strikes by the government on foreign soil threaten the sovereignty and security of the neighboring country and are likely to provoke a wider conflict. Limited attacks against TNRs can and do occur across national boundaries—for example, Cambodian troops exchanged artillery fire with Khmer Rouge forces in Thailand, and Ugandan forces occasionally crossed into Sudan in pursuit of the Lord's Resistance Army. In these examples, however, the government whose sovereignty had been violated objected strongly and moved to fortify their borders against further raids. Thus, conflict with neighbors is one cost of cross-border counterinsurgency.

As another example, in December 2004, Colombian authorities bribed Venezuelan National Guardsman to arrest and return Rodrigo Granda, a leading operative of the rebel group Fuerzas Armadas Revolucionarias de Colombia (FARC), who had been residing in Caracas. Venezuela strongly protested the maneuver, insisting that its sovereignty had been violated. This incident caused a major diplomatic rift between the neighboring countries, as Venezuela temporarily recalled its ambassador in Bogotá and suspended commercial relations. In March 2008, Colombia sent troops into Ecuador to hit a rebel camp and kill a FARC commander, Raul Reyes. This sovereignty violation led both Ecuador and Venezuela to break diplomatic ties with Colombia and move troops near their respective borders.[14] Thus, even relatively minor intrusions or domestic interference by the security forces of another country in pursuit of TNRs have the potential to escalate into international crises.

A second reason a base in a neighboring state is desirable is that, even if a state is strong enough to extensively penetrate another country's territory and attempt to rid it of rebel groups, it would still incur significant governance costs in doing so.[15] To be successful, the invading state would have to take, hold, and police part or all of the neighboring country's territory, which is usually prohibitively costly. Thus, there are few clear examples of

14. See Simon Romero, "Crisis at Colombia Border Spills Into Diplomatic Realm," *New York Times*, March 4, 2008, section A.

15. Governance costs refer to the costs borne by a state in managing the affairs of a subordinate or occupied polity. For a discussion, see Lake 1996.

states that have attempted this strategy; when they have, it is usually at a significant cost to themselves. In an attempt to destroy the Palestinian resistance in 1982, for example, Israel invaded and held southern Lebanon after repeated attacks by the Palestine Liberation Organization across the border; in doing so, it quickly fell into conflict with local Lebanese militias, namely Hezbollah, for decades. In a similar manner, Rwanda invaded Zaire in pursuit of Hutu fighters, many of whom participated in the Rwandan genocide. In so doing, Rwanda became involved a protracted conflict in Zaire/Democratic Republic of the Congo—first it intervened against Mobutu Sese Seko and then again against Laurent Kabila—which proved to be extremely costly. In both of these examples, the governments viewed the rebels across the border as a threat to their existence and so were willing to bear the enormous costs of entering and occupying foreign territory.

Finally, although it is difficult to assess the importance of norms in the behavior of states,[16] the international community—through the UN Charter and several treaties—has repeatedly promulgated the principles of national sovereignty and territorial integrity. Border violations, even in pursuit of rebels, elicit international condemnation. For instance, in 1976 Rhodesian forces attacked the Nyadzonia refugee camp in Mozambique in pursuit of rebels who were allegedly mobilizing there, and in so doing drew substantial fire from the international community. Border violations have also been the focus of numerous UN Security Council resolutions, demonstrating the international consensus against such acts. For instance, after Israel's invasion of Lebanon, UN Resolution 509 (June 6, 1982) states, "Reaffirming the need for strict respect for the territorial integrity, sovereignty and political independence of Lebanon . . . [the Council] demands that Israel withdraw all its military forces forthwith and unconditionally to the internationally recognized boundaries of Lebanon." In a similar resolution against Rwanda and Uganda, UN Resolution 1304 (June 16, 2000) demanded that, "Uganda and Rwanda, which have violated the sovereignty and territorial integrity of the Democratic Republic of the Congo, withdraw all of their forces . . . without further delay." In these examples, the offending government clearly did not withdraw their troops. Faced with serious threats across their borders, these states were willing to put up with disapproval of their actions; but international censure is certainly one cost that such tactics entail, and it can often be coupled with more concrete international sanctions.

---

16. For a discussion of international norms in the foreign policy behavior of states, see Katzenstein 1996 and Rosenblum and Salehyan 2004.

The argument is not an absolute one: international borders are not sacrosanct. Nevertheless, it is quite costly for state forces to cross national boundaries in pursuit of transnational rebels, and doing so may not even be an option for governments that lack the ability to confront their neighbors. Therefore, extraterritorial bases provide rebel groups with substantial cover in evading security forces, both while mobilizing insurgents and during combat operations.

Neighboring States as Sanctuary for Rebel Groups

Refugees

Under what conditions are neighboring states likely to be used by rebel groups? As mentioned earlier, access to *neighboring* territory will be especially important for organized rebellion. Although protest activity against the state may take place more broadly, proximity to the target is important for the military operations of rebel groups. First, migrants in neighboring countries, particularly refugees, may contribute to opposition activities. Oppressive governments and political violence have been demonstrated to be an important cause of refugee outflows (Azam and Hoeffler 2002; Davenport, Moore, and Poe 2003; Moore and Shellman 2004; Schmeidl 1997; Weiner 1996), and the vast majority of the world's refugees end up in states near their country of origin. Refugees in particular exit the state because of a direct experience of persecution or political violence and therefore have strong reasons to oppose the regime from which they have fled.[17] Although refugees are of course victims of violence, they are also prime candidates for recruitment involvement in rebel factions. Rather than simply being a *consequence* of fighting, they may also be contributors to conflict.[18] Because they have suffered violence and have often endured substantial losses—their livelihoods,

17. Refugees flee their origin country for a variety of reasons that are not limited to direct government persecution. Many individuals flee a region because of general conditions of violence in their origin country and have no particular stake in the politics between the government and opposition. However, a substantial subset of any refugee exodus is likely to include people who flee because of *direct* grievances against the state. For a discussion, see Lischer 2005.

18. Several theoretical works suggest a number of ways in which refugees, and migrants in general, can cause conflict. First, refugees may foster conflict in the *host country* through their direct involvement in violent activities or through their impact on the economy and ethnic relations. Second, refugees may cause conflict *between sending and receiving countries*, because providing shelter to refugees may be seen as harboring dissidents and implicates the sending country in the commission of human rights violations. Finally, refugees may cause conflict in their *home country* through participation in armed factions. For examples of this literature see Lischer 2005, Loescher 1993, Teitelbaum 1984, and Weiner 1992–1993.

property, family members, and homeland—refugees have clear grievances or motives for opposition activities. Moreover, because of these losses, refugees have low opportunity costs for fighting. Those refugees residing in squalid camps and who are dependent on foreign assistance have very few productive alternatives to joining rebel organizations, which may offer a better quality of life and a sense of purpose.[19] Finally, because they are not within their home state's political jurisdiction, the state cannot directly monitor or repress refugee communities.

This should not detract from the legitimate humanitarian concerns that refugee migration entails. The majority of the world's refugees never engage in fighting and are rightly characterized as victims. However, refugees are also not passive actors. Rather, they can and do participate in politics in both their home and host countries, including through violence (see Salehyan 2007b). Understanding security risks potentially resulting from refugee crises will assist in developing more effective policy responses.

A large body of case-study literature and qualitative accounts demonstrate this "refugee warrior" phenomenon (Lischer 2005; Stedman and Tanner 2003; Teitelbaum 1984; Weiner 1992–1993; Zolberg, Suhrke, and Aguayo 1989), but systematic quantitative research on this topic has been lacking.[20] A number of anecdotal cases serve to illustrate the relationship between refugee communities and violence: Cuban exiles in the United States organized the Bay of Pigs invasion of 1961; refugees from Rhodesia in Mozambique and Zambia supported the ZANU and ZAPU rebels; and Nicaraguan Contras turned to refugee communities in Honduras for resources and recruits. More recently, the Rwandan Patriotic Front organized among Tutsi refugees in Uganda; refugees in Chad from the Sudanese region of Darfur have backed various armed factions; and the United Tajik Opposition conducted significant operations among refugee camps in Afghanistan. Thus, although refugee camps are often thought of as shelters for the displaced, they may also serve a double purpose as bases where TNRs find relief and gather supplies and recruits.

To give a sense of the pervasiveness of refugee migration, figure 1.3 displays the countries of origin of refugees in 2000, with darker regions indi-

---

19. A number of authors have begun to examine the issue of rebel recruitment. See, for example, Gates 2002 and Weinstein 2005. Achvarina and Reich (2006) argue that refugee camps are especially attractive locations for the recruitment of child soldiers.

20. Although the argument here is that refugees contribute to conflict in their *home* countries, Salehyan and Gleditsch (2006) have found through large-N empirical testing that refugees often lead to the onset of civil conflict in their *host* countries, confirming the expectation that refugees are one mechanism of conflict diffusion across regions.

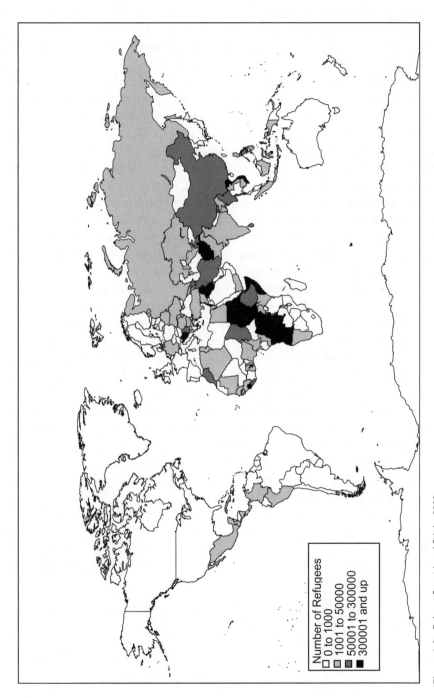

Figure 1.3. Refugee Countries of Origin, 2000.

Number of Refugees

☐ 0 to 1000
☐ 1001 to 50000
▨ 50001 to 300000
■ 300001 and up

cating greater numbers. Countries such as Afghanistan and Israel/Palestine each generated millions of refugees, who overwhelmingly resided in adjacent countries (Iran and Pakistan for Afghans; Lebanon, Jordan, and Syria for Palestinians). Other significant refugee source countries included the Democratic Republic of the Congo, Iraq, Sudan, and Burma. Roughly 10 percent of Afghans resided outside of their country in 2000; in the same year, approximately 22 percent of the non-Arab Sudanese population were refugees. Figure 1.4 graphs the number of refugees worldwide from 1980 to 2002. There was a significant peak in the early 1990s, which was largely due to new conflicts at the end of the Cold War—in, for example, Yugoslavia, Azerbaijan, Georgia, and Tajikistan—and the elimination of exit restrictions in Eastern Europe, which prompted a rise in the number of asylum seekers in Western countries. The number of refugees during this period ranged between 10 and 18 million, which is larger than the population of several countries. Although the vast majority of these refugees never engage in violence, a politically significant subset is recruited into, or supports, TNRs.

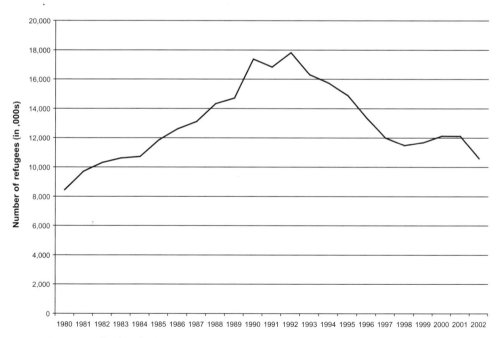

Figure 1.4. Number of refugees worldwide, 1980–2002. *Source:* United Nations High Commissioner for Refugees

Rival States

During periods of civil war, scholars have noted that rebel organizations and governments often receive substantial external support by foreign patrons who have a stake in the conflict (Byman 2005; Elbadawi and Sambanis 2002; Forman 1972; Regan 2000; Rosenau 1964). However, external support during "proxy wars" is not limited to the provision of resources and direct military intervention. Hostile neighbors may also allow rebel groups to establish extraterritorial bases on their soil in order to undermine their opponents. Rebel groups strategically form alliances with hostile neighbors to fight a mutual enemy across the border. Foreign rivals may delegate conflict to nonstate actors as a foreign policy tool. Thus, although many rivals attack their foreign enemies with their own forces, others substitute direct confrontation with acting through a proxy (Salehyan 2008). Destabilizing neighbors can be a goal in itself or it can be used to weaken a state in order to gain the upper hand in international disputes. Therefore, sanctuary is an important strategic asset that rival governments can offer rebel groups.

This relationship between civil and international conflict becomes even more intertwined in cases of irredentism, when the neighboring country supports ethnic rebels in order to annex disputed territory. For instance, Pakistan has backed Kashmiri insurgent groups and Somalia has supported Ethiopian rebels in the Ogaden region in order to assume control over areas populated by ethnic kin. In such cases, the rival state and the insurgents share overlapping agendas, and these disputes may be particularly hard to resolve if the patron state views the territory as particularly important for strategic reasons or as part of the national identity. Nonetheless, state actors choose to empower rebel organizations as a tactic toward securing territory rather than relying exclusively on their own military efforts.

Moreover, international borders between rival governments are likely to be especially "hard," or defended against incursions by neighboring state security forces. Hostile states view one another with suspicion and will fortify their borders against any intrusion, however limited. Because states cannot be sure of one another's intentions, actions taken to increase military presence near the border—even if only to limit movements by TNRs—are likely to be seen as threatening and will invite countervailing measures.[21] Additionally, in order to damage their rivals, host governments may provide resources, training opportunities, and logistical support to rebel groups; some

21. This presents security dilemma worries (see Jervis 1978).

even go so far as to use their own troops in joint operations with the rebels, blurring the line between civil and international war.

For example, during the Iran-Iraq War, Iran offered sanctuary to members of the Supreme Council for the Islamic Revolution in Iraq; likewise, Iraq was host to the Iranian militant group the Mujahedin-e-Khalq (see chapter 3). Long after their war ended, these two states continued to back one another's rebels, substituting direct hostilities with support for insurgents. Pakistan, a long-time enemy of India, offered training grounds and rear bases to Indian rebels in both Punjab and Kashmir. In the early 1970s, India had backed separatists in East Pakistan (Bangladesh). Although these states sometimes fought directly, they also used indirect means to destabilize each other. Finally, Thailand allowed Cambodian opposition forces to establish extraterritorial bases on its territory and provided them with substantial protection against Cambodian government forces by fortifying its borders. More directly, several rival governments have invaded their enemies alongside rebel movements that they had supported and trained on their soil. Libya invaded Chad along with Frolinat rebels who had organized on Libyan territory, and Tanzania invaded Uganda to oust Idi Amin along with rebels of the United National Liberation Front. In these cases, the invading state worked along with domestic insurgents, who had better local knowledge and domestic legitimacy.

Weak States

Several states lack adequate resources, personnel, and infrastructure to be able to police their territory effectively. These so-called "weak states" come to play reluctant hosts to TNRs because of their inability to rid their soil of such groups. Several governments only effectively control their capital cities but lack any substantial presence in, or ability to penetrate, peripheral areas. In the context of transnational terrorism, scholars have observed that terrorist groups often find opportunities for mobilization in failed or collapsed states (Bapat 2006; Dorff 2005; Rice 2003). Weak neighbors provide strategic opportunities for TNRs because although the host government may not welcome the TNR, it faces high opportunity costs for trying to deal with what is perceived as another state's problem. These host states will be reluctant to redirect significant resources away from more pressing domestic concerns, including monitoring and suppressing *local* dissent.

In some cases, provided that the host does not sympathize with the rebels, the target and host state may work together to limit TNR activity. The host state may offer some policing of its own, allow limited cross-border strikes against the rebels, and may not feel threatened by troop mobilization near the border with its neighbor. In addition, as opposed to rival neighbors, weak states do not necessarily have an interest in prolonging conflicts in neighboring countries. But although there may be limited security cooperation, more extensive counterinsurgency campaigns across the border by the target state are not likely to be welcomed because they necessarily threaten sovereignty of the host government and the security of local populations. The target government is limited in its response to TNRs by its diplomatic relations with its neighbor, and rebels are relatively safer in such countries as opposed to within the target state itself. Moreover, cooperating with host states involves transaction costs, as states must negotiate the acceptable range of action, the function of each nation's forces, and limitations on cross-border counterinsurgency. Frictions may also arise if counterinsurgency actions by other states unduly threaten locals in the host country.

After the collapse of the government in Somalia, the Ethiopian rebel faction Al-Ittihad Al-Islami established bases there. The government of Bhutan, despite trying to maintain friendly relations and cooperating with India, found it difficult to rid its territory of Assamese rebel groups. After the U.S. invasion of Afghanistan, Taliban forces have regrouped in remote areas of Pakistan, despite Pakistan's outward cooperation with U.S. forces. Attacking combatants in the tribal areas of Pakistan has been difficult as U.S., NATO, and Afghan forces cannot cross the border, and the Pakistani government lacks power and authority in these regions, where local leaders are strong.

The Conditional Effect of Refugees

Although refugee encampments may be used by rebels in their efforts to conduct an insurgency, the effect of refugees may be contingent on their location. In particular, well-governed countries that are on good terms with their neighbors can work to prevent the militarization of refugee communities (Lischer 2005). Efforts to provide security and productive livelihoods to refugees, screen against combatants, and integrate refugees into host countries can mitigate the security risks of refugee camps. For example, Malawi received over one million refugees from Mozambique, but worked with aid agencies to limit the militarization of camps and to move the refugees toward self-sufficiency. Providing long-term refugee communities with their basic needs and allowing them to access local employment options is likely to be especially important, because such efforts raise the opportunity costs for recruitment into rebel organizations.

By contrast, disorderly camp conditions in which the host government is unable to prevent rebel infiltration will be more conducive to violence, as will cases where rival governments actively encourage rebel mobilization among refugees (Stedman and Tanner 2003). As an example of the latter, Honduras—which was opposed to the Sandinista government in Nicaragua—encouraged Nicaraguan refugees to reside in camps along the border and allowed various Contra factions to mobilize within these camps, even as it placed restrictions on Salvadoran refugees thought to be sympathetic to leftist groups (Hartigan 1992). Humanitarian NGOs and the United Nations High Commissioner for Refugees are limited in their ability to provide security without the cooperation of the host government, as responsibility for security largely falls on the asylum country. Thus, refugees located in weak or rival states will be more likely to contribute to violence than refugees located in states that are friendly and capable of governing camps effectively.

Extraterritorial Mobilization and Conflict Bargaining

States and rebels should prefer a negotiated settlement—thus avoiding a long and bloody war—which would leave them both better off. War is costly and can be avoided if actors agree on a suitable distribution of benefits. Opportunities for external mobilization raise the bargaining power of opposition groups by making it more difficult for the government to win a decisive victory and by giving rebels time to mobilize forces in relative safety. Weak neighbors, rival neighbors, and refugee communities in which to mobilize can improve bargaining outcomes for rebels, but these factors are common knowledge to both parties. States and rebels should simply update their beliefs about the probability of victory and adjust their demands accordingly. Commonly known information should not lead to war (Fearon 1995). In addition, once fighting breaks out, information revealed on the battlefield should facilitate a negotiated settlement (Filson and Werner 2002; Wagner 2000).

One source of bargaining failure occurs when actors do not agree on the distribution of realized or potential power between them (Fearon 1995; Powell 1999); actors believe that they can do better through fighting than by accepting a proposed settlement. Uncertainty about the end-point of rebel mobilization is a common feature of all civil conflicts, whether or not rebels are transnational. Rebels must mobilize strength in order to win concessions. But there may be disagreement about the mobilization potential of the rebels at some future point, and gathering resources and recruits may itself be a violent process (e.g., through theft and conscription). Early on in a conflict, governments may not offer formal negotiations to weak rebels, hoping that they can secure a decisive victory (Bapat 2005). Yet even in early stages, there is a *tacit* bargain between governments and rebels over the distribution of benefits. Governments can offer aggrieved groups enough concessions or reforms to avoid or stop violence. If both sides agree on the *future* power of the challenger and its ability to survive government attacks, the state should be able to offer sufficient concessions, but the future is inherently more uncertain than the present. Therefore, uncertainty about the future power of the challenger makes civil conflict considerably more difficult to resolve through an *ex ante* bargain.

Transnational rebellions introduce another important source of uncertainty. States have greater capacity to monitor activities at home than they do abroad. They devote significant resources toward establishing domestic intelligence and surveillance capabilities; have networks of informers; and access to sophisticated monitoring equipment. Information on the external operations of rebels is inherently difficult for states to monitor and verify because the state often lacks the ability to gather intelligence abroad, particularly in unfamiliar areas. As Byman (2005, 70) writes, "In general, it is far easier to place spies and informants in areas where the government controls territory." Thus, information about transnational rebels is relatively scarce. This lack of rich information has typically been viewed as an obstacle to effective counterinsurgency. Although this is certainly true, poor information is also an impediment to bargaining because it becomes difficult for actors to gauge their relative capabilities.

Rebels may try to signal their strength to the government, but because the state knows that the opposition has an incentive to overstate its capabilities in order to win more than they would otherwise, such information is not reliable and cannot be verified (see Fearon 1995). Furthermore, rebels cannot reveal too much about their operations and tactics, because doing so would leave them at a military disadvantage. Thus, the first source of bargaining failure in transnational insurgencies is that they exacerbate informational problems commonly associated with conflict.

A second source of bargaining failure is that transnational rebellion makes credible commitment problems more difficult to resolve. As opposed to an international war, peace deals to end a civil war require rebels to demobilize and disarm their fighters and, by extension, to disband their external bases (Walter 2002). Because of difficulties in gathering information abroad, however, the state cannot be certain if full compliance with demobilization agreements has taken place. Just as it is difficult for states to monitor and verify rebel mobilization in other states, it is also difficult to verify compliance with demobilization agreements. Rebels may be able to hide armaments and supplies across the border in order to regroup at some point in the future, and the state has little reliable information about the extent of compliance. Offering concessions to the opposition without being confident that it will abide by its part of the bargain would leave the state worse-off than continuing to fight. Thus, verification of demobilization abroad is difficult to conduct without the cooperation of host governments. As long as permissive conditions in neighboring countries persist, rebels can reestablish their forces across the border.

Third, external rebel mobilization introduces new actors—rebel host states—into the bargaining environment. Multiple actors in the bargaining processes complicate negotiations by introducing a new set of preferences that must be satisfied and that can block progress on peace negotiations (Cunningham 2006; Stedman 1997). As Bapat (2006) argues, states have little reason to believe promises made by transnational nonstate actors, making negotiations difficult. Therefore, in order for rebel promises to be credible, host states must offer credible commitments of their own to limit rebel activities on their soil and ensure that these groups live up to their part of the deal. These states may be unwilling or, because of weakness, unable to provide necessary guarantees to the target state and can block negotiations between combatants. They can use rebel access as bargaining leverage to advance their own agendas, particularly if international rivalries exist. Thus, the bargaining environment becomes more complicated as two-actor bargains are expanded to include rebel hosts; these hosts can block agreements if the underlying permissive conditions allowing rebel access are not resolved.

Additionally, external signals of support for opposition groups may in fact make internal conflicts worse. Erin Jenne (2006) finds that when ethnic kin in neighboring states threaten to come to the aid of their brethren, emboldened minority groups are more likely to make extreme demands, risking an escalation of violence. Similarly, Thyne (2006) argues that domestic opposition groups increase their bargaining strength if foreign actors promise to assist them but that such signals may provoke conflict by leading rebels to issue stronger demands than the government is willing to accept. Thus, the inclusion of additional parties to the bargaining environment can make it more difficult to find an acceptable settlement because external patronage alters expectations about the domestic balance of power.

Although bargaining processes have become central to the study of international and civil war, empirically testing propositions about bargaining failure is inherently difficult. It is difficult for outside observers to gauge the level of information available to actors or to assess the perceived credibility of promises (see Gartzke 1999). For quantitative analyses (see chapters 2 and 3), we may, however, observe background conditions that are more likely to contribute to bargaining problems. These conditions, in turn, raise the probability that war will occur, even if we cannot make deterministic statements about whether or not war will break out. Case studies (see chapters 4 and 5) can then shed light on additional features of the bargaining process.

The Internationalization of Civil Conflict

Transnational rebellion has important implications for relations between target and host states. Indeed, transnational rebellions are fuelled by international rivalries and, in turn, contribute to regional conflicts. When TNRs have access to extraterritorial bases across the border, domestic conflicts necessarily become the subject of state-to-state relations at the regional level. Once bases are established in neighboring territories—with or without the consent of the host—tensions are likely to arise between states. Target governments will blame hosts for harboring dissidents and creating security risks. Target governments cannot be entirely certain of host governments' motivations or degree of support for the rebels and may launch retaliatory attacks. Weak neighbors may not be trying hard enough to combat rebels on their soil; rival neighbors may be contributing arms and resources in addition to sanctuary. Cross-border counterinsurgency attempts may also spark international hostilities if the host objects to border violations.

Therefore, civil wars and international disputes are intrinsically linked rather than separate processes. They are part of an endogenous, regional conflict nexus whereby international hostilities are generated by rebel sanctuaries and support, and preexisting animosities between states empower rebel organizations. The whole is greater than the sum of its parts. Civil wars and international conflicts combine to create broader, interlinked processes of contention and violence. Despite the pervasiveness of TNRs, most research on the causes of international disputes fails to take into account issues arising from civil conflicts (for exceptions see Davies 2002; Gleditsch, Salehyan, and Schultz 2008; Salehyan 2008; Walt 1996). The large body of international relations research on the causes of war typically focuses on dyadic relations between pairs of states while ignoring the role that transnational actors play in conflict processes. Moreover, most research focuses on constraints on the use of force among a particular dyad when disputes arise rather than on the issues at stake. Such constraints include joint democracy, trade interdependence, and power asymmetries (see e.g. Bueno de Mesquita et al. 1999; Oneal and Russett 2001; Bennett and Stam 1998; Bremer 1992; Scheider, Barbieri, and Gleditsch 2003; Schultz 2001). But this literature does little to elucidate the sources of international tension.

Bargaining models (e.g., Fearon 1995; Powell 1999) typically assume that states come into conflict over the distribution of some resource such as territory, but this is not tested explicitly. A growing empirical literature recently has examined the types of issues that lead to war. Yet these studies have also tended to focus on distributional issues, particularly the allocation of territory and water resources (Hensel 2001; Hensel, Mitchell, and Sowers 2006; Vasquez 1995). But this research also ignores linkages between civil and international conflicts and fails to consider nonstate actors as contributors to disputes between states.

One important exception is the research on transnational ethnic ties as a source of international conflict (Cetinyan 2002; Davis and Moore 1997; Jenne 2006; Saideman 2001, 2002; Trumbore 2003; Woodwell 2004). This research finds that states will often intervene in other countries' civil conflicts in order to protect their ethnic kin when ethnic groups span national boundaries. By introducing transnational actors as a source of interstate disputes, this literature makes an important contribution to the study of international conflict, but it is limited to ethnic groups that span borders.

Despite work on foreign intervention in civil war (see, e.g., Regan 2000), scholars have not considered the possibility that external support for rebel organizations, whether tacit or explicit, may lead to international hostilities between states. Hosting rebel organizations on one's territory is a quite common form of external support for insurgencies and is especially likely to lead to interstate armed conflict because, as opposed to material resources that can be delivered across long distances, external bases are typically located in contiguous countries. Thus, rebel hosting provides opportunities for violent interactions, whereas distant patrons may be outside of the target state's reach.

Thus, transnational rebellions are a major source of international conflict and can sometimes lead to armed violence between states. First, the rebel home state may retaliate against the host for providing sanctuary to dissident groups. Home countries will demand that the host state expel TNRs, or at least restrict their activities, and can threaten to use force in order to gain compliance. At times, rebel host states do cooperate to evict rebel organizations. For instance, after several incidents of cross-border fighting between Palestinian groups and Israel and Israeli threats against Jordan, the government of Jordan agreed to expel militant organizations from its territory in 1970. Yet weak rebel hosts may not have the capacity to evict TNRs on their territory, despite target state threats (the choice for rival hosts is different and will be discussed in the next section). Such states are faced with difficult options. They can take costly actions to drive out foreign rebels, which are likely to involve aggressive military assaults, cost lives and resources, and divert attention away from domestic policing. Otherwise, they risk attacks by their neighbors. Rebel home governments, for their part, may attack the host in order to increase the costs for continued hosting and, at the extreme, replace the government with one of its liking. Thus, weak rebel hosts may be drawn into international conflicts that are not of their choosing. Because of rebel hosts' inability to comply with demands to evict TNRs, effective bargaining to resolve the international dispute is not feasible.

For instance, after Palestinian militants left Jordan, they established bases in Lebanon, which the Lebanese government was too weak to prevent because of internal divisions in the government. This prompted Israel to invade Lebanon in 1982 in order to root out their bases and support their preferred government. Similarly, although Al-Qaeda may be unique for its global reach, the United States invaded Afghanistan after the Taliban government proved unwilling or unable to hand over Al-Qaeda leaders. In these cases, bargaining with the rebel host state was difficult because it was not able to comply with the target government's demands. The costs of expelling rebels exceeded the potential costs of retaliatory strikes.

Transnational rebellion can also lead to international armed conflict when governments launch limited strikes on foreign territory, despite the costly nature of cross-border counterinsurgency. Although they present a substantial impediment to the extension of state power, borders are not completely inviolable. Cross-border fighting, stray fire, damage to infrastructure near the frontier, and "hot pursuit" raids are likely to provoke international tensions, as the security and stability of the host government are threatened. Unlike direct retaliation against the host government, incursions across borders are directed at rebels themselves, although border violations and conflict spillovers affecting local populations will often be protested and sometimes responded to forcefully. For instance, on several occasions, Venezuela complained about Colombia's violations of their mutual border as Colombian armed forces attacked FARC rebels. Chadian soldiers also clashed with Sudanese forces after pursuing rebels across their frontier.[22] In sum, international conflicts are likely to arise between states

22. BBC News Online, "Chad Admits Battle Inside Sudan," April 10, 2007.

when neighbors threaten or use force against rebel hosts and when cross-border attacks generate protests over sovereignty violations.

Rival Hosts and International Conflict

Unlike weak rebel hosts, which may be drawn into wars not of their own choosing, rival host states deliberately choose to support TNRs. In these cases, hosting rebel organizations is indicative of preexisting conflict between states, although support for insurgency will exacerbate international tensions. There is a large body of literature on international rivalries and reoccurring conflict among particular dyads (Colaresi and Thompson 2002; Diehl and Goertz 2000; Thompson 2001). Usually it is assumed that in cases of rivalry, states will confront one another directly, using their own military forces. Yet in many instances states choose to foment insurgencies in their international opponents rather than directly use force. During the Cold War, for instance, the superpowers often did not invade hostile governments directly, but rather provided material support to insurgent groups and pursued wars by proxy forces. Thus, foreign support for insurgencies is an example of security delegation, where a principal (the patron state) empowers an agent (the rebel group) to carry out some foreign policy objective (on delegation, see Kiewiet and McCubbins 1991). Instead of, or as a complement to, directly using force against their enemies, states can choose to support rebel groups, including by providing sanctuary on their territory.

Delegation to a rebel organization entails costs and benefits. There is a trade-off between use of the state's own military resources and maintaining control over foreign policy. International military disputes cost resources and lives for the state, and they may invite the intervention of the target's international allies and supporters. Acts of direct state aggression are also likely to draw wider international condemnation. In many cases, states deny supporting rebel groups as a way to avoid these costs and diplomatic problems, as well as to avert potential criticism by domestic actors. In addition, if a state does not intend to govern the country after a successful invasion, it can delegate to a rebel organization, which will assume command of the invaded state after the incumbent regime is removed. The rival will not have to bear governance costs. Finally, rebel groups may have informational advantages over foreign troops. Rebels typically have better knowledge about the terrain, population, and government strategies as compared with foreign forces that lack local roots.

On the other hand, states lose some foreign policy discretion when they delegate conflict to a rebel group. They frequently have greater resources and military capabilities relative to rebel groups, and so direct invasion may entail a greater likelihood of defeating the enemy. More important, delegation may lead to "agency slack," in which the agent takes actions that are not consistent with the principal's preferences. By delegating conflict to a rebel organization, particularly if it is not feasible to effectively screen groups to ensure reliability *ex ante*, states lose foreign policy autonomy and the ability to direct the conflict. The rebel group may not be competent, may engage in actions which are seen as too extreme, may adopt strategies or policies not to the patron's liking, or may even turn on the patron completely using the resources that it had been provided.

As an example of delegation gone awry, Rwanda supported Laurent Kabila's rebel forces to remove the government of Mobutu Sese Seko in Zaire/Congo. Rwanda hoped to install a friendly regime, but Kabila turned on his former patron, which led Rwanda to invade the Congo once more. This book will not examine the choice between direct military contests and delegation to rebel groups, focusing instead on the implications of rebel hosting once the decision to host has been made. Suffice it to say that rebel empowerment can be a very useful foreign policy tool, and one that many states employ.

Tensions between states will arise if and when the rebel home state demands that the host evicts or limits the TNR. Rebel hosting serves to further fuel the international rivalry. Target states threaten to launch reprisal attacks against the host state in order to gain compliance with its demands. Here, bargaining fails because the benefits of maintaining domestic instability in one's rival outweigh the potential costs of retaliatory attacks (see Byman 2005; Bapat 2007). As Byman (2005, 260) writes, "Many of the possible punishments are accepted in advance, making it less surprising that the application of these punishments often fails to change the sponsor's behavior." Rival states anticipate the costs of retaliation and choose to host rebel groups anyway. By expelling rebels, rival states give up an important foreign policy tool and means of weakening their opponents, which they may not find acceptable.

In addition, rival states are especially likely to view one another with suspicion. The rebel target state may move troops near the international border to combat rebel organizations, yet these troop deployments are likely to be seen as threatening and may escalate to international conflict, even if they are not intended as such. Moreover, cross-border counterinsurgency raids, however limited, will be seen as provocative and can ignite direct state-to-state military clashes.

Delegation to rebel groups and hosting TNRs rather than confronting one's international enemies through the direct use of force suggests a substitution effect between international conflict and patronage of rebels (on substitution, see Morgan and Palmer 2000; Most and Starr 1984). Therefore, somewhat counterintuitively, we may witness less *direct* violence between the armed forces of rival states when governments shift some or all of their aggressive behavior to rebel agents. For instance, Honduras and Nicaragua—considered to be international enemies during the 1980s—never fought a war against one another, but Honduras empowered the Contra rebels to attack the Sandinista government from bases across the border. This is not to say that armed conflicts between rivals that delegate to rebels never occur, only that a share of the conflict behavior is conducted through proxies. We may still witness international violence in these cases, but less than we would otherwise see if hostile governments only relied on their own forces. In short, fewer direct clashes between the armed forces of rival states will take place when some military operations are delegated to rebel groups.

In addition to pure substitution effects, insurgent groups may also complement the state's military forces during an international invasion, as foreign troops and domestic rebels fight side-by-side. Rival states may support rebel groups in order to weaken their opponents in preparation for an international attack, and the invading government can benefit from the rebel's knowledge of the local terrain and population. Fighting alongside domestic groups can also add legitimacy and a local "face" to the operation. In such a manner, Tanzanian troops, alongside a Ugandan rebel force—the National Liberation Army—invaded Uganda in 1979 to oust the government of Idi Amin. But even when serving in complementary roles, delegation to rebel organizations still shifts some of the international conflict behavior to the agent, and we should witness fewer direct battles between government troops. Rather than wholly employing state forces, joint operations between states and rebel groups mean that some of the conflict is not directly between state personnel.

Possibilities for Conflict Resolution

This book focuses mainly on the causes of civil conflict, its duration, and the internationalization of rebellion. Based on the discussion above, however, what can be said about conflict resolution? Under what conditions do conflicts involving TNRs come to an end, either through outcomes on the battlefield or negotiations at the bargaining table? Conflict can either end in rebel victory, government victory, or a negotiated settlement (Mason, Weingarten, and Fett 1999). Although this book does not include quantitative empirical testing of conflict resolution processes because of limitations on data, it is important at least to consider the possible implications of the theory for ending civil wars and to develop a set of plausible hypotheses. This can aid in future research as well as in developing appropriate policy responses. In subsequent case-study chapters, I will come back to the topic of conflict resolution and probe the plausibility of the claims made here.

The empirical and theoretical scholarship on the resolution of civil conflict (Fortna 2004; Hartzell, Hoddie, and Rothchild 2001; Mason, Weingarten, and Fett 1999; Walter 1997, 2002; Zartman 1985) has normally looked at rebel-government interactions. Although Walter (1997, 2002) argues that third-party security guarantees make negotiated settlements more likely by alleviating the security fears of combatants under demobilization plans, the focus has primarily been on bargaining problems between governments and rebels. As argued above, however, for transnational rebellions it is more appropriate to characterize negotiations as a three-actor bargain between rebels, governments, and host states (see also Bapat 2006, 2007; Jenne 2006). To end civil wars, therefore, regional cooperation involving rebel host states is critical. Armed conflict is more likely to come to an end when host states agree to limit rebel access to their territory or if they cooperate in implementing a peace deal. Peace negotiations including TNRs entail multiple levels of interaction involving bargains between rebels and their target state, rebels and their host state, and agreements between the states themselves.

The preferences of the target government and the rebels are fairly clear. The target government prefers to fight the rebels on its own territory, where it has a comparative advantage in repressive capabilities. They will pressure the host government to push rebels off of its soil, thereby removing their tactical cover. Rebels wish to maintain bases across the border from which to continue mobilizing and attacking the target government. The preferences of the host government, however, will vary depending on its relationship with each side, the costs of allowing rebels access, and the costs of attempting to expel them. Thus, the preferences and commitments of the rebel host state are critical for negotiations. Agreements between rebels and their target government will only be credible if the host cooperates to limit rebel activities, verify the demobilization process, and provide guarantees of nonuse of its territory. In other words, the rebel host must demonstrate its willingness and capability to disallow sanctuary.

Important factors influencing this decision are the foreign-policy relationship between the target and the host country and the host's affinity for the rebel's aims. When the host country is hostile to the target state (and sympathetic to the rebels), its preference for a government victory is low.

Under these conditions, rival neighbors have a strong incentive to continue to allow rebels access to their territory in order to undermine their opponents. In contrast, host governments that are friendly but perhaps too weak to prevent rebel access will not side with the rebels very strongly, if at all.

In addition to preferences for a rebel or government victory, states must consider the relative costs of expelling or continuing to harbor TNRs. Attempting to expel rebels can provoke direct fighting between the rebel faction and the host government[23] and will entail a diversion of resources toward that end. However, continuing to allow rebel access to the state's territory leads to bilateral tensions and conflict between neighbors, and any cross-border attacks by the target government in pursuit of rebels jeopardizes the security of the host country and the safety of local populations. Quite simply, rebel host countries will agree to limit TNR activities when the benefits of hosting rebels are outweighed by the costs. The expected benefit of hosting rebels is a function of the host's preference for a rebel victory (or distaste for government victory) minus the costs of conflict with neighbors; the expected benefit of evicting rebels is a function of the state's preference for a government victory (or distaste for a rebel victory) minus the costs of expulsion.

Conflict can end in several ways. First, the rebels may reenter their own country, successfully defeat the government, and gain power, or in the case of a secessionist movement, win independence. Yet, for victory, rebels will not be able to rely on external sanctuary alone. Extraterritorial bases can provide relatively weak rebel groups a period of incubation while they gather strength. Yet if they are to succeed, rebels must at some point be able to take and hold significant areas of their country's territory. This will mainly be a function of the local support that rebels enjoy, the weakness of the target state, and conditions on the battlefield (see Kalyvas 2006).

Barring this, a second possible ending is for the government to defeat the rebels. As long as rebels have continued access to extraterritorial bases, the probability of successful repression is low and conflict will endure. Therefore, conflict is more likely to end in government victory if the host decides to expel rebels from its territory, which allows the target to wield its power more effectively. This may happen if several conditions change in the host state:

1. The target and host governments improve relations with one another. If states end their mutual antagonism and improve bilateral

---

23. For example, in 1970 Jordan and various Palestinian militias fought over continued rebel access to Jordanian soil. This event, known as Black September, caused hundreds of deaths on each side but forced the PLO and other groups out of Jordan.

relations, the host state will be less inclined to work toward a rebel victory and will cooperate to limit TNR presence.
2. The host government improves its capacity to restrict TNR activities, thereby lowering the costs of expulsion. In this case, the host government may engage in joint operations with the target state to oust rebel units on its soil, or call on international actors such as the UN for assistance.
3. The target government is able to increase the costs of continued hosting through negative sanctions, including by threatening (or engaging in) an international war. The target state may in extreme cases invade the host state to rid it of rebel groups; or, through threats and intimidation, pressure the host to expel rebels on its own.

Situations 1 and 2 entail positive efforts at cooperation by neighboring states, whereas the third scenario involves coercion.

Finally, conflicts may end in negotiated settlements. Here as well, the cooperation of the host government will be a critical determinant of negotiation success. Host governments can either block peace agreements, pressure parties to come to the bargaining table, or work to ensure that an agreement is honored. Sometimes, host states may prefer continued fighting over a peace negotiation and will prevent the implementation of a deal; thus, the host government may act as a "spoiler" or "veto player" during peace negotiations (Cunningham 2006; Stedman 1997). By refusing to limit rebel presence on its soil and continuing to provide resources to rebel groups, host governments can make continued fighting more attractive and impede the progress of negotiations.

Host states may, on the other hand, play a more positive role and encourage parties to come to the negotiating table. Here, they have bargaining leverage over both sides of the conflict: they have leverage on the rebels because they can provide (more or less) easy access to their territory, and they have leverage on the target government because they can assist insurgents. Thus, hosts can increase the costs of continued conflict for either side—by allowing or disallowing rebel bases—and can encourage warring groups to come to the bargaining table. Hosts states will find a negotiated resolution to the conflict more desirable if continued cross-border fighting and poor relations with their neighbor is costly to them and if their preference for a decisive rebel victory is not particularly deep.

For example, Zambia, Mozambique, and Botswana, which hosted rebels from neighboring Rhodesia (Zimbabwe), were critical in pressuring combatants to the negotiating table. Early on in the conflict, these "front-line" states supported the principle of black majority rule in Rhodesia, although they believed that negotiation with the white settler government was desirable. As the war progressed, the conflict became increasingly costly for the host governments. Zambia, for instance, lost its access to the Indian Ocean through Rhodesia, which created a heavy economic toll as the conflict continued. A Zambian foreign minister remarked, "We have been much too preoccupied with Rhodesia. Our economy, our growth has been severely retarded. We must now turn to fulfill our national aspirations."[24] Additionally, the Rhodesian government increased the costs of continued hosting during the final years of the conflict by intensifying sporadic attacks on rebel bases in Zambia and Mozambique, several of which killed locals as well. Weary of the fighting, the front-line states pressed all parties to come to a negotiated settlement, and in particular threatened the rebels with expulsion if they did not bargain seriously with the government (see Preston 2005; Stedman 1991; Walter 2002, chap. 6).

Rebel host states can play an important role in securing compliance with a peace deal. For a negotiated settlement to occur, there must be a process of rebel demobilization—rebels must credibly commit to cease fighting and lay down their arms, and governments must credibly commit to not attacking after disarmament occurs (Walter 1997, 2002). Disarming must include the promise to discontinue the use of extraterritorial bases and eliminate weapons stockpiles across the border. Because the informational environment in other countries is relatively poor, it is difficult for the target state to independently verify compliance with demobilization plans without the assistance of the host. Rebels can hide weapons abroad and remobilize in the future as long as permissive conditions in neighboring countries persist. Governments would be made worse-off by offering concessions to the opposition while the latter continues to maintain a fighting ability that would allow it to renege on a deal later. Therefore, in order for peace to hold, host governments must cooperate to limit rebel activities on their territory and ensure compliance with demobilization agreements among units on their soil. They must provide reliable information that demobilization is taking place and credible assurances that future access will be forbidden. Hosts can employ costly signals that their commitments are sincere, such as moving against foot-dragging rebels with force, inviting neutral monitors to gather information about rebel compliance, and making public commitments to international and domestic audiences. Thus,

---

24. Quoted in Gergory Jaynes, *New York Times*, December 17, 1979, "Zambia Finds that Life as Rhodesia Neighbor Isn't Sunny."

neighbors can assist by making promises to fully demobilize more credible and by preventing future rearmament.

In short, regional cooperation is necessary to bring conflicts to an end when extraterritorial bases are present. The host state and the target state may work together to eliminate extraterritorial bases and drive rebels back across the border, where the government's ability to combat them is greater. Alternatively, during peace negotiations the cooperation of the host government is vital. Host states can pressure rebels and the target government to come to the bargaining table and ensure that rebels lay down their arms after a peace deal. Although rebel access to external bases allows fighting to erupt and sustain itself, lack of these opportunities will cause conflict to end, either through a decisive victory or by forcing groups to negotiate peace.

THIS theory of transnational rebellion makes three overarching claims that can be assessed empirically. First, rebellion is more likely to occur when conditions in neighboring countries favor the establishment of extraterritorial bases. International borders constrain the use of force by governments, and so access to external territory should embolden rebels. This proposition will be tested in the next chapter. Second, hosting foreign rebels will bring the host and target countries into conflict with one another. Therefore, the probability of international disputes will increase when civil wars display transnational characteristics. This proposition will be tested in chapter 3. Third, the cooperation of rebel host countries will be needed in bringing civil wars to an end. Host states can either assist in defeating the rebels or work to make negotiated settlements more likely to succeed. This will be explored in the case study chapters: chapters 4 and 5. The following chapters will develop specific hypotheses relating to these claims; discuss ways of operationalizing key concepts; and conduct a series of empirical studies to probe the validity of the argument.

2 Transnational Rebels and Civil Violence

In the previous chapter, I argued that rebellion will be more likely to occur when conditions in neighboring countries allow rebels to take up extraterritorial bases. International borders and safe havens in neighboring countries allow rebels the opportunity to mobilize their supporters and sustain their forces while being less susceptible to government repression. External rebel bases make conflict more likely to erupt and to endure.

I also argued that while mobilization in other countries raises the bargaining power of rebel groups that lack sufficient domestic opportunities, it also exacerbates informational and commitment problems, making negotiation more difficult. Although the beliefs of actors, their level of information, and the credibility of promises are difficult to observe for a large set of cases, we can observe features of the bargaining environment—or broader background conditions—that make compromise more difficult and conflict more likely. This chapter will explore the observable implications of the theory for conflict patterns in general. The case studies in chapters 4 and 5 will shed light on the microfoundations of bargaining and negotiations.

For purposes of analysis, this chapter focuses primarily on conditions and processes relating to civil conflict. The following chapter analyzes how transnational rebellions give rise to international disputes. For tractability, these empirical chapters look at civil and international conflict separately; however, as emphasized in chapter 1, these modes of conflict are linked and mutually reinforcing. They are part of a larger regional conflict nexus that spans the internal/external divide, and the choice to conduct separate analyses of each form of conflict should not obscure this relationship.

Empirical Implications of the Theory

This section develops a series of propositions concerning transnational rebels and civil conflict that serve as the basis for the empirical analysis. The first set of propositions relates to neighboring country conditions that provide opportunities for establishing external bases. Under what conditions are rebels most likely to find sanctuary in neighboring states? First, rival governments may encourage and aid transnational rebels by allowing them access to their territory. Although many states choose to confront their enemies with their own forces rather than delegating to rebel proxies, some rivals work to foment instability in their neighbors by harboring transnational rebels. In addition, borders between hostile states are especially likely to be hardened, and any incursions across the border by state security forces are likely to be challenged, providing cover for rebel groups. Such states are also more likely to pursue their own agendas during negotiations and block peace settlements. This hypothesis is stated as follows:

> *H1 (rivalry): Rebellion is more likely to occur when the state is bordered by a rival state.*

Second, as argued in the previous chapter, weak or failed states are likely to be used by transnational rebels because the host government is unable to stop them. Such states do not have sufficient resources or capabilities to prevent transnational rebels from taking up positions on their soil. Furthermore, weak governments face high opportunity costs for dealing with another state's rebels, particularly if the host government must divert resources away from policing domestic dissidents. Therefore, this hypothesis is formally given as:

> *H2 (weak state): Rebellion is more likely to occur when the state is bordered by a weak state.*

With respect to weak neighboring states, it may be possible for governments to devise better counterinsurgency strategies. Given that a weak neighboring state is not hostile, the target government may be able to move troops toward the border and implement better border controls without provoking its neighbor. Some security cooperation between states may be possible, although this still creates transaction costs for counterinsurgency operations. Moreover, such hosts are less likely to play an active role in blocking settlements than rival hosts. Therefore, weak neighboring states may have less of an effect on the duration of civil conflict that on its onset.

Third, refugees located in nearby states are likely to contribute to rebellion. Refugees who flee oppressive and inept governments have strong incentives to join insurgents, and since life in refugee camps is often dismal, refugees have few opportunity costs for fighting. Refugee encampments therefore provide recruits and resources for rebel organizations. Hypothesis 3a states that:

> H3a (refugee diasporas): Rebellion is more likely to occur
> when there are refugees in neighboring states.

Additionally, the location of refugee communities is important. Capable and friendly governments can manage refugee communities effectively to preserve their noncombatant status. Refugees should not pose a security threat if the host government maintains order in refugee encampments. Conversely, refugees in countries where the government is either weak or a rival are more likely to provide support to rebel organizations.Therefore, a subhypothesis states:

> H3b (refugee location): Refugees are more likely to contribute
> to rebellion if they are located in weak or rival states.

Each of these hypotheses relates to the occurrence of conflict, which includes both conflict onset and continuation. Refugees in neighbors, rival governments, and weak states nearby may lead to a new conflict and, once underway, lead to longer conflicts. Weak states may play less of a role in prolonging conflicts, however, since they may cooperate with the target state and not actively impede negotiations. In addition, although some rivals choose to support nascent rebel groups, others confront their enemies directly, and so rivalry may have less of an effect on civil war onset. At the same time, once a rebellion has erupted, rival states may choose to use it to their advantage by prolonging the war. These potential caveats—which can be tested—should not detract from the general claim that weak and rival neighbors will contribute to conflict.

Once fighting has begun, it is possible to directly observe whether rebels are using extraterritorial bases. I collected data on insurgencies during the post-World War II period to determine whether or not rebels did in fact have access to external territory. It is expected that when they do, governments will have a difficult time suppressing them, and therefore rebellion will endure longer. It is not possible to observe whether rebels are mobilizing in external bases *prior* to the onset of conflict, since these are typically clandestine; therefore we are left with observing their effect on the duration of conflict alone. Therefore, a second test is developed, which focuses on conflict duration. This hypothesis is stated as follows:

> *H4 (extraterritorial bases): Conflicts will endure longer when rebels have access to extraterritorial bases.*

It should be noted that this hypothesis presents a more direct test of the propositions made in the previous chapter. Other regional conditions, such as rival states, weak states, and refugees, are said to contribute to the emergence of external bases. In addition, these regional factors may cluster in space for reasons unrelated to the theory, leading to spurious findings. Directly observing the use of external bases circumvents this potential problem. Thus, in combined models, the inclusion of an extraterritorial base variable should outperform other, indirect indicators.

It is also important to be clear about links in the causal chain suggested by these hypotheses. Hypotheses 1–3 pertain to neighborhood conditions in general that are likely to favor rebel sanctuary. Rebel sanctuaries, in turn, are conducive to conflict. These background conditions can be observed prior to conflict onset and their impact on the outbreak of a new episode of violence can be assessed, as can their impact on conflict continuation, although such tests are indirect. Once conflict has erupted, however, hypothesis 4 directly tests the impact of extraterritorial bases on the duration of fighting. Therefore, "bad neighborhoods" lead to conditions ripe for transnational rebel bases, and the bases themselves—which are only observable after conflict breaks out—are responsible for conflict. As an additional check on these causal linkages, below I will present a set of diagnostic tests confirming that weak neighbors, rival neighbors, and refugee communities are associated with external sanctuaries.

Finally, rather than looking at civil wars in the country as a whole, the final hypothesis relates to the propensity of ethnic groups to rebel. Since many civil conflicts take on an ethnic dimension, we can observe which ethnic groups rebel and which do not. Many ethnic groups are territorially concentrated in particular regions. The theory of transnational rebellion implies that, in contrast to ethnic groups that are dispersed or confined to the interior of a country, ethnic groups that are located near international borders are more likely to rebel because they have greater access to external territory and resources. This test is attractive because it allows for within-country variation in conflict patterns. Rather than looking at conditions pertaining to a country as a whole, we may assess the likelihood of conflict among particular subnational social groups, which leads to the following hypothesis:

> *H5 (ethnic rebellion): Ethnic groups that are located near an international border are more likely to rebel.*

Measuring the Concepts

The main dependent variable—or outcome to be explained—in this analysis is the incidence of civil conflict. The data are comprised of annual country observations spanning the period from 1951 to 2000—the years for which reliable data were available. Two points of clarification are needed. First, as opposed to several studies that treat conflict onset and conflict duration as distinct phenomena (see, e.g., Balch-Lindsay and Enterline 2000; Fearon 2004; Fearon and Laitin 2003; Hegre et al. 2001; Regan 2002), this study examines conflict *incidence*. Much of the literature has adopted the practice of dropping from the analysis subsequent years of violence after the initial year (in the case of onset), or only of looking at periods of ongoing war with conflict resolution as the dependent variable (duration). As discussed by Ibrahim Elbadawi and Nicholas Sambanis (2002), however, although it is sometimes important to look at conflict onset and continuation separately, it is also important to study in tandem with onset the reasons why conflicts endure.

The theoretical framework presented in chapter 1 generally applies to the occurrence of conflict within a country rather than conflict initiation or duration alone. External mobilization makes the outbreak of conflict more likely and also makes conflict more difficult to resolve through force or negotiations once fighting is under way. The initial conditions that lead to war may also be associated with how long a war lasts—war persists until these factors are no longer present; but if onset and continuation are driven by different processes, we should like to know this as well. Furthermore, as will be discussed below, certain estimation techniques can account for both types of events. Therefore, the dependent variable in this study is conflict incidence, or *spells of conflict*, which is dichotomous and coded 1 for years in which a country experienced a civil war or internal violence and 0 otherwise. More precisely, conflict incidence is defined as the probability of observing a war onset at time t given peace at time -1, *as well as* the probability of observing continued war at $t+1$ given that there was a war at time t.

A second point of clarification is also needed: much of the literature has looked at the phenomenon of civil *war*, which is normally defined by a somewhat arbitrary classification of conflicts based on the number of battle deaths (usually 1,000 or more). Typically, authors offer no good explanation for limiting their analyses to conflicts that reach a certain death threshold and therefore artificially truncate the number of violent incidents in their datasets. Simmering, low-level conflicts such as the decades-long conflict in the Indian state of Assam or the conflict in the Angolan province of Cabinda would never appear in datasets that define civil wars as conflicts that exceed 1,000 deaths. Rather than looking exclusively at *war*, which is an imprecisely defined concept, this study examines lesser armed conflicts—rebellions, insurgencies, terrorist acts, guerilla wars, and so forth—in conjunction with larger-scale conflicts such as full-blown wars and revolutions.[1] On theoretical grounds, moreover, there is no good reason to expect low- and high-intensity contests between governments and rebels to be driven by an entirely different set of factors.

The list of civil conflicts used here is drawn from the Uppsala/Peace Research Institute of Oslo Armed Conflicts Dataset (U/PACD), which was developed by the department of Peace and Conflict Research at Uppsala University and the Peace Research Institute of Oslo. The countries used in the statistical analysis below conform to the list of countries for which data is available on the dependent variable; however, because of data limitations on the independent variables (namely, refugees), the initial year of analysis for this study is 1951, not 1945, which is the start year for the U/PACD. For inclusion in the U/PACD, a conflict must meet the following characteristics: (1) *armed* force must have been used during the conflict; (2) there must be at least *twenty-five battle-related deaths* in a given year; (3) the conflict must occur between the *government* of a country and an *organized opposition* group; and (4) the *incompatibility* between the government and the opposition must be over the control of the *central government* or *territory* within the state (N. P. Gleditsch et al. 2002).[2]

A few modifications were made in order to account for the meanings of "conflict" and "insurgency" in the context of this study. First, all cases of coups or instances of violence in which a faction of the military was listed

1. A high threshold for classifying binary events also has important methodological limitations when using either a lagged dependent variable or counts of years at "peace." With a 1,000-death threshold, an event that falls just short of the cutoff point would not be counted as a conflict and would be assumed to have no impact on the subsequent probability of violence. In practice, however, low-intensity conflicts are likely to be systematically associated with a higher likelihood of future large-scale conflict. See Gates and Strand 2004 for a related discussion.

2. For those familiar with this data, I include all intrastate and internationalized intrastate disputes (type 3 and type 4 conflicts) that occur on a state's territory.

as the opposition group are not included. Theoretically, contests for power between rival factions within the ruling elite are distinct from conflicts that emerge from popular forces. The processes that occur during the rebellions analyzed here of popular mobilization, rebel recruitment, and securing sanctuary in neighboring countries are markedly different from revolts launched from within the barracks.

The second modification relates to the question of what to do with brief lulls in the violence. Should a brief period with little or no violence followed by the resumption of fighting be coded as a new war altogether or as one ongoing period of conflict? I adopt the latter approach and consolidate spells of conflict in which there are three or fewer interim years of "peace" between parties fighting over the same incompatibility.[3] In reality, although active fighting may have ceased, the underlying conflict has not been resolved. Therefore, ceasefires and temporary truces of three or fewer years followed by renewed conflict are not counted as "peaceful" periods but are included within the larger conflict (i.e., they are coded 1).

Several examples will clarify this coding decision. From 1990 to 2001, the government of Senegal fought a minor armed conflict against the Movement of the Democratic Forces of the Casamance. However, no fighting was reported in the U/PACD for the years 1991, 1994, 1996. Rather than code four separate armed conflicts (1990, 1992–93, 1995, and 1997–2001), I consolidate this conflict into one long spell from 1990–2001. It is not appropriate to think that the issues at stake in the underlying clash were "resolved" in 1991, 1994, and 1996—there simply was no reported fighting during these years, but the dispute continued nonetheless.

As a second example, take Nicaragua. The U/PACD data lists one conflict between the government of Luis Somoza Debayle and the Sandinistas from 1978 to 1979 and a second conflict between the newly empowered Sandinista government and the Contra rebels from 1981 to 1989. There is no fighting reported in 1980. For the purposes of this book, these are counted as one continuous spell of conflict from 1978 to 1989. Although many may be tempted to count this conflict as two distinct civil wars, it may just as well be considered one long period in which control over the central government was contested by various factions. In fact,

3. As with many data coding decisions, sometimes one is forced to make arbitrary distinctions in the data. Lulls in the fighting that last three or fewer years are subsumed under one long period of conflict, but ceasefires that last four or more years are coded as periods of peace. There are no good theoretical grounds for deciding on a three-year interim period: it is entirely a decision made for expediency. Alternative codings (i.e., with no consolidation, with five-year gaps) made no difference in the results.

many of the Contra rebels were ex-Somoza military personnel. Because the issue of incompatibility remained unchanged between the rounds of fighting—that is, control of Managua—this is considered to be the same civil war.[4]

Lastly, take the case of Russia during the early 1990s. In 1990–1991, the USSR (Russia) fought against rebels in the break-away region of Armenia. Three years later in 1994, Chechen rebels decided to launch their own insurrection against the central government. Although these conflicts are separated by just two years of peace (1992–1993), the issues at stake were distinct—the separatist conflict in Armenia was over a different incompatibility than the separatist conflict in Chechnya. Russia therefore is coded as having two conflicts 1990–1991 (Armenia) and 1994–2002 (Chechnya), with a two-year period of peace in between.

A final modification was also included. As an addendum, U/PACD has a list of unclear cases in which a conflict was not included in the final dataset either because: (1) the opposition group did not meet the level of organization needed; (2) the number of deaths was not confirmed; or (3) the issue of incompatibility was not clearly about control over the central government or territorial autonomy. The first two exclusions are reasonable: to exclude riots, mob violence, or petty criminality, there must be an organized opposition group and the number of deaths must meet their minimal definition.

However, excluding cases in which the incompatibility is unclear is a bit more problematic. Some issue incompatibilities may defy traditional classifications but are nonetheless real disputes in which governments fight armed opposition groups. If an analyst compiling the data could not be certain of the reasons behind the conflict or if the conflict did not fall into a predefined incompatibility category, there is no reason to eliminate it from a dataset. Three wars in the U/PACD list are excluded from their final dataset for the reason of unclear incompatibility but are included here: (1) Indonesia versus communist insurgents, 1965; (2) Jordan versus the Palestine Liberation Organization, 1970–1971; and (3) Zimbabwe versus RENAMO, 1987.[5] In the cases of Jordan and Zimbabwe, the government fought

---

4. Alternative codings were also considered in which a change in the central government creates a new civil war. This alternative specification does not significantly change the main results.

5. These country-years of conflict constitute less than one-half of one percent of the total number of civil war years (4 out of 1157). They are included for theoretical reasons, but eliminating them from the estimation did not significantly change the results presented below.

against foreign rebels who had taken up bases on its soil and who did not necessarily contest control over the central government or a region. In the Indonesian case, it was not clear if the group demanded territorial autonomy or control over the central government. Nevertheless, these were real conflicts between a government and an organized opposition, and so these cases are included in the dataset used in this book.

Independent Variables

The first hypothesis is that countries that border rival states are more likely to experience internal armed conflict. Rival governments are expected to provide sanctuary and support to rebel groups as a means to destabilize the regime across the border. To test this hypothesis, I use the rivalry data compiled by William R. Thompson (2001). This data is based on qualitative accounts, particularly foreign policy histories of governments, belligerent public statements, and acts of aggression between countries. To be included as rivals, two countries must "regard each other as (a) competitors, (b) the source of actual or latent threats that pose some possibility of becoming militarized, and (c) enemies" (Thompson 2001, 560). The Thompson data differs from other rivalry datasets (see, e.g., Diehl and Goertz 2000) in that it does not require a minimum dispute duration between countries, and it does not rely on counts of open armed hostilities (see Thompson 2001 for details).[6]

Some of the rivalries listed in the Thompson dataset occur between noncontiguous countries, for example, China and the United States. Because the theory pertains to the use of *neighboring* territory (rebels lack the capability to project force), cases of nonneighboring rivals are excluded from the analysis. The rivalry indicator used here is a dichotomous variable coded 1 for years in which the state in question neighbors at least one state which is considered a rival (and 0 otherwise). Neighbors are defined as states falling within 100km of the borders of the country in question, including strict contiguity based upon the Gleditsch and Ward Minimum Distance Dataset (Gleditsch and Ward 2001). This practice ensures the inclusion of neighboring states that are not strictly contiguous but that are separated by short spans of water that can easily be crossed by combatant groups. Rivalries are also lagged one year since issues relating to the civil war itself may give rise to international tensions.

The second hypothesis considered is that weak neighboring countries—those with poor policing, infrastructural capacity, and administrative

6. I thank William Thompson for providing me with an electronic version of this dataset.

resources—are more likely to be used as cover for transnational rebel groups. Measuring state weakness is extremely difficult, both conceptually and practically. What does it mean for a state to be "weak"? What aspects of policing, the military, infrastructure, and so forth are the most important? Which indicators cover a sufficient number of countries for a sufficient number of years to make statistical analyses worthwhile? This study uses two measures for state weakness. The first is a binary variable coded as 1 if the country in question borders (within 100 km) at least one state which is experiencing armed conflict as defined by the U/PACD and 0 otherwise. Neighboring a country experiencing a civil war has been found to be an important predictor of domestic conflict (Hegre and Sambanis 2006; Salehyan and Gleditsch 2006; Sambanis 2001), although authors usually attribute such clustering to opaque mechanisms such as "diffusion" or "spillover" effects. The explanation for conflict clustering offered here is that civil wars in neighboring countries expose security weaknesses and divert resources toward combating domestic insurgents.[7] Under these circumstances, rebels from neighboring countries seek to benefit from this condition of relative "anarchy" by positioning themselves inside the neighbor's territory. The expectation, therefore, is that countries with neighbors at civil war are more likely to experience war themselves.

A state may be weak even if not experiencing a civil war. It may simply lack the resources to maintain effective control over its territory. Although measures of infrastructure such as roadways and communications networks, of police personnel, of equipment, of tax extraction, and so on would be ideal indicators of state strength, such data is not readily available for all country-years. This is especially true for the poorest governments, which lack the capacity to gather adequate records. Therefore, as a proxy for state capacity, I use data on the neighboring countries' GDP per capita drawn from Kristian Gleditsch's expanded GDP data; this dataset includes estimates for countries not covered by traditional data sources such as the Penn World Tables (K. S. Gleditsch 2002). Countries that are wealthier overall are expected to have better communications, administration, police resources, and infrastructure, which may in part be captured by GDP per capita (Fearon and Laitin 2003). A binary variable is included if the state in

7. This of course is not the only explanation for conflict clustering. Salehyan and Gleditsch (2006) find that refugees from neighboring countries significantly raise the probability that the host country will experience a violent conflict. This may be due to direct hostility between the refugee group and the host government; the exchange of personnel, resources, and ideas among combatant groups; changing demographics; and economic competition.

question borders at least one country that falls below the 10th percentile on GDP per capita for the given year.[8]

Finally, this study will assess the role of refugees in neighboring states in facilitating conflict in their home countries. Refugee communities can contribute to conflict by providing resources and safe-havens to insurgent groups and are prime locations for recruitment into rebel organizations (Zolberg, Suhrke, and Aguayo 1989). To test this hypothesis, I include data from the United Nations High Commissioner for Refugees Population Data Unit.[9] This data contains dyadic entries for annual refugee stocks by origin and destination countries.[10] Data on Palestinian refugees were collected by the United Nations Relief and Works Agency and the U.S. Committee for Refugees and were used to supplement the UNHCR data. Using the same definition as above for neighboring states, all refugees from the country of observation in all neighboring states were added together. The distribution of this variable is highly skewed, as the vast majority of countries and years have no refugees in immediate neighbors, and the data has a long right tail with countries such as Afghanistan and Mozambique sending over 1,000,000 refugees to neighboring states. Furthermore, the effect of refugees may not be strictly linear, but diminishing with size. Therefore, the natural log of the number of refugees is taken to eliminate much of the skewed nature of the data and account for diminishing marginal impact.

Clearly, there is inherent endogeneity in the refugee measure. Several statistical studies have confirmed that refugees are a *consequence* of civil war (Davenport, Moore, and Poe 2003; Neumayer 2004; Schmeidl 1997), whereas the argument here is that refugees may also cause or exacerbate conflict. In using refugee data as a *predictor* of conflict, there are several conceptual and methodological issues to be aware of. First, current refugees may be a consequence of the conflict and will therefore be correlated with the dependent variable, although there may be no causation (type 1 endogeneity).

---

8. A number of alternative measures based on neighboring country GDP per capita were used, but as with this measure, none were found to be important. A vector of all neighboring countries was created and data on the minimum GDP per capita in this vector was included in regressions. As another indicator, mean GDP per capita for the vector of neighboring states was included. Finally, data on road coverage was included, but because of the large number of missing observations and lack of temporal coverage, this was also not ideal.

9. I thank Bela Hovy of the United Nations High Commissioner for Refugees for providing me with this data.

10. Refugee figures are not without problems. In particular, Jeff Crisp (1999) notes how the politicized nature of many refugee crises leads some actors to distort refugee numbers in order to advance a political agenda. Although not perfect, these figures are the best currently available and have been used widely.

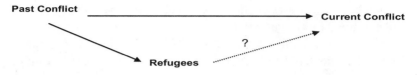

Figure 2.1. Type 2 Endogeneity

Therefore, I lag the refugee variable and include a lagged dependent variable as well. This way, I can assess the effect of refugees at *t*-1 while controlling for conflict in the same period; last year's refugees should contribute to this year's conflict even when taking into account past fighting.

Second, taking into account conflict at *t*-1 may not be sufficient; conflict in earlier periods may matter as well. A conflict may cause a significant number of refugees, fighting may cease for a few years, and then conflict could resume again for reasons totally unrelated to refugees but as a direct result of attributes of the past conflict (type 2 endogeneity) (see figure 2.1).

A number of steps are taken to account for this type of endogeneity. The first, discussed above, relates to how the dependent variable was coded. Brief lulls in fighting of three or fewer years are subsumed under the larger conflict and not counted as peace years. During these brief interim periods, there may be refugees in neighboring states at *t*-1 but no actual fighting during this period, which would show up as a positive "hit" in the regression if these years were coded as peaceful. Coding these interim years of no active fighting as "conflict years," partially corrects for this type of endogeneity.

Because three years may be too brief as an interim period, a variable for peace years—the number of years the country has been without conflict—is included. If a recent war led to a significant number of refugees, this is accounted for by such a variable. This method also controls for duration dependence in the dependent variable; peace and war may be self-sustaining processes. However, this presents a hard test with respect to conflict onset, since past conflict and refugees are likely to be highly related to one another, and there may not be sufficient independent variation in the indicators.

The third potential problem in using refugees as an independent variable arises from the conflict deaths threshold (figure 2.2; type 3 endogeneity). Conflicts appear in any given dataset if they cause a sufficient number of fatalities. An insurgency may simmer below this threshold for a number of years, generating a large number of refugees, and then explode into a larger

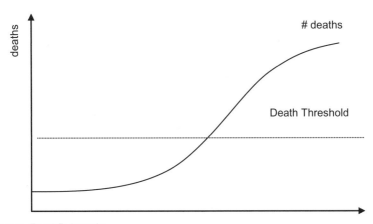

Figure 2.2. Type 3 Endogeneity

civil war that crosses the requisite number of deaths. It would appear as though the refugees generated during the low-intensity phase (coded as peace) were responsible for the war, but it may simply be that the escalation of conflict-years was not coded in the dataset. This would indeed be problematic if the threshold were set too high—at 1,000 or even 100 deaths—however, the low conflict intensity threshold in the U/PACD (25 deaths) greatly reduces such concern. Very low-level violence, causing fewer than 25 deaths, is not likely to generate a significant number of refugees.

The final type of endogeneity, simultaneous causation, is not so easily accounted for. Although lagged values of the independent and dependent variables can account for the effect of last year's refugees, it may be the case that annual records are simply too coarse if events unfold more rapidly. Refugees generated in February, for example, may join a rebel organization by October, and annual observations would not account for this possibility. This should have the effect of biasing the results *against* a positive finding for refugees, however, and so, is a conservative method.[11]

Refugees may have a larger impact in certain countries and a smaller impact in others. Another hypothesis to be explored is that refugees are most likely to contribute to conflict if they are located in weak or rival states. Refugees in neighbors that have the capacity to adequately regulate migrant communities and that do not wish to encourage rebellions are less likely to be

11. Also see table 2.3 in the appendix to this chapter. One way to account for endogeneity is to consult the cases themselves. It is possible to observe whether rebels were also based in countries where there were significant refugee communities. A careful reading of cases reveals that several large refugee communities also harbor rebel groups.

active in armed opposition groups. To test this possibility, I include a variable for refugees located within neighboring countries that are *either* rivals (as defined above) or are themselves experiencing an internal conflict.[12]

Control Variables

The main variables of interest, listed above, relate directly to the broader regional environment in which a state is situated. However, domestic conditions are also expected to be relevant. A number of domestic variables found to be important in other studies of conflict must therefore be included as control variables. These factors include wealth, population, regime type, and ethnic relations.

To begin with, a variable is included for the country's GDP per capita (logged). Conflict is expected to be less likely in wealthier countries because citizens have fewer economic grievances and high opportunity costs for fighting and because the state may be better able to deter challengers through a strong and well-equipped security force (Collier and Hoeffler 2004; Fearon and Laitin 2003). GDP data are drawn from Gleditsch's (2002b) expanded GDP data, which has the best temporal and geographic coverage. This measure is lagged to account for possible reverse-causation, as conflict may cause a decline in economic conditions. Second, I include a control for total population size (logged). It may be the case that countries with larger populations are more difficult to govern because state security forces are stretched thin when they must monitor dissent among a large population. I include a once-lagged value because conflict may affect population size (either through deaths or emigration).

Third, several studies have demonstrated that regime type is an important predictor of civil conflict. It has been argued that the most democratic and the most autocratic countries are least susceptible to a violent challenge. Democracies encourage nonviolent means of dissent, whereas authoritarian regimes can effectively deter opposition. Mixed regimes, or "anocracies," which are not fully democratic but not extremely repressive, are most likely to experience conflict (Hegre et al. 2001; Muller and Weede 1990). There should be a parabolic, inverted-U shaped relationship between continuous measures of democracy and conflict. Regime data for this study comes from the combined democracy-autocracy score from the Polity IV data project (Marshall and Jaggers 2002). This widely used data

---

12. I have also disaggregated the measure into its component parts; that is, refugees in civil war countries, refugees in rival countries, and all others. However, these measures are highly related to one another and do not independently vary enough for use in statistical analyses.

consists of a 21-point scale ranging from most autocratic (-10) to the most democratic (+10) regimes.[13] Because conflict is likely to affect regime type, I use once-lagged rather than contemporaneous values for the Polity score. To test for the nonlinear effect of democracy, I include a squared Polity term as well.

Finally, many have argued that the ethnic composition of a country may be an important predictor of conflict, yet there is little agreement as to what measure of ethnicity is most appropriate (Fearon and Laitin 2003; Reynal-Querol 2002; Vanhanen 1999; see Cederman and Girardin 2007 for a discussion). Various measures of fractionalization, polarization, and ethnic dominance have been proposed, with very little consensus on what aspects of ethnicity really matter. Rather than engage in this debate at length, I include the ethnolinguistic fractionalization index used by Fearon and Laitin (2003). This index gives the probability that two randomly drawn individuals are from different ethnolinguistic groups and is included as a measure of ethnic heterogeneity.

Methods

The data are in time-series cross-sectional format, with country-years as the units of observation and a binary dependent variable indicating the presence or absence of conflict as defined above. Instead of looking at conflict onset or duration as separate research questions, this analysis looks at incidence, or spells of conflict. A number of methods have been proposed in estimating models with such a structure (Beck et al. 2001; Beck, Katz, and Tucker 1998; Elbadawi and Sambanis 2002). Two different estimation techniques are used to check the robustness of the results: a time-series cross-section logit regression with random effects and an autoregressive term, and the transition model (Beck et al. 2001).

The first approach, proposed by Elbadawi and Sambanis (2002), is a random effects model. This model separates the individual-specific part of the error term, υ, from the error term itself, ε. In the case of the data used here, country-level effects are estimated: it may be the case that there are unmodeled attributes specific to the country in question that drive conflict. A lagged dependent variable is also used to account for serial autocorrelation.

$$P(y_{it} \mid X_{it}) = \frac{1}{1 + \exp^{-(X_{it}\beta + \varphi\, y_{c-1} + \upsilon_i + \varepsilon_{it})}} \qquad (1)$$

13. Countries with special indeterminate codes are assigned a value of 0 according to the standard practice in the literature and the recommendation of the Polity project.

Random effects models assume—as with the error term, ε—that υ is randomly drawn and uncorrelated with each of the explanatory variables. As an alternative to random effects models, fixed effects models do not make such assumptions and directly estimate the individual-level effect by including variables for each grouping. However, fixed effects models do not permit time-invariant independent or dependent variables, as they would be perfectly collinear with the effect terms and are therefore not feasible.

The second estimation technique is one proposed by Beck et al. (2001)—the transition model. We can think of spells of conflict as two different "transitions" in the data. The first is the transition from no conflict to conflict, and the second is the transition from conflict to peace. Formally, the transition model is given as a pair of logit equations:

$$P(y_{i,t} = 1 \mid y_{i,t-1} = 0) = \frac{1}{1 + \exp^{-(X_{i,z}\beta + \delta d_{y-0})}} \tag{2}$$

$$P(y_{i,t} = 1 \mid y_{i,t-1} = 1) = \frac{1}{1 + \exp^{-(X_{i,z}\gamma + \lambda d_{y-1})}} \tag{3}$$

More concretely, the transition model is simply a pair of logit models. The first model estimates the probability of a new conflict onset given that there was peace in the previous year; the second model estimates the probability of conflict continuation given that there was conflict in the previous year. In practice, two logit models are run with the sample being split into two groups based on the value of the lagged dependent variable (DV). The random effects model accounts for an intercept shift based on the value of the lagged dependent variable while assuming that the effect of the covariates remains the same. The transition model, by contrast, allows for differences in the parameters of the right-hand side variables based on whether onset (β) or continuation (γ) is being estimated.[14] In addition, we can account for duration dependence by including a count of war years (for the group where $y_{t-1} = 1$) and peace years (for the group where $y_{t-1} = 0$), in a procedure identical to the Beck, Katz, and Tucker (1998) method for binary time-series cross-sectional data.

---

14. Some readers may be more familiar with the dynamic probit (or logit) model favored by Elbadawi and Sambanis (2002). In the dynamic probit model, a lagged dependent variable and interaction terms between each independent variable (IV) and the lagged DV are included on the right hand side. In effect, the transition model is identical to the dynamic probit model. Splitting the sample is easier to read and interpret than interaction terms, so this approach will be used here.

Quantitative Results

Table 2.1 reports the results for the random effects logit model (model 1) and the transition model (model 2). The difference in these models is that model 1 assumes that the factors behind the onset and continuation of conflict are the same, and model 2 allows us to test whether or not onset and continuation are distinct processes.[15] Although the hypotheses fare reasonably well, there are interesting differences among the two estimation techniques.

First, let us consider hypothesis 1, that countries with rival neighbors are more likely to experience civil conflict. In model 1, international rivalries are shown to be a positive and consistent predictor of civil conflict, confirming expectations. In the transition model, however, international rivalries are shown to have a less statistically significant effect on conflict onset but having a significant effect on conflict continuation. Although this finding deserves further research, we may speculate as to why this may be the case. International rivals sometimes choose to attack their enemies with their own military forces but at other times choose to substitute direct conflict with support for rebel organizations (Salehyan 2008). Therefore, there may not be a consistent, regular relationship between rivalry and the initial outbreak of insurgency if various means of confronting international foes are chosen. Nevertheless, the positive finding for continuation suggests that once a civil war has begun, international rivals may make such disputes more difficult to resolve through their support for rebel groups. After a conflict is underway, rivals may try to use it to their advantage.

Hypothesis 2 claimed that weak neighboring states are likely to contribute to civil conflict. One indicator of state weakness—a neighbor with low GDP per capita—was not shown to have a significant influence on conflict in either model; indeed, the sign is in the wrong direction. Perhaps this measure of state weakness is too crude to capture the policing capabilities of

15. The coefficients and standard errors are given along with p-values for the z statistics instead of the more traditional use of stars, allowing readers to draw their own conclusions about the statistical strength of the associations. There is a debate in the statistics literature, however, on the utility of using tests of statistical significance for apparent populations. Normally, significance testing is used to give a measure of how confident the analyst or reader can be that the relationship in the sample holds true for the population being generalized to. In the current study, nearly all country-years since 1945 are analyzed, so the sample size approaches the entire universe of cases that the theory addresses. If readers accept that the entire population is being analyzed, then standard errors are not used to understand true population parameters, but rather to determine the consistency of the statistical relationship in the observed data. In other words, they reveal how often the expected (probabilistic) relationship between the DV and IV occurs in practice. For a discussion, see Berk, Western, and Weiss 1995 and Bollen 1995.

Table 2.1 Regression results: Neighboring country conditions and civil conflict incidence

	1. Random Effects Logit		2. Transition Model			
	Coefficient (Standard error)	p-value	Coefficient (β: onset) (Standard error)	p-value	Coefficient (γ: continuation) (Standard error)	p-value
Rival neighbor (NB) (t-1)	0.359	0.037	0.090	0.345	0.348	0.081
	(0.201)		(0.227)		(0.249)	
Low GDP per cap. NB	−0.046	0.426	−0.150	0.294	−0.151	0.301
	(0.244)		(0.276)		(0.289)	
Civil war NB	0.605	0.001	0.645	0.002	0.221	0.207
	(0.192)		(0.217)		(0.270)	
Refugees in NB (t-1)	0.040	0.024	0.004	0.449	0.047	0.019
	(0.020)		(0.029)		(0.022)	
Population (t-1)	0.219	0.002	0.244	<0.001	0.013	0.446
	(0.077)		(0.068)		(0.098)	
GDP per cap. (t-1)	−0.205	0.070	−0.180	0.128	−0.291	0.055
	(0.138)		(0.158)		(0.182)	
Polity (t-1)	0.022	0.065	0.015	0.200	0.036	0.028
	(0.015)		(0.018)		(0.019)	
Polity squared	−0.009	0.002	−0.011	0.002	−0.002	0.304
	(0.003)		(0.004)		(0.004)	
Ethnic fractionalization	0.846	0.020	1.172	0.002	−0.135	0.378
	(0.412)		(0.403)		(0.435)	
Conflict (t-1)	5.317	<0.001	—	—	—	—
	(0.182)					
Peace (war) years	—	—	−0.009	0.153	0.071	0.001
			(0.009)		(0.024)	
Constant	−4.665	<0.000	−4.717	0.001	3.587	0.024
	(1.333)		(1.366)		(1.804)	
N	5896		4920		976	
Wald Chi squared	1072.83		71.50		24.55	
P> Chi squared	<0.001		<0.001		0.006	
Rho	0.155[a]		—		—	

[a] indicates .05 significance for Rho
Robust standard errors reported
P-values are of one-tailed significance tests

neighboring states adequately. However, model 1 shows a positive (and significant) relationship between neighboring civil wars—another weak state indicator—and civil conflict in the country itself. This confirms earlier studies that demonstrate the tendency for civil conflicts to be geographically clustered. The explanation offered here is that states weakened by civil war are likely to serve as safe-havens for rebel groups from other countries; according to this measure of state weakness, hypothesis 2 receives good support.[16] In model 2, an interesting difference between conflict onset and continuation emerges. A civil war in the neighborhood increases the likelihood of conflict onset, although it does not have a consistent relationship with respect to conflict continuation (although the sign is positive). Although conjectural at this point, it is plausible that states confronting TNRs in weak neighbors can devise better counterinsurgency and border control measures as well as engage in some security cooperation with their neighbors. Moreover, weak hosts may not actively attempt to block negotiated settlements since they do not have much at stake in the conflict.

Hypothesis 3a states that refugees in neighboring countries are likely to contribute to conflict. Not only are refugees a consequence of conflict, but they may also provide shelter, resources, and recruitment opportunities for TNRs. In the random effects model, refugees are shown to be a strong predictor of civil conflict in the sending country. This result holds even when factoring in the effects of both past refugees and prior conflicts to correct for potential endogeneity. In the transition model, refugees are shown to be a positive and significant predictor of conflict continuation, but have a less consistent effect on conflict onset. This may be due to high methodological hurdles, as past conflicts are accounted for by the inclusion of a counter of years since previous conflict. With this estimation technique, it is difficult to untangle the independent effect of refugees—who flee from earlier fighting—from that of the previous spell of civil war. Nonetheless, hypothesis 3a receives generally strong support across the models.

The control variables behave largely as expected across the models. First, population size is shown to increase the likelihood of civil wars in the random effects model as well as in the onset cut of the transition model. Second, higher GDP per capita reduces the probability of a civil conflict, confirming several previous studies. The Polity index and its square reveal a curvilinear relationship between the level of democracy and the likelihood of civil conflict across the models, confirming the expectation that anocracies are more conflict-prone. Contrary to Fearon and Laitin's research (2003), the models

---

16. See the appendix to this chapter for further examination of causal relationships.

show a positive relationship between ethnic fractionalization and conflict; ethnic fractionalization, however, is shown to have less of an effect on conflict continuation.

Table 2.2 reports the results regarding the location of refugees. Hypothesis 3b claimed that refugees have a stronger effect on civil conflict if they are located in states that are weak or in states that are rivals. Thus, the refugee indicator is divided into two sets of refugee hosts. The first is the number of refugees located in countries that are experiencing a civil war or that are international rivals. The second is the number of refugees in all other neighboring states. Model 3 uses the random effects estimator while model 4 uses the continuation cut of the transition model, γ. In model 3, both groups of refugees are shown to have a positive and significant effect on civil conflict in the sending country, and the magnitudes of the coefficients are nearly identical. However, in model 4, refugees in rival or civil war neighbors are shown to have a positive and significant influence on conflict continuation, but refugees in all other states exhibit a less consistent effect, confirming hypothesis 3b.

How important are these variables and how much do they raise the odds of conflict? Table 2.3 computes the substantive impact of the variables on the predicted probability of violence using model 1 in table 2.1. To set the baseline category, all of the dichotomous independent variables were set at 0, all continuous variables are set at their means, and polity is set at 0. Because values of the lagged dependent variable have a large impact on the results, two different baseline comparison groups were used: one with the lagged DV set to 0, another with the lagged DV set to 1. Whereas the latter estimates the probability of conflict continuation, the former analyzes conflict onset.

The upper portion of table 2.3 reports the changes in predicted probabilities given an increase in the selected variables over the baseline case where there was no conflict in the previous year. Therefore, in our hypothetical country that had no civil war in the previous year, the chance of experiencing a civil war is approximately 1.7 percent. How do various values of the independent variables affect this baseline probability? A similar country with a rival has a 2.4 percent chance of experiencing a civil war. Although this probability may not appear to be very large in an absolute sense, in relative terms it is a 42.3 percent increase over the baseline. A country with a neighbor experiencing civil conflict has a 3.0 percent chance of experiencing a conflict, or an 81.4 percent greater probability of violence over the baseline. Given these estimates, a shift in the number of refugees from 0 to 100,000 (in log terms) increases the risk of civil conflict by approximately 55 percent, and

Table 2.2 The location of refugees and civil conflict

	3. Random effects logit		4. Transition model	
	Coefficient (Standard error)	p-value	Coefficient (γ: continuation) (Standard error)	p-value
Ref. in rival/Civil War (CW)	0.035	0.075	0.056	0.047
Neighbor (NB) (t-1)	(0.024)		(0.034)	
Ref in nonrival/CW NB (t-1)	0.035	0.094	0.023	0.252
	(0.026)		(0.034)	
Rival NB (t-1)	0.384	0.028	0.286	0.122
	(0.201)		(0.246)	
Civil war NB	0.559	0.002	0.169	0.254
	(0.188)		(0.256)	
Population (t-1)	0.208	0.003	0.027	0.389
	(0.075)		(0.097)	
GDP per cap. (t-1)	−0.193	0.065	−0.231	0.074
	(0.127)		(0.160)	
Polity (t-1)	0.020	0.079	0.032	0.041
	(0.015)		(0.019)	
Polity squared	−0.008	0.003	−0.002	0.294
	(0.003)		(0.004)	
Ethnic fractionalization	0.829	0.018	−0.009	0.492
	(0.396)		(0.427)	
Conflict (t-1)	5.320	<0.001	—	—
	(0.181)			
War years	—	—	0.064	0.002
			(0.022)	
Constant	−4.718	<0.001	2.918	0.038
	(1.256)		(1.638)	
N	6049		1007	
Wald Chi squared	1100.47		27.20	
P> Chi squared	<0.001		0.002	
Rho	0.142*		—	

[a] indicates .05 significance for Rho
Robust standard errors reported
P-values are of one-tailed significance tests

Table 2.3. Predicted probabilities of conflict given increases in selected variables

	Prediction	% Increase over baseline
New war onset		
Baseline[a]	0.017	
Rival	0.024	42.32
Civil war	0.030	81.39
Refugees 0 to 100k	0.026	55.41
GDP per capita	0.013	−20.09
War continuation		
Baseline[a]	0.774	
Rival	0.831	7.326
Civil war	0.863	11.482
Refugees 0 to 100k	0.843	8.872
GDP per capita	0.739	−4.610

[a] Baseline: all dichotomous variables set at zero, continuous variables set at their means, Polity set at zero. The estimated model is model 1 in table 2.1.

an increase in GDP per capita by $1,000 over its mean value decreases the risk of conflict by 20 percent. Although the *absolute* probabilities reported in the upper portion of table 2.3 may seem low, it is clear that the *change* in the probability of a new conflict over the comparison group is rather large.

The lower portion of table 2.3 sets the value of the lagged dependent variable in the baseline category to 1 and gives the probabilities of conflict continuation for a another year. The probability of continued rebellion given a conflict in the previous time period is rather high: 77.4 percent for the baseline. How do the variables of interest affect this underlying probability? First, a country with a rival neighbor is expected to have an 83 percent chance of conflict continuation, or a 7.3 percent increase in the expected probability. A neighbor with a rebellion increases the probability of conflict continuation by roughly 11.5 percent, and 100,000 refugees across the border raises the probability of continuation up to 84.3 percent. Clearly, as table 2.3 shows, there is an important substantive effect of each of the variables of interest, as rivalry, neighboring conflict, and refugees all lead to a substantial increase in the prevalence of rebellion.

Extraterritorial Bases and Conflict Duration

In the analysis above, neighboring state weakness, rivalry, and refugees are positively associated with conflict because of opportunities for TNRs to establish extraterritorial bases. Although it is not possible to observe the existence of rebel bases prior to the onset of an armed conflict—they are, after all, clandestine—it is possible to know whether a rebel organization has an extraterritorial base once fighting is underway. Thus, we can estimate the effect of external bases on the duration of armed conflict, which presents a more direct test of the theoretical propositions. Neighborhood conditions such as weak states, rival states, and refugee camps provide fertile ground for rebels to establish foreign sanctuaries; and we can ascertain their direct effect. In addition, there may be geographic clustering of these variables for reasons unrelated to the existence of external bases—leading to spurious findings—which this approach circumvents. Moreover, since it is argued that these neighborhood conditions give rise to extraterritorial sanctuaries, the base variable, which is a direct measure of TNR location, should outperform the other variables in combined models by sapping some of their explanatory power.

All of the conflicts in the U/PACD were researched to determine if any rebel party to a conflict had a presence outside of the boundaries of the target state during the period of conflict. A variety of primary and secondary sources were consulted to determine if insurgents used extraterritorial bases.[17] A three-part variable was developed and labeled as follows: *0* equals no extraterritorial presence; *1* signifies limited or sporadic use of external territory; and *2* indicates extensive and sustained use of extraterritorial bases.[18] Values of this variable were included for each country-year observation, and changes in these values, although not common, were included. Alternative codings were also estimated by combining the 0 and 1 categories as well as by combining the 1 and 2 categories, but these variations did not affect the results. In all, 55 percent of all rebel groups included in the U/PACD (159 of 291) had scores of 1 or 2. To estimate these regressions, the duration cut (γ) of the transition model is used.

17. These sources include: (1) the Uppsala University Armed Conflicts Database, http://www.pcr.uu.se/database/index.php; (2) the Minorities at Risk conflict histories; (3) Patrick Brogan, *World Conflicts: A Comprehensive Guide to World Strife, 1945–1998;* (4) The Keesings Record of World Events, www.keesings.com; (5) Lexis-Nexus News Archives; (6) *The New York Times* Archives; 7) the International Boundaries News Database, http://www-ibru.dur.ac.uk/; 8) the Federation of American Scientists listing of armed factions, http://www.fas.org/irp/world/para/; (9) http://Onwar.com; (10) U.S. Library of Congress Country Studies.

18. For methodological reasons, this variable was lagged. Because data on extraterritorial bases was only collected for country-years where the value of the dependent variable equals 1 (i.e., when there is a civil conflict), the model cannot be estimated with the variable itself because there is no variation on the DV. However, including lagged values of the extraterritorial bases variable eliminates this problem, and lagged values are very highly correlated with current values: R=.95.

Table 2.4 Extraterritorial bases and conflict duration

	Model 5		Model 6	
	Coefficient (γ: continuation) (Standard error)	p-value	Coefficient (γ: continuation) (Standard error)	p-value
External base	0.903 (0.158)	<0.001	0.881 (0.164)	<0.001
Rival NB (t-1)	—	—	0.291 (0.253)	0.125
Civil war NB (t-1)	—	—	0.177 (0.269)	0.255
Refugees in NB (t-1)	—	—	0.029 (0.024)	0.114
Population (t-1)	0.049 (0.093)	0.299	0.073 (0.095)	0.222
GDP per cap. (t-1)	−0.382 (0.157)	0.008	−0.335 (0.165)	0.022
Polity (t-1)	0.034 (0.019)	0.037	0.039 (0.019)	0.019
Polity squared	−0.004 (0.004)	0.175	−0.004 (0.004)	0.178
Ethnic fractionalization	−0.374 (0.452)	0.204	−0.355 (0.449)	0.215
War years	0.048 (0.022)	0.016	0.039 (0.022)	0.040
Constant	3.959 (1.524)	0.005	3.060 (1.698)	0.036
N	1007		1007	
Wald Chi squared	44.69		47.86	
P> Chi squared	<0.001		<0.001	

Robust standard errors reported
P-values are of one-tailed significance tests

As model 5 in table 2.4 shows, the effect of extraterritorial bases on conflict duration is positive and significant. Substantively the effect is large as well. Setting continuous variables to their means, war years to 1, and changing the value of extraterritorial bases from 0 to 1 increases the predicted probability of conflict continuation to 92 percent, up from a baseline probability of

Table 2.5 Neighborhood conditions as predictors of external bases (Dependent variable: external bases)

	Rival neighbor	Civil war neighbor	(log) Refugees (t-1)
Coefficient	0.098	0.169	0.049
Standard Error	0.051	0.054	0.004
T-statistic	1.930	3.160	11.730

82 percent; increasing the value of bases from 0 to 2 shifts the probability of war continuation to 96 percent. Thus, in both statistical and substantive terms, hypothesis 4 is confirmed.

Model 6 includes variables for regional refugees, civil wars, and rivals, along with the direct measure of extraterritorial bases. As expected, the external base variable retains its significance, though its coefficient is slightly reduced. More important, the other regional conditions lose much of their explanatory power, since most of their variation is soaked up by the base variable. The magnitude of the other coefficients are reduced (compared to models above), providing evidence that these factors work through the mechanism of creating areas in which TNRs can establish sanctuaries. Bivariate linear probability models with bases as the dependent variable and each of the neighborhood variables as independent variables (table 2.5) confirm expectations: these variables are significant predictors of TNR bases.

International Borders and Ethnic Conflict

The final hypothesis is that ethnic groups located near international borders will be more likely to rebel. As opposed to groups located in the interior or groups dispersed across the country, proximity to international boundaries gives ethnic rebels the opportunity to slip back and forth across the border in order to escape government repression. Although the theory is not specific to ethnic conflict per se, using ethnic groups as the unit of analysis is attractive because it allows for subnational variation in conflict patterns. Furthermore, given that many conflicts are characterized by contests between ethnic groups over control of the state or secession, it is reasonable to use ethnic groups—as opposed to some other subnational actor—as the unit of analysis. Thus, hypothesis 5 expects that, all else being equal, ethnic groups that are concentrated in regions along international borders are more likely to rebel than other groups.

The data used in this analysis comes from the Minorities at Risk (MAR) Project,[19] which collects information on ethnic group characteristics, group discrimination, and acts of protest and violence for ethnic groups throughout the world (for details, see Davenport 2004). An eight-part variable for the level of antiregime rebellion is included in these data. The value labels are as follows:

0 No violence reported
1 Political banditry, sporadic terrorism
2 Campaigns of terrorism
3 Local rebellions
4 Small-scale guerrilla activity
5 Intermediate guerrilla activity
6 Large-scale guerrilla activity
7 Protracted civil war

The dataset also has a variable for the concentration of ethnic groups near an international boundary. This is a four-part variable for: (1) no geographic concentration; (2) the group is concentrated away from an international border; (3) the group is concentrated along one international border; and (4) the group is concentrated along two or more borders. For this analysis, a dichotomous variable is created which is scored 1 for categories 3 and 4, above. Observations were collected by ethnic group in five-year periods from 1980 to 2000, therefore there are 5 observations per ethnic group.

Table 2.6 shows the bivariate relationship between the MAR rebellion score for each observation (ethnic group/year), divided between groups that are located along an international border and groups that are not. Comparing actual versus expected values indicates that there is a statistically significant difference among these categories. As can be seen from the table, although the modal category for both types of ethnic groups is no conflict, at each step in the rebellion index, groups located near an international border more frequently engage in violence. More specifically, only 17 percent of ethnic groups that were located away from an international boundary engaged in some form of political violence (70 of 406), but 42 percent of groups near an international border did so (265 of 637).

Others have suggested that transnational ethnic ties may explain relationship between proximity to a border and propensity for ethnic uprising, as borders often bisect ethnic communities and ethnic groups may

19. http://www.cidcm.umd.edu/inscr/mar/ (accessed January 15, 2007).

Table 2.6 Level of ethnic rebellion and location near a border

		International border		
		No	Yes	Total
Rebellion score	0	336	372	708
	1	20	55	75
	2	5	32	37
	3	9	29	38
	4	9	37	46
	5	9	38	47
	6	6	30	36
	7	12	44	56
	Total	406	637	1,043

$\chi^2 = 69.8825$
p-value $= <0.001$

come to the aid of their kin in other countries (Cetinyan 2002; Davis and Moore 1997; Saideman 2001; Woodwell 2004). Many cases of conflict may also be driven by irredentist motivations, where the ethic group is assisted by a foreign power seeking to annex territory. This mutual assistance may either embolden ethnic groups to rebel or make governments more likely to offer concessions and thereby dampen violent activity (Cetinyan 2002). A multivariate analysis that includes a number of statistical controls can take this relationship into account. It includes a binary variable, also taken from the MAR dataset, which is coded 1 for groups that have ethnic kin in other states.

I also include a binary variable for concentrated (as opposed to dispersed) ethnic groups that are not located near an international border to control for factors associated with group concentration. Monica Toft (2003) argues that territorial concentration in an ethnic homeland makes groups more likely to rebel because actors view territory as an indivisible issue. Using the same data sources used in this analysis she finds empirical support for the claim that group concentration is an important predictor of violence. Thus, the effects of simple group concentration must be controlled for. As additional controls, I include a seven-part variable (also from MAR), which indicates the degree of economic disadvantage a group faces—a measure of grievance—and regime data based on the Polity score.

Two alternative estimation techniques are used. First, a random effects GLS model is estimated that takes into account repeat observations for the same ethnic group.[20] This model treats the eight-point conflict scale as a continuous variable. Second, because the rebellion scale may reflect simple orderings rather than a truly continuous dependent variable, an ordered logit model is estimated with robust standard errors adjusted for clustering by ethnic group.

Table 2.7 shows the results for the multivariate analysis; the results are robust to the estimation technique used.[21] As can be seen from the table, even when including the control variables, groups that are concentrated near an international border are shown to be more likely to engage in rebellion. The coefficients show that the effect for location near an international border is larger and more significant than that of ethnic kin in other states. Transnational ethnic ties and potential irredentism may be important in particular cases, but simply being located near an international boundary appears to have a large independent effect. Furthermore, group concentration does not matter in and of itself; it only matters when groups are concentrated *and* located near a border. Therefore, Toft's (2003) hypothesized relationship between territorial concentration and violence only applies in cases where group concentration combines with international opportunities for mobilization.

The other control variables reveal that economic discrimination, a measure of grounds for grievance, increases violent activity and that the level of democracy—a state-wide attribute—decreases violent behavior. In sum, there is good evidence in support of hypothesis 5—ethnic groups are more likely to rebel when they are located near international boundaries.

Evaluating the Evidence

Based on the results offered above, what can be said about the hypotheses? Have any unexpected relationships emerged in the data? First, hypothesis 1 receives relatively good support from the models. The random effects logit model reveals a strong relationship between neighborhood rivals and civil conflict. The transition model, however, reveals that international rivals are more strongly associated with the duration of conflict than with its initial

20. In models not shown, country as opposed to group effects were estimated. Results do not vary with this alternative specification.

21. In additional GLS models (not reported), time "effects" were estimated by including dummy variables for each of the years (setting 1980 as the baseline). The results remain virtually unchanged, with the coefficient international border *increasing* in size.

Table 2.7 Ethnic conflict and international borders

	Generalized least squares		Ordered logit	
	B	p-value	β	p-value
International border	0.611	0.048	0.904	0.018
	(.366)		(.428)	
International kin	0.386	0.113	0.387	0.123
	(.318)		(.334)	
Concentrated group	0.124	0.333	0.183	0.264
	(.286)		(0.289)	
Economic discrimination	0.074	0.090	0.108	0.046
	(.055)		(.064)	
Polity	−0.037	0.001	−0.036	0.024
	(.012)		(.018)	
Constant	0.534	0.004	—	
	(0.200)		—	
Cuts: 1	—		1.770	0.275
2	—		2.166	0.287
3	—		2.387	0.297
4	—		2.624	0.301
5	—		3.003	0.318
6	—		3.493	0.354
7	—		4.073	0.397
N	963		963	
Number of groups	258		—	
Wald Chi squared	32.52		33.72	
P > Chi squared	<0.001		<0.001	
Rho	0.623		—	

Standard errors for ordered logit cuts reported in the "p-value" column
P-values are of one-tailed tests

outbreak. One reason for this may be that international rivals do not always choose to confront their enemies through rebel proxies. Given that rivals may choose between direct confrontation and support for rebellion, the effect on civil war onset may be somewhat indeterminate. However, once a rebellion has begun, rival countries may attempt to take advantage of instability in their neighbor by offering support to insurgents and by using their influence to block peace settlements.

Hypothesis 2 receives strong support for at least one of the indicators. Although neighboring a weak state, as measured by GDP per capita, is not a significant predictor of conflict, neighboring a state weakened by civil war does have a large substantive impact on violence. Failed states, therefore, can and do provide fertile breeding grounds for rebel organizations. Whereas the random effects model displayed a positive and significant effect, the transition model revealed that civil wars in neighbors are more clearly associated with the onset of conflict than with its duration. This may be because states can adopt better counterinsurgency measures under these circumstances. Troop deployments near the border and robust border security measures can be implemented without provoking neighbors. Moreover, there may be opportunities for security cooperation between states. Importantly, if states are simply too weak to prevent rebel access but are not sympathetic to the rebellion, they will not try to block peace agreements between combatant parties, but rather may play a constructive role in facilitating negotiated settlements.

Hypothesis 3a also finds strong evidence in the data. All models demonstrate that refugees are an important *cause* of conflict, not just the unfortunate victims of it. This lends support to the substantial case study literature on the role that "refugee warriors" play during civil wars. Yet the transition model demonstrates that refugees have an important effect on conflict continuation but have less of an effect on conflict onset. This is perhaps not surprising given that most refugees first flee from violence and only then engage in or facilitate it, and relatively few long-term refugee communities start rebellions later in time as compared with refugees that fight in contemporaneous conflicts.

Additionally, this absence of a finding for onset may be due to steps to mitigate concerns about endogeneity. Refugees are obviously correlated with prior conflict, and it is difficult to ascertain whether subsequent conflicts are related to attributes of a previous war or whether refugees are directly responsible for the resumption of fighting. This is not to say that this does not happen in practice: Cuban exiles fleeing the Castro regime launched the Bay of Pigs insurgency; ex-Somoza military personnel began the Contra rebellion against the Sandinistas from bases in Honduras; Iranians who fled the Islamic Revolution government began a civil war—under the Mujahedin-e-Khalq—against that regime, to name a few examples. However, to be on the methodological "safe-side" with regard to endogeneity, such incidents would not be picked up as cases where refugees began a new rebellion because the effects of the first round of fighting, which led to an exodus in the first place, are taken into account. Nonetheless, the transition model revealed that refugee communities prolong the duration of a conflict significantly.

Subhypothesis 3b which suggests that refugees are most likely to contribute to the duration of civil conflict when they are located in weak or rival countries, also receives support. This upholds the notion that not all refugees are security threats but only become militarized when rival governments, or militants with free access to refugee camps, are able to mobilize civilian refugees into TNR organizations.

Directly observing the opposition's use of extraterritorial bases and estimating their effect on conflict duration yielded positive results as well. Confirming hypothesis 4, the models show that extraterritorial sanctuaries have an important substantive impact on how long conflicts last. Notably, this provides more direct evidence about the role that TNRs play during armed conflicts. One may argue that the other neighborhood conditions are not truly *causal*; that is, neighborhood civil wars, rivalries, and refugees may be spuriously related to domestic civil wars and cluster geographically for reasons unrelated to the theory. However, the extraterritorial base variable is a clear indicator of the strategic use of foreign sanctuaries by TNRs. Moreover, this variable was shown to outperform the other neighborhood indicators when combined in a single model, and additional tests confirmed the expectation that these factors work through the mechanism of providing opportunities for the establishment of external bases.

Finally, hypothesis 5—that ethnic groups near an international border will be more likely to rebel—finds strong support. Groups that are territorially concentrated and near an international boundary are more likely to fight because they have access to neighboring territory. These models use a completely different set of data and different units of analysis to provide a useful additional test of the implications of the theory.

What does this imply for the theoretical framework presented in the previous chapter? I have argued that regional and border effects are integral to our understanding of conflict processes: when rebels have the ability to mobilize outside of their target state, fighting is more likely to erupt and rebel organizations can better escape repression. State boundaries constrain government forces to their sovereign jurisdiction, but rebels and opposition groups are less limited in their geographic scope. Border and regional effects matter—civil conflicts are not entirely driven by internal processes. Several other elements of the theory—most notably bargaining dynamics—which are not conducive to a quantitative study, will be examined in subsequent chapters.

Importantly, this chapter has demonstrated that nation-state "boxes" are too limited as units of analysis. Although some rebellions are fought entirely within countries, many civil wars are better characterized as regional or transnational phenomena. International borders clearly do not limit rebel organizations, and our theories and empirical studies of civil war likewise should not be confined to country-level factors. Understanding the nexus between internal and external factors is likely to substantially improve our analyses of conflict.

Chapter 2 Appendix
Exploring Cause and Effect Relationships
with Case Evidence

Most statistical analyses are plagued by indeterminate causal connections between the independent and dependent variables. It is axiomatic that statistics can prove correlation but not causation. For instance, in studies of civil conflict, GDP has been used by various authors as a measure of state capacity, grievances, and the opportunity costs for fighting. Causal inference in a statistical sense suggests that a one-unit increase in X has a particular effect on the Y variable, but it is difficult to determine if the proposed *theoretical* conditions are responsible for this relationship or if alternative explanations for the same correlation are more accurate.

In order to get a better sense of causation, it may be useful to dig a little deeper behind the statistical correlations presented in this chapter. Therefore, I conduct an analysis of civil conflicts during the period 1996–2000 to verify if positive "hits" in the statistical regressions hold for the theoretical reasons suggested in chapter 1. Namely, I ask, did neighbors actually host rebels when they were expected to? For this time frame, I look at cases of conflict where there existed: (1) a rival neighbor, (2) a neighbor experiencing civil war, and (3) neighbors hosting 10,000 or more refugees. In other words, since these variables are dichotomized and conflict is also a 0/1 variable, the cases analyzed here are those that are both are coded 1. Then, if there was a conflict in country A and neighboring country B was a rival (for example), I examined whether the rebels actually used the rival's territory as a base. Data on the presence of extraterritorial bases was used to determine whether the coincidence of independent and dependent variables is correctly accounted for by the theory—rebels should have external bases in these territories.

This is an additional diagnostic (supplementing table 2.5), which allows us to ascertain whether links in the causal chain—from regional conditions to external bases—are valid. This approach mimics Michael Ross (2004) with respect to natural resource abundance and conflict. It has been argued

Chapter 2, Appendix Table A Civil war and interstate rivalries, 1996–2000

	Civil war	Rival name	Rebel host?
1	Afghanistan	Iran	yes
2	Algeria	Morocco	yes
3	Angola	DR Congo	yes
4	Colombia	Venezuela	yes
5	DR Congo	Angola	yes
6	Egypt	Israel	no
		Sudan	yes
7	Ethiopia	Eritrea	yes
		Sudan	yes
8	India	China	no
		Pakistan	yes
9	Iran	Afghanistan	no
		Iraq	yes
10	Iraq	Iran	yes
		Kuwait	no
		Saudi Arabia	no
		Syria	no
11	Israel	Egypt	yes
		Syria	yes
12	Pakistan	India	no
13	Peru	Ecuador	no
14	Sudan	Egypt	no
		Eritrea	yes
		Ethiopia	yes
		Uganda	yes
15	Turkey	Greece	yes
16	Uganda	Sudan	yes
17	Uzbekistan	Kazakhstan	no
18	Yugoslavia	Bosnia	no
		Croatia	no

Percent correctly attributed: 78% (number of correctly attributed cases/total number of cases).

Chapter 2, Appendix Table B Civil war and neighboring civil war, 1996–2000

	Country	Neighbor Name	Rebel Host?
1	Afghanistan	Tajikistan	yes
		Pakistan	no
		Iran	yes
2	Algeria	Niger	no
3	Angola	Congo-B	yes
		DR Congo	yes
4	Burundi	DR Congo	yes
		Rwanda	yes
5	Chad	Niger	yes
		Sudan	yes
6	Colombia	Peru	no
7	Congo-B	DR Congo	no
		Angola	no
8	DR Congo	Angola	yes
		Burundi	yes
		Congo-B	no
		Rwanda	yes
		Sudan	no
		Uganda	yes
9	Egypt	Sudan	yes
		Israel	no
10	Ethiopia	Eritrea	yes
		Somalia	yes
		Sudan	no
11	Guinea	Liberia	yes
		Senegal	no
		Sierra Leone	yes
12	India	Myanmar	yes
		Nepal	no
		Pakistan	yes
13	Iran	Afghanistan	no
		Turkey	no
14	Iraq	Turkey	yes
15	Israel	Egypt	yes
16	Liberia	Guinea	yes
		Sierra Leone	yes

Chapter 2, Appendix Table B (*continued*)

	Country	Neighbor Name	Rebel Host?
17	Myanmar	India	no
18	Nepal	India	yes
19	Niger	Chad	no
		Algeria	no
20	Pakistan	Afghanistan	no
		India	no
21	Peru	Colombia	no
22	Rwanda	Burundi	no
		DR Congo	yes
		Uganda	no
23	Senegal	Guinea	no
24	Sierra Leone	Guinea	no
		Liberia	yes
25	Somalia	Ethiopia	no
26	Sudan	Chad	no
		DR Congo	no
		Egypt	no
		Eritrea	yes
		Ethiopia	yes
		Uganda	yes
27	Tajikistan	Afghanistan	yes
28	Turkey	Iran	yes
		Iraq	yes
29	Uganda	DR Congo	yes
		Rwanda	no
		Sudan	yes
30	Uzbekistan	Afghanistan	yes

Percent correctly attributed = 67% (number of correctly attributed cases/total number of cases).

that natural resource dependence leads to the outbreak of armed conflict because rebels seek the opportunity to gather lootable resources. Ross deliberately chooses thirteen cases of civil conflict where natural resources were plentiful to determine whether these conflicts were in fact fueled by the presence of such commodities. Through detailed process tracing, he is able to check the validity of the theoretical claims made by other scholars

Chapter 2, Appendix Table C Civil war and greater than 10,000 refugees in neighbors, 1996–2000

	Country	Refugee host (>10,000)	Rebel host?
1	Afghanistan	Iran	yes
		Pakistan	no
		Tajikistan	yes
2	Angola	Congo-B	yes
		DR Congo	yes
		Namibia	no
		Zambia	no
3	Burundi	DR Congo	yes
		Tanzania	yes
4	Cambodia	Thailand	yes
		Vietnam	no
5	Chad	Cameroon	yes
6	Congo-B	DR Congo	no
		Gabon	no
7	DR Congo	Angola	yes
		Burundi	yes
		Central African Republic	no
		Rwanda	yes
		Uganda	yes
		Zambia	no
8	Ethiopia	Sudan	no
9	Iran	Iraq	yes
10	Iraq	Iran	yes
11	Israel	Jordan	yes
		Lebanon	yes
		Syria	yes
12	Liberia	Cote d'Ivoire	yes
		Guinea	yes
		Sierra Leone	yes
13	Myanmar	Bangladesh	no
		Thailand	yes
14	Niger	Algeria	no
15	Russia	Kazakhstan	no
16	Rwanda	DR Congo	yes
		Tanzania	no
		Uganda	no

Chapter 2, Appendix Table C (*continued*)

	Country	Refugee host (>10,000)	Rebel host?
17	Senegal	Guinea-Bissau	yes
18	Sierra Leone	Guinea	no
		Liberia	yes
19	Somalia	Djibouti	no
		Ethiopia	no
		Kenya	no
20	Sudan	Central African Republic	no
		Chad	no
		DR Congo	no
		Ethiopia	yes
		Kenya	no
		Uganda	yes
21	Tajikistan	Afghanistan	yes
		Kyrgyzstan	no
		Uzbekistan	no
22	Turkey	Iraq	yes
23	Uganda	DR Congo	yes
24	Yugoslavia	Albania	no
		Bosnia	no
		Macedonia	no

Percent correctly attributed: 75% (number of correctly attributed cases/total number of cases).

(e.g., Collier and Hoeffler 2004) and propose alternative causal pathways. Although the analysis here is less ambitious in terms of rich detail, it serves as a similar "check" on the statistical methodology.

The "percent correctly attributed" tally at the bottom of each table divides the total number of cases of civil war by the number of cases where rebels were present in at least one of the listed neighbors. Table A looks at the presence of external bases during periods of civil war in which there existed a rival neighbor; table B looks at bases in neighboring countries that are also experiencing conflict; and table C looks at the relationship between refugee communities of 10,000 or more and the presence of rebel bases. In each case, there appears to be a strong relationship between these neighborhood factors and the location of rebel bases.

3 Transnational Rebels and International Conflict

In June 1982, after an assassination attempt on Shlomo Argov, Israel's ambassador to the United Kingdom, Israel invaded Lebanon. This war, code-named "Operation Peace in Galilee," was not fought over territory or economic resources but because Lebanon was host to the Palestine Liberation Organization (PLO), a transnational rebel organization responsible for a number of attacks on Israel. The PLO had established its headquarters in Lebanon after it was evicted from Jordanian territory in 1970 and had grown into a formidable insurgent army, primarily recruiting among refugee camps. Israel's response to the PLO presence in Lebanon initially took the form of artillery fire and aerial bombings across the border. Weakened by internal disputes and conflict among various religious factions, Lebanon's fragile government was powerless to move against the PLO forces in the south or respond to Israeli incursions. Israel invaded Lebanon to rout the PLO and occupied a security zone in the south, where it remained for nearly two decades. But this was not the end of Israel's troubles with militants in Lebanon. In summer 2006, Israel again attacked Lebanon in order to combat Hezbollah, a militant group that was established during the period of Israeli occupation and which calls for Israel's destruction.

The previous chapter demonstrated that the availability of mobilization opportunities abroad makes rebellion more likely to break out and to endure. As discussed in chapter 1, however, extraterritorial bases also serve to create or exacerbate tensions between rebel host and home countries. This was certainly the case between Israel and Lebanon. Therefore, there are endogenous and mutually reinforcing relationships between internal and international conflict: conditions in a neighborhood provide opportunities for rebel mobilization and, in turn, foster international disputes between states. Although many studies of international war focus on relations among state dyads alone, conflicts often involve "triangular" strategic bargains involving rebels, host governments, and home governments. This chapter develops and tests hypotheses regarding the implications of TNR activities for state-to-state relations. External bases should raise the probability of international disputes between states, but the path to conflict will differ depending on the type of rebel host. Rival governments support rebel organizations in order to weaken their international enemies, substituting the direct use of force with rebel patronage. Such states delegate at least some of their foreign policy prerogatives to rebel groups and may in fact be involved in less *direct* fighting. Weak states, by contrast, may be drawn into international wars that are not of their own choosing because they are unable to evict TNRs or prevent cross-border incursions.

Thus, a second major claim of this book—one that has been overlooked by traditional conflict research—is that civil conflicts frequently spill over into relations between states. Although there is now a large body of scholarly research on foreign intervention in civil wars, much of this work seeks to explain the causes of such intervention or its effect on conflict outcomes or duration (see e.g. Balch-Lindsay and Enterline 2000; Carment and Rowlands 1998; Elbadawi and Sambanis 2000; Meernik 1996; Regan 2000, 2002; Saideman 2002; Walter 2002). Yet scholars have largely ignored the possibility that foreign interference in another state's domestic conflicts—particularly on behalf of rebel groups—raises the probability of a violent *international* confrontation between states. This chapter presents statistical evidence that external rebel bases are associated with a higher likelihood of international conflict and that international rivals sometimes use support for insurgents as an alternative to direct fighting. I will also dig deeper behind the statistical associations by examining a number of cases in greater detail.

While this chapter focuses on the determinants of international conflict, these results must be viewed in light of the overarching theory about how civil and international conflicts are intertwined, multiactor interactions and processes. Rebels are sometimes aided by external enemies, but they can also provoke or deepen international hostilities and are part of multiple, simultaneous bargaining processes. Therefore, the results presented in this book paint a larger picture of "zones" of overlapping conflicts.

Empirical Implications of the Theory

As asserted in chapter 1, holding bases in neighboring countries will be especially important for the military operations of rebel organizations because they lack the ability to project force over long distances. Bases across the border provide strategic advantages to TNR groups. Yet hosting rebel organizations necessarily internationalizes "domestic" conflicts by drawing in external actors. Whether external states deliberately support TNRs on their soil or play reluctant hosts to militants, conflicts between rebel host and home countries are likely to arise, although, as discussed below, the consequences of their involvement differ depending on the type of rebel host.

All forms of support to rebel groups—including funds and arms—are likely to provoke international tension, but providing sanctuary to TNRs is particularly likely to spark a military confrontation between states. It is well-known that geographic contiguity raises the risk of an armed conflict in a dyad because proximity provides ample opportunities for violent interactions (Most and Starr 1989). Land transport is relatively easy to conduct, but moving military forces longer distances requires substantial air and sea capabilities. Although foreign patrons providing arms and finances to rebels may be far away and beyond the reach of the offended government, neighboring patrons are an easier target for retaliation.[1]

There are several reasons why international conflicts may arise from hosting rebels. First, the home state can retaliate against the host for harboring dissidents. Home countries will demand that the host rid its territory of rebels and can threaten to use force in order to gain compliance. Yet it may be difficult for weak rebel hosts to comply with these demands, because driving out foreign rebels may be just as costly as—or even more costly than—an international confrontation. This complicates negotiations because weak states, lacking the capacity to meet the target state's policy demands, cannot make credible commitments to evict insurgents. Thus, weak states are drawn into conflicts that are not of their choosing. Rival neighbors, by contrast, deliberately provide access to transnational rebels. These states continue to host foreign insurgents because the benefits of weakening their international opponents outweigh the potential costs of retaliation (for a formal treatment, see Bapat 2006).

---

1. This is not to say that international conflicts over rebel patronage never occur between distant states. A major reason for the U.S. military invasion of Afghanistan was to attack Al-Qaeda forces, which were hosted by the Taliban government. Nonetheless, most states do not have the capacity to attack distant countries.

Second, although the costs of counterinsurgency are higher, limited strikes across the border sometimes occur. Cross-border fighting, stray fire, and "hot pursuit" raids into foreign territory are likely to provoke tension because they jeopardize the security and sovereignty of the host country. Unlike retaliation against the host government, these attacks are targeted at the TNR group, but they still violate the sovereign territory of the neighbor. Third, concern over the negative effects of conflict spillovers—such as economic disruptions, health effects, and refugee flows—can spark international incidents (Ghobarah, Huth, and Russett 2003; Murdoch and Sandler 2004; Salehyan and Gleditsch 2006). Finally, the target country may deploy troops near the international boundary to block insurgents at the border, but such troop mobilization may be threatening to neighbors and create security-dilemma worries about the true intent of such actions.

This discussion leads to the following hypothesis:

> H6 (international conflict). External rebel bases in neighboring territories increase the probability of a militarized interstate dispute between rebel host and home countries.

Rival States and Substitution Effects

Rival neighboring states deliberately choose to host rebel organizations and support opposition movements in order to undermine their enemies. Although international animosity certainly precedes rebel support, rebel support can further exacerbate the rivalry. In many cases states confront their opponents with their own military resources. Yet in addition, states can attack their international opponents indirectly by supporting insurgent groups. Delegation to a rebel organization spares the state the costs of direct military engagement but can also lead to agency problems if the rebel group takes actions that are not fully consistent with the preferences of the patron. Thus, there is a trade-off between avoiding costs and foreign policy autonomy. The choice between strategies is an interesting subject in-and-of itself, but for the time being will be left for future research.

This discussion suggests a possible substitution effect (on substitution see Most and Starr 1984; Morgan and Palmer 2000). International rivals are known to be more conflict-prone than other dyads, yet they may substitute direct state-to-state military action with support for rebels. Some—although certainly not all—of the conflict is carried out through proxies rather than conducted directly. Therefore, we should see a *decrease* in international military disputes when rival states support and shelter rebel organizations. This leads to a further hypothesis:

> *H7 (rivals and substitution effects). International rivals are less likely to use direct force against one another when transnational rebel bases are located on their territory.*

Note that this hypothesis is a conditional one. Hypothesis 6 holds that the presence of extraterritorial bases independently increases the probability of international conflict. Hypothesis 7 claims that *for cases of rival dyads,* such bases will be associated with fewer direct uses of force than would otherwise be expected. Although international rivals engage in disputes more regularly than other dyads, the joint effect of rivalries and sanctuaries is not simply an additive one. Rather, there is an *interactive* effect, where direct force between rivals is somewhat attenuated by transferring armed conflict to rebel organizations.

Measuring the Concepts

A statistical analysis of international conflicts during the latter part of the twentieth century will help to test these hypothesis. The units of analysis are dyad-years from 1946–1999 and are restricted to contiguous states because rebel bases, for the most part, are located in neighboring territories. Additional models that do not impose such a restriction are examined below. For the dependent variable, international disputes, I employ a dichotomous variable from the Militarized Interstate Dispute (MID) dataset (Ghosn, Palmer, and Bremer 2004), which is coded 1 for category 4 or 5 MIDs.[2] The MID categories indicate the level of hostility, with category 4 and 5 disputes involving the actual use of force.[3] Because the dependent variable is binary (namely, Binary Time-Series Cross-Section, BTSCS), I use the Beck, Katz, and Tucker (1998) event-history estimation method by including a count of peace years among states and three cubic splines on

2. In alternative models, which I do not report for the sake of space, I include a different indicator of international conflict from the International Crisis Behavior (ICB) Dataset (Brecher, Wilkenfeld, and Moser 1988). The ICB dataset does not require the actual use of force. They include international crises that have a substantial potential to escalate to an international war. The results do not change significantly when using this alternative measure.

3. The MID data is a 0 to 5 variable that ranges from no hostility to full-blown war. A dichotomous variable for category 4 and 5 MIDs has become standard in the literature. In an alternative specification, I run an ordered logit model on the full range of the MID data. The main findings are unchanged with this model.

the right hand side of the equation.[4] Accordingly, only the initial year of conflict, or onset, is recorded, and ongoing years are excluded from the analysis.

The main independent variable of interest is a dichotomous indicator coded 1 if at least one state in the dyad is host to a transnational rebel group from the other state. This is the external bases variable described in the previous chapter. I have also considered variables for mutual and one-sided hosting of rebel groups; the main effects are quite similar.

Second, I include a variable which indicates the presence of an international rivalry in a dyad. This variable comes from William R. Thompson's (2001) dataset on international rivalries and is coded 1 for rivals (and 0 otherwise). This is the same rivalry indicator described in chapter 2. Using this measure is attractive given the hypothesis about substitution effects, since it is not based on a minimum number of international conflict events. To test hypothesis 7, an interaction term between external bases and rivalries is included. Since both of these variables are dichotomous (0, 1), this interaction takes the value of 1 for cases in which external bases *and* rivalries are present and 0 otherwise. The sign on the interaction is expected to be negative, and its constituent components are expected to be signed positively.

In addition to foreign sanctuaries used by transnational rebels, other forms of support to opposition groups are also expected to be relevant to international conflict dynamics. Previously, scholars have focused primarily on transfers of arms and finances to rebel groups, and such assistance may also increase conflict behavior between states. For comparison purposes, therefore, I estimate models including data compiled by Patrick Regan (2000) on external intervention in civil war. This is a dummy variable coded 1 for cases where external states provided military or economic assistance to rebel organizations. This was also interacted with the rivalry indicator to test for substitution. A finding that other forms of support to rebels also increase conflict behavior would serve as a useful extension of the theory. Yet direct transfers are somewhat different from external bases because such support is a voluntary choice by the patron and is necessarily given by hostile states, whereas sanctuaries can be found in passive neighbors. Additionally, resources can be supplied by distant states, but neighbors are needed for external bases.

I also include a number of control variables. First, power ratios may affect the likelihood of conflict, as overwhelming power preponderance may deter armed conflict. The power ratio variable included here is taken from the Composite Index of National Capabilities (CINC) of the Correlates of

---

4. In the results section below, the cubic splines are not reported in the regression tables.

War (COW) data and is the natural logarithm of the stronger party's CINC score divided by the sum of the two nations' CINCs.[5] The CINC index is based on military personnel, military expenditures, economic production, and population data. The COW project's alliance data is also included (Singer, Bremer, and Stuckey 1972). This is a dichotomous indicator coded 1 if the members of the dyad are part of a mutual defense pact.[6] Finally, I include data from the Polity project to control for dyadic democracy. Several scholars have shown that democracies are less likely to fight one another (Jaggers and Gurr 1995). The Polity score of the least democratic state in the dyad was included to test the democratic peace hypothesis.

As an additional test, I replicate the results reported in Russett and Oneal (2001), a well-established model of international conflict. This model specification includes information on all dyads, contiguous or not, from 1946 to 1991.[7] As above, the dependent variable is a dummy variable for category 4 and 5 MIDs. The variables in this model include indicators for dyadic democracy, bilateral trade, and joint membership in international organizations. Each of these "liberal" factors are expected to decrease the probability of an international dispute. Additional variables include the dyadic power ratio, alliances,[8] distance, contiguity, and whether both states are minor powers (see Russett and Oneal for a full description of variables used). These models were also estimated using the Beck, Katz, and Tucker (1998) method for BTSCS data. All models employ robust standard errors clustered by dyad to account for additional nonindependence of observations.

Quantitative Results

Table 3.1 reports the results using contiguous dyads. The first model includes the variable for external bases by itself, and model 2 includes the interaction between rivals and bases. Model 3 compares these results with Patrick Regan's indicator of foreign support for rebel groups. Except for

5. As an alternative specification, I include the natural log of the stronger state's CINC divided by the weaker state's CINC. Results do not change substantially.

6. The MID, ICB, alliance, and CINC data were generated using EUgene software. See Bennett and Stam (2000).

7. Because data on external bases is only available for the post-World War II period, the full time span of the Russett and Oneal data cannot be used.

8. The Russett and Oneal alliance indicator is coded 1 for any form of alliance, which is different from the defense pact indicator described above.

Table 3.1 International conflict regression results, contiguous dyads

	1. Coefficient (Standard error)	p-value	2. Coefficient (Standard error)	p-value	3. Coefficient (Standard error)	p-value
External base	1.147 (0.168)	<0.000	1.672 (0.194)	<0.000	—	—
Rival's external base	—	—	−1.172 (0.257)	<0.000	—	—
Intervention (Regan)	—	—	—	—	0.912 (0.251)	<0.000
Rival's × external intervention	—	—	—	—	−0.389 (0.328)	0.118
Rivals	1.243 (0.145)	<0.001	1.552 (0.155)	<0.001	1.365 (0.158)	<0.001
Power ratio	0.265 (0.325)	0.208	0.190 (0.312)	0.272	0.200 (0.353)	0.285
Defense pact	−0.147 (0.129)	0.129	−0.148 (0.126)	0.121	−0.258 (0.131)	0.025
Democracy	−0.016 (0.012)	0.095	−0.012 (0.012)	0.162	−0.010 (0.012)	0.210
Peace years	0.047 (0.047)	0.156	0.046 (0.046)	0.164	0.029 (0.044)	0.256
Constant	−3.371 (0.186)	<0.001	−3.499 (0.195)	<0.001	−3.155 (0.176)	<0.001
N	10197		10197		10197	
Wald Chi squared	298.02		333.9		283.07	

Standard errors clustered on dyads.
P-values are of one-tailed significance tests.
Cubic splines not reported.

the results for defense pact in model 3, the control variables do not reach statistical significance at conventional levels.[9] Given that these variables predict the existence of an international rivalry quite well, the lack of statistical significance should not be surprising, and indeed democracy

9. As an alternative specification, I include a dummy variable coded one for cases where both countries have a Polity score of 6 or greater. In such models, joint democracy has a negative and significant effect on conflict, supporting the democratic peace hypothesis. I include the Polity score of the least democratic state (the "weak link") in order to be consistent with work by Russett and Oneal. In this alternative model, the findings for the main variables of interest are substantively unchanged.

becomes significant when rivalry is excluded from the model. However, since these indicators are mainly included as controls, this should not be a major concern.

Turning to the main independent variable, the external rebel base indicator is positive and significant, providing strong evidence in support of hypothesis 6 that external rebel bases in neighboring territories increase the probability of a militarized interstate dispute between rebel host and home countries. Interstate rivalries are also shown to increase the likelihood of a MID significantly, as expected. In support of hypothesis 7 that international rivals are less likely to use direct force against one another when transnational rebel bases are located on their territory, model 2 displays a statistically significant interactive effect between interstate rivalries and external bases, and the sign on the interaction is negative. Therefore, these variables cannot be considered in isolation of one another, but their combined effect must be taken into account. A simple additive model would suggest a very high probability of conflict if both variables take on the value of 1. Yet while the individual coefficients for external bases and rivalries are positive, when both factors are present the coefficient for the interaction term must be added to the base estimate. The negative sign on the interaction indicates a reduction in the log-odds of conflict when both conditions apply. This provides evidence in support of the claim that there is a substitution effect between rebel support and state-to-state military engagements; the odds of interstate armed conflict are reduced when rivals host TNR groups. This does not imply "peace" in any meaningful sense; only that enemies use unconventional means of striking their opponents.

Model 3 compares these results with the Regan coding of foreign intervention. The intervention variable is positive and significant, indicating that military and economic support for rebels is also associated with a higher likelihood of international conflict. In addition to external sanctuaries, transfers of finances and arms to rebels also increase the odds of a MID. As before, the interaction term is negative, although the strength of the statistical association is not as strong.[10] These results extend the potential applicability of my theory to other forms of foreign patronage of rebel groups.

To aid in the interpretation of the results and to illustrate the findings, figure 3.1 displays substantive effects on the predicted probability of MIDs using these estimates. To construct a baseline probability, the power ratio was set at its mean, defense pact and Polity were set to 0, and the number of peace

---

10. When the Regan intervention variable is included in a model along with external bases, the former loses its statistical significance, but the latter retains significance.

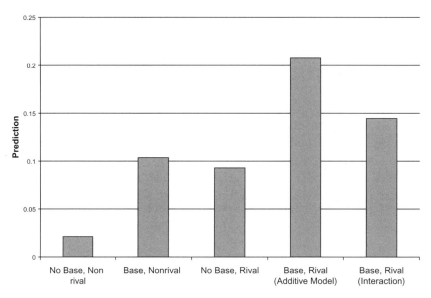

Figure 3.1. Predicted probabilities of interstate conflict

years was set to 5. Figure 3.1 displays increases in predicted probabilities given independent shifts in the rivalry and external base variables along with the combined effects of these factors. In the absence of bases or rivalry, the predicted risk of conflict in a given dyad is roughly 2 percent. External bases and international rivalries independently raise the probability of conflict in a given year to approximately 10 percent and 9 percent, respectively.

The final two categories represented in figure 3.1 show the estimated probabilities when rivalry and external bases are present. The simple additive effect of rivalries and international bases is rather large, raising the predicted probability of conflict to 20 percent. Yet this would be misleading, since there is an interaction between the two variables, mitigating their combined effect. When both conditions are present, the predicted probability of conflict rises to about 14 percent—lower than the additive model. This indicates moderate support for the substitution hypothesis. If there were perfect substitution, then rivals would never fight directly when they provide support to rebel groups. This is clearly not the case; the joint presence of both conditions still raises the likelihood of conflict significantly, yet not as much as would be expected if there were a simple additive effect.[11] States will typically (i.e., on

11. In models not shown, the effect of one-sided versus mutual rebel hosting is estimated. One-sided and two-sided rebel support both raise the probability of conflict, and there is a negative interaction with rivalries. Thus, there is little difference between one-sided and mutual rebel support.

average) substitute between rebel support and direct hostilities against rivals. Some, but not all, conflict behavior is delegated to rebel proxies rather than conducted by the state's own military forces. Thus, there is no perfect substitution between these modes of warfare. Clearly, more research is needed to disentangle complex relationships between rebel patronage and international conflict.

As an alternative model specification, I replicate Russett and Oneal's analysis in their seminal book, *Triangulating Peace* (2001). This model has now become a widely accepted standard in the international relations literature; however, I use the Binary Time-Series Cross-Section estimation technique proposed by Beck, Katz, and Tucker (1998) and thus include a count of peace years and three splines (splines not reported). This alternative specification contains information on all dyads in the world, 1946–1991, and includes a variable for contiguity. This model also includes a larger set of control variables. Table 3.2 presents the regression results. Model 1 in table 3.2 includes variables for rivalry, external bases, and their interaction, and model 2 includes the variable for economic or military support for rebels from the Regan dataset.[12] The main Russett and Oneal findings are unchanged in these models, except that trade dependence and inter-governmental organization membership are no longer significant.

The main results are robust to this alternative specification. Both international rivalries and external bases are shown to have a positive and significant effect on the likelihood of conflict. As before, the interaction between these variables is negative and significant, again supporting the notion that delegation to a rebel organization somewhat reduces the odds of witnessing a direct military confrontation between rivals. Model 2 also shows the Regan intervention variable to be an important predictor of militarized disputes, and the interaction term between rivals and intervention displays the expected negative sign. This analysis again supports hypotheses 6 and 7.

Exploring the Relationship through Case Narratives

Statistical correlations are good for identifying broad empirical patterns, but they are only suggestive of causal relationships (see the appendix to chapter 2). Correlations may be spurious, or they may hold for reasons other than those proposed by the theory. For example, debates rage over the

12. The basic Russett and Oneal model was compared with the current models using the Bayesian Information Criterion (BIC) scores. Comparison of BIC scores indicates strong support in favor of including variables for rivalry and external bases.

Table 3.2 International conflict regression results, Russett and Oneal replication

	1. Coefficient (Standard error)	p-value	2. Coefficient (Standard error)	p-value
External base	1.384	<0.000	—	—
	(0.179)			
Rival's external base	−1.200	<0.000	—	—
	(0.305)			
Intervention (Regan)	—	—	0.770	0.004
			(0.284)	
Rival's × external intervention	—	—	−0.296	0.196
			(0.346)	
Rivals	1.334	<0.001	1.198	<0.001
	(0.135)		(0.135)	
Power ratio	−0.126	0.001	−0.120	0.002
	(0.041)		(0.041)	
Democracy	−0.039	<0.001	−0.037	<0.001
	(0.011)		(0.011)	
Trade	−7.474	0.256	−8.173	0.228
	(11.361)		(10.969)	
IGO membership	−0.001	0.358	−0.001	0.362
	(0.004)		(0.004)	
Allies	−0.397	0.002	−0.463	0.001
	(0.135)		(0.138)	
Distance	−0.180	0.002	−0.183	0.002
	(0.062)		(0.062)	
Noncontiguous	−1.134	<0.001	−1.200	<0.001
	(0.207)		(0.201)	
Minor powers	−0.486	0.005	−0.382	0.019
	(0.186)		(0.184)	
Peace years	−0.054	0.082	−0.061	0.054
	(0.039)		(0.038)	
Constant	−2.648	<0.001	−2.505	<0.001
	(0.511)		(0.516)	
N	27412		27412	
Wald Chi squared	899.14		860.72	

Standard errors clustered on dyads.
P-values are of one-tailed significance tests.

true causal story behind the democratic peace—is the relationship due to institutional or normative factors? Is it in fact spurious? Although statistical analyses repeatedly demonstrate that democracies are less likely to fight one another than nondemocracies, there is little consensus as to why this is the case, or if omitted variables are really at work (Gartzke 2007; Gowa 1995; Rosato 2005). One way of examining causality is to look at the cases in greater depth in order to trace the processes by which the variables are linked. This exercise is particularly important for the analysis here, because I have argued that there is an endogenous relationship between transnational rebellion and interstate conflict. If rival states host rebel organizations, then we must assess whether subsequent conflicts are due to rebel hosting or preexisting animosities. Alternatively, if weak states host rebel groups, then perhaps porous borders and inability to deter foreign aggression, rather than rebel bases themselves, drive international conflict. Although the statistical analysis confirmed that there are independent effects for each variable, it is important to explore causal patterns.

New MID narratives available from the Correlates of War project[13] for the 1990s provide a better sense of the issues that create tensions between states. These narratives give a short description of the events surrounding disputes. When appropriate, the information in the MID narratives was complemented with additional research through Lexis-Nexis[14] news searches and secondary sources. Table 3.3 lists all MIDs described in the online narratives in which at least one state was hosting the other's rebel organization(s). In other words, this analysis deliberately selects cases that are coded 1 for both disputes and external bases. The narratives then allow us to ascertain whether the coincidence of variables in the regression is for the reasons specified by the theory or whether the relationship is due to unrelated factors. The objective here is not statistical inference (which was done above), but rather to look at the underlying processes that generate international conflict.

The MID narratives overwhelming support the claim that issues arising out of transnational rebel activities are directly responsible for several interstate conflicts. Table 3.3 demonstrates that in 83 percent of the cases where external bases and MIDs coincided with one another, the presence of rebels was cited as a major factor leading to conflict. In only four of the twenty-three listed cases was the relationship spurious or simply coincidental. Although conflict histories are only available for recent MIDs, this set of cases provides strong preliminary evidence that the violent conflicts

13. Available at http://www.correlatesofwar.org/ (accessed August 4, 2008).
14. http://web.lexis-nexis.com (last accessed July 6, 2007).

Table 3.3 External bases and MIDs: Case narratives

Country A	Country B	Start year	MID number	Rebel involvement?	Notes (spurious attribution in parentheses)
India	Pakistan	1993	4007	yes	Dispute over bombings by Kashmir militants
Afghanistan	Tajikistan	1993	4054	yes	Afghanistan supporting rebel forces from Tajikistan
Niger	Chad	1993	4067	yes	Chadian border guard killed while pursuing rebels in Niger
Lebanon	Israel	1993	4182	yes	Israel attacks Hezbollah in Lebanon and Syria
Syria	Israel	1993	4182	yes	Israel attacks Hezbollah in Lebanon and Syria
Greece	Turkey	1994	4040	no	(coastal dispute)
Uganda	Sudan	1994	4078	yes	Both sides accuse one another of supporting rebels
Colombia	Venezuela	1994	4219	yes	Spillover from guerilla war in Colombia
Myanmar	Thailand	1995	4002	yes	Burmese rebels operating in Thailand
India	Bangladesh	1995	4005	no	(incidental shooting)
Turkey	Iraq	1995	4158	yes	Turkey enters Iraq to attack PKK (Kurdish) forces
Congo	Angola	1995	4168	no	(brief border clash)
Eritrea	Sudan	1996	4124	yes	Each side accuses the other of supporting rebels
DR Congo	Uganda	1996	4170	yes	Cross-border clashes between rebel forces and Uganda
Iran	Turkey	1996	4191	yes	Turkey enters Iran and attacks a Kurdish village
Iran	Iraq	1996	4192	yes	Iran enters Iraq to attack Kurdish rebel forces
Tanzania	Burundi	1997	4123	yes	Cross-border fight between Burundi and refugees in Tanzania
Colombia	Venezuela	1997	4172	yes	Spillover from Colombia conflict, Venezuela enters Colombia
Congo	Angola	1997	4246	yes	Angola intervenes in Congo in support of rebels
DR Congo	Angola	1998	4339	yes	Failed peace negotiations in DRC, Angolan support for rebels
DR Congo	Uganda	1998	4339	yes	Failed peace negotiations in DRC, Ugandan support for rebels
Myanmar	Thailand	1999	4138	no	(territorial water dispute)
Iran	Turkey	1999	4289	yes	Turkey attacks Iran over PKK bases

Percent Correctly Attributed: 83% (number of correctly attributed cases/total number of cases)
MID number refers to the Militarized Interstate Dispute code in the Correlates of War dataset.

shown in the statistical findings are in fact due to the impact of transnational rebel groups.

Many of these incidents involved cross-border counterinsurgency operations that violated the sovereign territory of the rebel host state. Turkey, for example, has launched numerous attacks on both Iran and Iraq in pursuit of Kurdish rebel forces (MIDs 4158, 4191, 4289). Occasionally, hot pursuit raids into neighboring territory cause clashes between government forces. For instance, several Chadian border guards were fired on by security forces—killing one—when they crossed the border into Niger in pursuit of rebels (MID 4067).

Beyond cross-border counterinsurgency operations, several armed conflicts between states have occurred when countries retaliate against their neighbors for supporting insurgents. For instance, Burundi and Tanzania were involved in a clash in 1997, killing dozens, after Burundi accused its neighbor of harboring militant factions within refugee camps (MID 4123). Sometimes foreign governments have launched full-scale invasions of neighboring countries in support of rebel factions during a civil war; in these cases, rebel and government forces fight alongside one another and serve complementary roles. For example, Angola attacked Congo-Brazzaville in 1997 to support rebel factions loyal to Denis Sassou Nguesso and installed him as president (MID 4246).

A few additional examples will serve to verify these causal connections. In MID 4124, Eritrea accused Sudan of supporting an Islamic militant organization—the Eritrean Islamic Jihad Movement—which was trying to overthrow President Isaias Afwerki.[15] In turn, Sudan accused Eritrea of providing shelter to Sudanese rebel groups from the south. Indeed, in interviews with the press, Afwerki repeatedly expressed his support for the Sudanese opposition.[16] As a result, several military clashes occurred between the two governments between 1996 and 1998.

At first, both governments moved troops near the international border, and in a July 1996 speech the Sudanese vice president warned Eritrea not to provoke a war. Then on July 23, a Sudanese newspaper reported that the government had beaten back an invasion force comprised of rebels backed by Eritrean regular troops; subsequently, a state of emergency was declared

15. This conflict summary is supplemented by news searches from the International Boundaries News Database, http://www-ibru.dur.ac.uk/resources/newsarchive.html (accessed December 10, 2005).

16. See, for example, "Eritrean president on readiness to give military support to Sudanese opposition,"*Al-Hayat (London)*, January 22, 1996. Also reported in the BBC Summary of World Broadcasts, January 25, 1996.

in the Sudanese province of Kassala. Over the following months, Sudanese opposition groups, notably the Sudanese People's Liberation Army, frequently launched attacks from Eritrea, and in January 1997 made a major advance into Sudan near the town of Dawazin. In response, the Sudanese Information Minister said that Eritrean support for rebel groups amounted to a declaration of war on his country. Then on February 26, 1998, Eritrean media sources reported that Sudan had launched air and artillery attacks on several villages in the Gologue region of Eritrea. A few days later, it was reported that Eritrean forces were shelling the Sudanese villages of Awad, Galsa, and Hadra. Further deployment of troops to the border by both governments threatened an escalation of the conflict into a full-scale war; but war was averted by a summit in Qatar in May 1999, when the presidents of both countries agreed to end hostilities and resume diplomatic relations.

In another case (MID 4002), Burma and Thailand clashed several times over the issue of ethnic Karen rebels from Burma operating across the border in Thailand. These incidents took place around the Burmese village of Kawmoora and the Thai village of Mae Sot, which lie directly across the border from one another. On several occasions, the Burmese government pursued rebels on the other side of the border, violating Thailand's sovereignty and prompting a Thai military response and troop deployment to defend the border against further encroachment. Stray Burmese shells landing on Thai territory also threatened Thailand's security, and in response the Thai government demanded that Burmese forces stay at least five kilometers away from the border.

MID 4182 refers to a series of incidents between 1993 and 2001 in which Israel clashed with Lebanon and Syria over Hezbollah's presence in those countries. Hezbollah had been receiving significant military and economic support from the Syrian government as a means of influencing internal Lebanese politics and of continuing to pressure Israel. Cross-border attacks by Hezbollah often provoked Israeli retaliation against forces on Lebanese and Syrian territory, which in turn elicited a response from these governments. Lebanese and Syrian troops sometimes fought alongside Hezbollah guerillas when Israel launched attacks on their soil, threatening a regional war.

These cases suggest a direct causal relationship between extraterritorial rebel bases and international conflicts. In some cases, the operations of TNR groups create new tensions between states. In other cases (examined below), the emergence of TNRs reflect standing hostilities between governments but serve to exacerbate these hostilities and to further escalate the conflict.

Rivalries, International Conflict, and TNR Support

Additional case analysis can provide useful insights into mutually constitutive relationships between transnational insurgencies, state-to-state conflict, and the development of international rivalries. These cases can give us some, albeit preliminary, evidence of substitution effects between direct confrontations among a particular rival dyad and support for TNRs. Although it is inherently difficult to test counterfactual claims that the prevalence of direct interstate hostility would have been higher were it not for delegation to rebel organizations, looking at additional cases can give us some clues to the complex relationships between rivalries, interstate disputes, and rebel patronage. In two pairs of states, Mozambique-South Africa and Iran-Iraq, the states viewed one another as international rivals, supported rebel organizations fighting against their rivals, and sometimes directly used force against one another. An exploration of interrelationships between rivalries and support for TNRs, as well as how states variously utilized rebels and their own military forces to undermine their opponents, reveals that what is normally thought of as international armed conflict—that is, military contests between the security forces of nation-states—does not adequately capture the range of tactics and tools that countries use in their foreign relations with their enemies.

Mozambique-South Africa

Relations between South Africa and Mozambique were seriously strained after the latter gained independence from Portugal in 1975. The independence movement, the Front for the Liberation of Mozambique (FRELIMO), installed a Soviet-allied, Marxist regime after the Portuguese withdrawal, earning the enmity of Rhodesia and South Africa, which were both dominated by white minority governments. Shortly after FRELIMO established control over Mozambique, these neighboring states funded and trained a reactionary rebel organization known as the Mozambican National Resistance, or RENAMO, which was known for its exceptional brutality. In response, the FRELIMO regime gave sanctuary to black nationalist rebels from Rhodesia and South Africa. In 1980, the Rhodesian government fell to the forces of the Zimbabwean African National Union and the Zimbabwean African People's Union, but South Africa's whites-only government retained power until the end of the apartheid regime in 1994. South Africa continued its support of RENAMO while at the same time fighting a low-level insurgency against the African National Congress (ANC) and its military wing, Umkhonto we Siswe (Spear of the Nation), which were largely based in Mozambique.

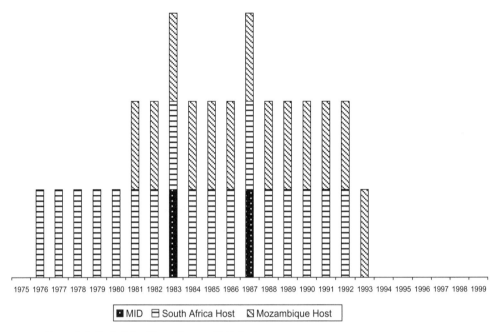

Figure 3.2 South Africa-Mozambique conflict behavior

It is important to note that despite bitter animosity between South Africa and Mozambique and South Africa's clear military superiority, the two never fought a full-scale war against one another. Figure 3.2 displays relations between South Africa and Mozambique since 1975. According to the Thompson rivalry dataset, these states were considered rivals from 1976, after FRELIMO took power, until 1992, when the civil war in Mozambique came to an end. The dark regions in the figure show incidents of militarized interstate disputes between these neighbors. Two category 4 MIDs were fought in 1983 and 1987, both of which caused fatalities, but neither came close to a full international war (category 5 MID). Also depicted are periods in which each state hosted rebel organizations from the other. These hash-marked areas only show time-periods when the rebels were active, that is, years in which they engaged in conflicts that reached the twenty-five battle-deaths threshold given by the Uppsala/PRIO Armed Conflicts Dataset.

The two MIDs involving these states both took the form of South African cross-border attacks against ANC bases in Maputo, Mozambique. Thus, in neither case did the military forces of the two states confront one another on the battlefield. In May 1983, South African jets bombed ANC headquarters in Maputo: dozens of people were killed and a Mozambican antiaircraft installation was destroyed.[17] This assault was in retaliation for an ANC car bomb attack in Pretoria a few days earlier. In May 1987, South Africa again launched a raid against ANC headquarters in Maputo, killing three civilians and prompting a diplomatic outcry by Mozambique and widespread international condemnation.[18] These so-called militarized "interstate" disputes were thus not fought between the armed forces of the two governments but between South Africa and the ANC, on Mozambican territory.

Instead of direct clashes, South Africa and Mozambique sought to undermine one another by supporting rebel organizations trained and supplied on their territory. This became a source of severe friction in bilateral relations. In 1984, the two governments attempted to establish peace between them through a nonaggression pact—the Nkomati Accord—which called for an end to support for rebel organizations. Yet despite the formal agreement, South Africa continued to provide covert support for RENAMO guerillas until the end of the civil war. Mozambique was more serious about cutting off support for the ANC and did expel key operatives, but ANC forces continued to use its territory for several years. After the Cold War came to an end, drying up funding for the combatants, FRELIMO and RENAMO agreed to a peace settlement and the deployment of UN peacekeepers. South Africa also began to relax its apartheid laws, and in 1994 the first elections with universal suffrage brought ANC leader Nelson Mandela to power. For both states, then, the inability to militarily defeat TNRs—which relied heavily on external sanctuaries—lead the respective governments to offer political concessions to the opposition.

Iran-Iraq

Iran and Iraq have been bitter rivals for several decades owing to a number of longstanding territorial disputes between the two countries. The most prominent dispute regards control over the Shatt al-Arab waterway (Arvand Rud in Persian), where the Tigris and Euphrates rivers flow into the Persian Gulf. Iraq also at times has claimed sovereignty over the Iranian province of Khuzestan, where a significant Arab minority resides, and over several small islands in the Persian Gulf, which Iran occupied after the British colonial administration withdrew in 1971. For its part, Iran has significant historical

17. Alan Cowell, "Damage in Mozambique Raid Looks Surprisingly Light," *New York Times,* May 25, 1983, A12, Late City Final Edition. See also "South African Jets Bomb Mozambique," *New York Times,* May 23, 1983, A1, Late City Final Edition.

18. William Claiborne, "Commandos Kill 3 in Mozambique Raid," *Washington Post,* page A17, Final Edition.

and religious ties to Iraqi Shias, who, despite being a majority of Iraq's population, were largely excluded from power under Saddam Hussein's regime. As figure 3.3 shows, these neighbors fought one another repeatedly over their territorial disputes.[19] Whereas several low-level clashes occurred between the two countries in the 1950s, 1960s, and 1970s, the conflict became a large-scale war after the Iranian Revolution of 1979. With internal Iranian politics in disarray following the deposal of the Shah, Iraq opportunistically launched a full invasion of Iran in 1980 but was unable to win a decisive victory. Instead, the Iran-Iraq War lingered on until 1988, when the two nations agreed on a ceasefire.

Prior to 1980, these two rivals provided support and sanctuary to one another's dissidents. Thus, even when they were not directly fighting each other, they continued to act through rebel proxies. The Shah of Iran supported the Iraqi Kurdish Democratic Party (KDP), a militant organization fighting for an independent Iraqi Kurdistan (Library of Congress Country Studies 1989, 1990). In fact, the KDP was founded in Iran in 1946 under the leadership of Mustafa Barzani.[20] The Shah's stepped up support for the KDP in the 1960s allowed the organization to engage in more significant operations. Meanwhile, the Iranian dissident cleric Ayatollah Khomeini was granted asylum in Iraq in 1965, where he fomented anti-Shah sentiment until Saddam Hussein expelled him in 1978. With Iranian backing, the KDP fought several large battles against Iraqi forces and proved to be a formidable security challenge for Saddam Hussein's regime. In 1974, in an attempt to end the insurgency, Saddam Hussein offered an autonomy deal to the KDP, which was rejected (Library of Congress 1989, 1990). The following year, on March 6 in Algiers, the two neighbors signed an agreement over the Shatt al-Arab in which Iraq capitulated to Iran's demand to set the border at the thalweg (the deepest point of the river) in exchange for Iran discontinuing its support of the KDP. A short period of peace followed in which the two states did not engage one another and Iran ended formal links to the KDP, although the KDP and a new Iraqi Kurdish rebel faction—the Patriotic Union of Kurdistan—continued to use Iranian territory, slipping back and forth across the porous border.

After the Iranian Revolution, Saddam Hussein used this moment of weakness to renege on agreements with the Shah. When the Iran-Iraq War broke out in 1980, each nation sponsored and supported the other's rebel

---

19. As before, the periods of rebel hosting are only listed if the rebel organization were at least minimally active (causing at least twenty-five battle-deaths).

20. KDP website, http://www.kdp.se/ (accessed July 9, 2007).

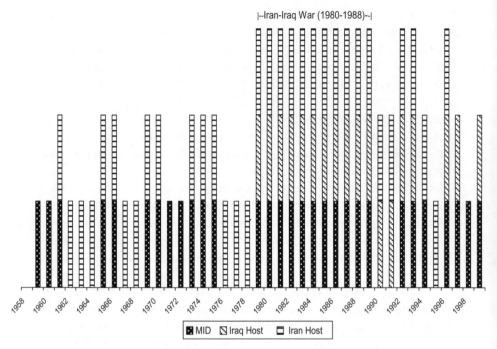

Figure 3.3 Iran-Iraq conflict behavior

organizations, encouraging the establishment of a "fifth column" against its enemy. Thus, in addition to direct military engagement, both sides utilized TNRs as an additional strategic tool. Iran again provided support to Iraqi Kurdish rebels in the north, while Iraq granted sanctuary and support to Iranian Kurds, who launched their own insurgency under the banner of the Kurdish Democratic Party of Iran (KDPI). Iran also supported Iraqi Shia insurgents, and in 1982, the Supreme Council for the Islamic Revolution in Iraq (SCIRI), which advocated an Iranian-style regime, was founded.[21] With several thousand fighters, SCIRI would become a significant political force and is active to this day.

Iraq backed two additional Iranian rebel organizations. The first—and by far the most significant armed opposition movement—was the Mujahedin-e-Khalq (MEK), whose ideology blended elements of Islamism and Marxism. Despite being longtime opponents of the Shah and one of the key forces behind the revolution, the MEK did not support the Islamic regime led by

21. Federation of American Scientists, http://fas.org/irp/world/para/sciri.htm (accessed July 7, 2007).

Khomeini. The MEK maintained military bases in Iraq at the invitation of Saddam Hussein's government and has had offices throughout Europe and North America. The second militant group was a small and short-lived Arab insurgency based in Khuzestan, the Arab Political Cultural Organization (APCO). Despite Saddam Hussein's attempts to mobilize them, however, Iranian Arabs largely remained loyal to the regime in Tehran.

During the Iran-Iraq War, both countries blended direct military engagements with patronage of TNRs. Yet despite several years of war and the crippling toll the conflict took on both nation's economies, the conflict ended in an indecisive ceasefire in 1988, at which time the prewar status quo was restored. As figure 3.3 shows, there was a temporary lull in fighting between the two countries after the ceasefire was implemented. Although there have been MIDs between Iran and Iraq since 1988—discussed below—these did not reach the level of full-scale war.

Notwithstanding the cease-fire agreement and an end to large-scale military operations, it would be incorrect to assume that armed hostilities between the two countries stopped; rather, the rivals simply continued their conflict through rebel proxies. After 1988, Iraq continued to harbor the MEK, which launched several attacks on Iran throughout the 1990s and has attacked Iranian embassies and interests overseas. Iran also provided safe-haven and support to SCIRI, which was responsible for a number of attacks on Iraq during the 1990s and became a major player in Iraqi politics after the U.S. invasion of 2003. Both countries also provided support for various Kurdish opposition groups.

The MIDs that did occur between the two countries during the 1990s were mostly the result of Iranian cross-border counterinsurgency strikes against various rebel groups rather than direct state-to-state confrontations. Iraq, for its part, was constrained in its ability to respond in kind because of its defeat to the United States in the first Persian Gulf War. For instance, between March and July of 1993, Iran attacked several KDPI and MEK positions within Iraqi territory. In July and August of 1996, Iranian forces again crossed into Iraqi territory to attack Kurdish militants and launched several cross-border artillery strikes on rebel strongholds. Iraqi government officials called the maneuver an invasion, and in response Iraq deployed three army divisions to the border to prevent further Iranian incursions. Despite Iraqi protests, in September of 1997, Iran proceeded to bomb MEK bases on the Iraqi side of the border, creating further diplomatic tension and prompting the United States to engage in stricter enforcement of the southern Iraqi no-fly zone. Iran nevertheless continued to occasionally attack MEK operatives within Iraq, and in 1999 fired SCUD missiles at an MEK base 100km north of Baghdad.[22] Thus, as can be seen in figure 3.3, Iran and Iraq have been continuously engaged in direct or indirect armed confrontation with one another for several decades. Focusing only on periods of state-to-state clashes would be misleading, as a significant part of each nation's foreign policy strategy vis-à-vis the other was to support TNRs.

Evaluating the Evidence

Foreign interventions in internal conflicts have received a great deal of scholarly attention in recent years. Many civil conflicts have become important *international* events wherein external parties support combatant groups. This chapter demonstrates, however, that foreign interventions not only affect events in the target country itself, but also have important implications for state-to-state relations. Support for insurgent groups in other countries frequently leads to conflict between states; this relationship is confirmed through a statistical analysis of MIDs during the post-World War II era. Although financial and military transfers to rebels increase conflict between states, hosting transnational rebels on one's territory has a particularly large effect. A closer look at several cases confirms the causal relationship between foreign patronage of rebel organizations and international conflict.

In addition, hostile governments frequently act through rebel organizations to weaken their international enemies. Rather than using their own military forces, states sometimes choose to support TNRs as a way of avoiding the costs and risks associated with direct confrontation. In support of this claim, the statistical results demonstrate that when rival states host TNR groups, there is a somewhat decreased incidence of interstate armed conflict. Exploring the substitution of the direct use of force for delegation to rebels, as well as potential complementarities between these modes of conflict, is an interesting topic for future research. Although some preliminary case evidence was given here, more work needs to be done to analyze such substitution effects.

This and the preceding chapter present substantial evidence that the lines between domestic and interstate conflict are frequently obscured by TNRs. Civil conflicts are often not confined to the boundaries of the nation-state. Foreign sanctuaries and international support for opposition groups are common to many so-called "domestic" disputes. But in addition, many in-

22. These events were described in the MID narratives.

ternational conflicts are rooted in the actors and events surrounding civil wars. Therefore, rather than mutually exclusive forms of conflict, inter- and intrastate wars are often linked in a complex nexus. Moreover, privileging states as the primary actors in international politics can be misleading, as several disputes involve multifaceted relationships between governments, domestic opposition groups, and transnational rebels. Frequently, dyadic bargaining processes and relationships between states—or between states and rebels—do not adequately capture multiactor conflicts involving state and nonstate entities. A greater understanding of the role that transnational actors play in bridging the domestic and international realms will greatly improve our analyses of world events.

Introduction to the Case Studies

The quantitative results presented in the previous chapters reveal strong statistical relationships between neighborhood conditions and civil war and between transnational rebellion and interstate conflict. Nevertheless, it is useful to examine a few cases in greater depth in order to look at the underlying causal processes behind the statistical correlations, assess elements of the theory that are difficult to test in a quantitative study, and shed light on additional empirical implications of the theory. The following chapters examine the civil wars in Nicaragua and Rwanda and how these conflicts spread throughout Central America and the Great Lakes region of Africa, respectively. These "civil" conflicts are better understood as complex "systems," where domestic and international disputes overlapped in multiple ways. These cases elucidate the dynamics of transnational conflicts—namely, how they begin, how governments attempt to combat TNR groups, their implications for regional relations, and how they were ultimately resolved.

As argued in chapter 1, transnational rebellions are more difficult to resolve through negotiations because external mobilization poses special challenges for conflict bargaining. External mobilization exacerbates informational problems, draws external actors into the bargaining process who can block negotiations, and makes credible commitments to demobilize fighters more difficult secure. However, it is difficult to test bargaining theories in a quantitative analysis of many cases, as this requires knowledge about the actual decision-making processes. The following chapters examine negotiations between states and rebels and between host and home countries. If the theory I have developed is indeed plausible, then the actors themselves must perceive that negotiations are complicated by the transnational nature of the conflict. Although we cannot actually "look into the heads" of the actors, we can examine public statements and key junctures in negotiations to understand the fears and motivations of decision-makers.

An additional implication of the theory is examined here; conflict termination—or the end to armed violence—will be unlikely unless broad regional cooperation is achieved. Neighboring states must commit to limit rebel activities on their territory. Rebel hosts can either push insurgents off of their territory and cooperate with counterinsurgency efforts, making conflicts more likely to end in government victory, or they can facilitate negotiated settlements by ensuring that rebel units on their soil comply with demobilization agreements and by providing guarantees of future abandonment of their territory. Thus, conflicts are more likely to end when TNRs no longer have access to external bases and when regional governments demonstrate their ability and resolve to limit rebel activities. For successful counterinsurgency or negotiated settlements, the cooperation of rebel hosts is needed. A full test of this conjecture must await further data collection and a more comprehensive analysis. However, the cases presented here can at least probe the plausibility of this additional aspect of the theory.

These case studies should be seen as complementing the statistical analyses presented in the previous chapters. The quantitative studies made causal inferences based on statistical associations among large amounts of data. The case analyses seek out the process by which transnational rebellion unfolds. In particular, they address: (1) the strategic choice by rebels to locate abroad; (2) the state's difficulties in repressing rebels; (3) the motives of the host country in facilitating or preventing rebel activities; (4) state-to-state frictions and tensions; and (5) multiactor bargains and conflict resolution efforts. The case studies also provide rich empirical detail that large-N studies gloss over.

Nicaragua and Rwanda

Why select Nicaragua and Rwanda for in-depth analyses? First, relatively good information is available on these conflicts through published materials, news accounts, and online sources. Second, the Nicaraguan conflict ended through a negotiated settlement, whereas the Rwandan conflict ended after counterinsurgency operations. These different endings are not considered "dependent variables" in this analysis, and so I will not attempt to explain the variation in the type of conflict termination. Instead, the case studies provide evidence that these modes of conflict termination followed a similar logic, where agreements by rebel hosts to limit TNRs were important preconditions for ending these wars. This variation will also highlight interesting nuances in the role that host states play in cooperating with counterinsurgency efforts (Rwanda) and in facilitating credible commitments after peace agreements (Nicaragua). Finally, these conflicts vary in their geographic context, motivations, and time period. The Nicaraguan civil war was an ideological struggle, whereas the Rwandan conflict was an ethnic one; one war was fought during the Cold War, and the other occurred following the Cold War; one was fought in Latin America, one in Africa. Therefore, these differences cannot explain the common outcome of conflict termination.

That said, comparisons across the cases are not as important as comparisons over time *within the same conflict*. Rather than comparing these cases to one another, it is more important to understand how these conflicts evolved over time: how they began, how they were fought, and why they finally ended when they did. By looking at the same conflict longitudinally over several years, we can understand key moments and events that lead to significant shifts in the conflict and the preconditions for conflict resolution. Therefore, dynamic processes, rather than cross-sectional variation, are the main focus of the following chapters.

In Nicaragua, the Sandinista government, despite being able to prevent the Contra rebels from establishing a lasting presence on Nicaraguan territory and threatening the capital, was not able to pursue the rebels into Costa Rica and Honduras for fear of provoking a war with these states and their military supporter, the United States. The Sandinistas refused to engage in direct talks with the Contras, believing that the support of the United States and neighboring governments was critical to the rebels' continued viability. Importantly, during the initial rounds of peace negotiations to end Nicaragua's civil war, the rebels were excluded altogether; instead, talks were conducted between the governments in the region. Only after agreements were signed between Nicaragua and its neighbors did serious negotiations between the government and the rebels begin. When neighboring states provided Nicaragua credible assurances that Contra units—particularly in Honduras—would be disbanded, the peace process moved forward.

In addition to illustrating the causal pathways to conflict resolution, the exploration of this case also demonstrates that the "conventional" view of the Contras and of Central American governments as pawns of the United States is too simplistic. This view suggests that the end of the Cold War and the withdrawal of U.S. support ended the Contra insurgency. Rather, Honduras and Costa Rica began to assert their independence even as Washington pressured them to continue their support for the rebels. Although the waning of Cold War concerns was not irrelevant, the commitment by Contra hosts to enforce demobilization agreements, despite opposition from the administration of President George H.W. Bush, allowed peace to move forward.

Rwanda presents a harder case for the theory. As argued in chapter 1 international borders protect TNRs because it is costly for the home state to strike rebel positions in host territories where it is not sovereign. However, borders are not completely inviolable: although crossing a border increases the costs of counterinsurgency operations significantly, sovereignty violations can and do occur. Rwanda after the 1994 takeover by the Rwandan Patriotic Front (RPF) presents an instance of a government that was willing and able to extensively penetrate the territory of a neighbor, Zaire/Democratic Republic of the Congo (DRC). This territorial violation occurred because the Hutu rebels included those responsible for the 1994 genocide and therefore presented an existential threat to the Tutsi-led government of Rwanda.

In support of the theory, however, the Rwandan government faced considerable costs in pursuing such a strategy and was ultimately unable to defeat rebel forces by itself. Although the government established military superiority over its own territory, it was not able to defeat insurgents hiding across the border—demonstrating that *despite* substantial sovereignty violations, governments are still limited in their ability to combat TNR groups. Rwandan armed forces were hampered by war with the DRC and its regional allies, their lack of local knowledge, and their inability to maintain control over such a vast territory. Marginalization of the Rwandan rebels followed an agreement between the DRC and Rwanda that called for the withdrawal of Rwandan forces in exchange for the DRC's cooperation in forcibly disarming the Hutu rebels. Thus, conflict termination did not occur as a result of Rwandan actions alone—even with extensive penetration of Congolese soil—but after the DRC agreed to cooperate in preventing rebel access.

4 The Nicaraguan Civil War

Decades of economic mismanagement and authoritarianism under the Somoza regime in Nicaragua led to widespread popular discontent and the formation of the leftist Frente Sandinista de Liberación Nacional (FSLN) in the early 1960s. The Sandinistas' name came from a revolutionary, anti-imperialist figure, Augusto César Sandino, who during the 1920s and 1930s opposed the conservative regime of Emiliano Chamorro and U.S. interference in Nicaraguan affairs. The FSLN was formed in 1961 out of a number of leftist organizations, including the Nicaraguan Socialist Party, the Nicaraguan Patriotic Youth, and the Frente Revolucionario Sandino, and received inspiration from the recent success of the Cuban revolution (Miranda and Ratliff 1993). The FSLN advocated broad economic reforms to address income inequality in Nicaragua and an end to the oligarchy of a handful of economic and political elites with extensive ties to the United States. Such demands were echoed elsewhere in Central America, where conflicts in Guatemala and El Salvador were also brewing (Booth 1991).

The FSLN was an underground movement largely based in urban areas, particularly Managua, and launched its initial attacks in the early 1970s. Responding to this growing threat, Anastasio Somoza engaged in a campaign of repression, including censorship of the media, the arrest of political opponents, and widespread torture and executions. Such repressive measures backfired, however, as public resentment against the Somoza regime grew and international condemnation of human rights violations intensified.

U.S. support for the Somoza regime waned as President Jimmy Carter, who championed the cause of international human rights, demanded political reform and an end to the state of siege in Nicaragua. During this time, the Sandinistas grew rapidly in strength as arms flowed in from Cuba, Venezuela, and Panama and recruits from broad segments of Nicaraguan society joined the revolution. Battles between the Nicaraguan National Guard and the FSLN intensified in 1978 after the killing of a popular anti-Somoza newspaper editor, Pedro Joaquín Chamorro, led to a series of mass protests and general strikes. The Sandinista rebels also benefited from the support of Costa Rica and the use of its territory, where they trained soldiers, stockpiled weapons, and formed a government in exile (Walker 2003). Although their roots were in the urban underground, the FSLN became a transnational rebel organization with significant external operations and support from across the region. The FSLN "government in exile" declared itself the rightful government of Nicaragua on June 18, 1979. With the combination of military setbacks, popular protests, and international pressure, Anastasio Somoza fled the country a month later, on July 17. Two days later, the FSLN marched on Managua and established a new revolutionary regime.

Soon after the revolution, however, opponents of the new government surfaced and took up arms. Supporters of the old order, particularly members of the former National Guard, comprised one of the main components of this anti-Sandinista front, which would come to be popularly known as the Contras. Yet it would be incorrect to characterize the Contras as simply a counterrevolutionary force comprised of right-wing Somoza supporters. As several scholars have noted (Brown 2001; Horton 1998), peasants in Nicaragua's rural highlands—including many who fought with the FSLN against the Somoza government—rose up in opposition to the Sandinistas' radical reform agenda, particularly agricultural expropriation and redistribution. Moreover, Nicaragua's indigenous Miskito population formed their own opposition groups in response to widespread discrimination and marginalization.

The first serious battle between the Sandinistas and the rebels (who had not yet organized under the "Contra" banner) was fought in the Nueva Segovia region in November 1979 when rebels attacked a military outpost outside the town of Quilalí, located near the Honduran border (Brown 2001, 14). Although the Nicaraguan resistance would later benefit from extensive U.S. aid, these initial campaigns were fought without foreign help. Therefore, although the Contras were often accused of being a U.S. "mercenary" force, they originated independently of foreign assistance. In fact, during the first several months of the Sandinista revolution, the United States—under the Carter administration—sought to work with the new government. Initially the United States provided foreign aid to the Sandinistas in the hope that it could head off a further shift to the left and alignment with the Soviet Union. For the most part, these early rebel activities were poorly organized and ad hoc.

As the Sandinista regime continued its program of socialist economic reform and deepened its ties with Cuba and the Soviet Union, several actors in U.S. foreign policy circles began to view the regime as a regional threat. With conflicts gathering steam in El Salvador and Guatemala, it was feared that governments across Central America could fall and align with the Soviet Union. When Carter lost the 1980 presidential election to Ronald Reagan, the United States took a much more active role in organizing, equipping, and training the various opposition groups, now referred to collectively as the Contras. The right-wing government in Argentina, also fearing a leftist turn in the region and wishing to bolster ties with Washington, provided extensive assistance to the Contras as well. With a much stronger opposition force and fears of a possible U.S.-sponsored invasion, the Sandinistas increasingly relied on Cuba and the Soviet Union for military assistance and augmented their armed forces significantly (Walker 2003). Thus, Nicaragua had become a prime Cold War battle ground.

The Significance of Extraterritorial Bases

Although the Contra forces clearly benefited from the support of the Reagan administration, they were never strong enough to take and hold significant parts of Nicaraguan territory. Unable to establish a lasting presence within the country, the Contras relied on access to bases in Honduras and Costa Rica, two countries that played pivotal roles in the Nicaraguan civil war. As Lynn Horton notes, the border region had long been strategically important to several rebel groups throughout Nicaragua's conflict-ridden history: "Quilalí's strategic location near the Honduran border as well as its rugged terrain continued to make the municipality attractive to guerilla movements" (1998, 33). Thus, not surprisingly, the earliest and most significant battles with the Sandinistas occurred along Nicaragua's porous borders.

Under the military rule of Policarpo Paz García, Honduras and the Reagan administration took active roles in opposing the Sandinista regime. Honduras was not simply a pawn in the U.S. camp, but rather it actively sought to undermine the Sandinista regime, which it viewed as a threat. In 1981, Colonel Gustavo Alvarez Martínez, a fierce anticommunist military official, approached U.S. Ambassador Jack Binns to propose a direct attack on Nicaragua; the United States viewed this option as too extreme and rejected the plan (Schultz and Schultz 1994, 64–65). Instead, the military junta in Honduras, in conjunction with the U.S. Central Intelligence Agency under William Casey, orchestrated a covert war against Managua by equipping and training Contra forces, including ex-Somoza Guardsmen and former Sandinista peasants who defected from the revolution. After the Honduran elections, which ended military rule and brought President Roberto Suazo Córdova to power in 1982, the Honduran government continued its policy of hosting the Contras and allowing U.S. intelligence and military personnel access to the rebels. For its part, Honduras received millions of dollars in U.S. foreign assistance. By 1983, an estimated 7,000 Contras were operating in Honduras (Brogan 1998, 506),[1] with the largest faction, the Fuerza Democratica Nicaragüense (FDN), operating under the command of Enrique Bermudez, a former member of the National Guard.

Granting extraterritorial bases to the Contras did not come without cost for Honduras. The border regions of Choluteca and El Paraíso became de facto military zones. Relations between local Hondurans and foreign fighters and refugees were often tense. In contrast to refugees from El Salvador, who were believed to sympathize with leftist insurgents in that country and whose activities were restricted, Nicaraguan refugees were encouraged to reside in camps along the border, where the Contras could easily recruit among them and gather supplies (Hartigan 1992). Locals complained of lawlessness in these camps and the destruction of private property. Additionally, the Nicaraguan government sometimes attacked positions on Honduran territory in "hot pursuit" of the rebels, further souring relations between neighbors and jeopardizing the safety of locals. As one example of frequent border violations, the Sandinista army crossed into Honduras in February 1987, killing one Honduran soldier and injuring three;[2] several Hondurans were also injured or killed by landmines placed within the country.[3] Such incidents, and the militarization of the border region, led several thousand Hondurans to flee the area for the interior (Zolberg, Suhrke, and Aguayo 1989, 211).[4]

1. Although estimates vary, sources indicate that the Contras reached 15,000 troops located in Honduras and Costa Rica. See Hartzell 2002.

2. British Broadcasting Corporation, "Honduras Reports Nicaraguan Army Incursion," February 16, 1987.

3. Julia Preston, "Honduras Feels Impact of Contra War: Government Cedes Border Strip To Nicaraguan-Rebel Fighting," *Washington Post*, November 11, 1986, A1.

4. See Tova Maria Solo, "Contra Rebels Forced them to Flee Land, Hondurans Say," *Toronto Star*, August 10, 1986, B5.

Along the southern frontier, Costa Rica hosted other Contra factions, the largest of which was led by Eden Pastóra Gomez (known popularly as Co-mandante Zero), a former Sandinista commander. Pastóra had been part of the FSLN march on Managua, but for personal or ideological reasons he turned on his former comrades. Relations between Pastóra and Bermudez were strained as Pastóra, the anti-Somoza revolutionary, did not want his former National Guard enemies to regain control of the country. Unlike rebel units led by ex-members of the National Guard, however, the United States was more hesitant to provide resources to rebels led by former San-dinista leaders, whose anticommunist credentials were lacking (Schultz and Schultz 1994).

In contrast to Honduras, Costa Rica—the only stable democracy in the region—was more reluctant to allow extensive Contra/United States access to its territory due to popular suspicion regarding U.S. intentions in the re-gion. Nonetheless, under pressure from the Reagan administration and the promise of millions of dollars in aid, Luis Alberto Monge Álvarez, president of Costa Rica, tacitly provided bases to the Contras while publicly denying they existed.

Extraterritorial bases were critical for the Contras' operations and longevity. Initially the Contras claimed they could quickly mobilize a large army and defeat the government on its own turf. Despite several of-fensives, they could neither establish territorial control over sigificant parts of Nicaragua nor threaten to take major urban areas. As one diplo-mat observed, "The Contras don't stand much chance of defeating the Sandinistas on their own. While they can retreat into Honduras they will survive. But if they move into Nicaragua in force, they'll be stopped."[5] Af-ter a number of early setbacks trying to establish a rebel presence on Nicaraguan territory, Contra Commander Edgar Chamorro decided to change tactics and engage in a war of attrition, stating, "We know that militarily we cannot defeat the Sandinistas. . . . They have reserves which seem inexhaustible."[6] Thus, the Nicaraguan government was able to estab-lish military supremacy over its own territory and was not likely to be de-feated through conventional battles on its own soil. Without safe havens inside the country, the Contras' ability to flee into Honduras and Costa Rica prevented their demise.

5. Alan Riding, "Guarded by AK-47's, Sandinistas Take to the Fields," *New York Times*, Jan-uary 26, 1983, A2.
6. "Nicaragua: Contras React to Setback by Switching Strategies," *Latin America Weekly Re-port*, September 16, 1983, 5. Also see "Nicaragua's Contras Face a Rough Road," *U.S. News & World Report*, August 29, 1983, 27.

Recognizing the strategic advantage the Contras enjoyed as long as they had access to bases in neighboring countries, in 1986 Nicaragua attempted to pressure these host states to evict the Contras and discredit them internationally by filing a suit in the International Court of Justice.[7] Such pressure did little to change Honduran and Costa Rican policies as long as they had U.S. support in international forums. Nonetheless, Nicaragua continued to work through international legal channels, at least as a way to bring international attention to external patronage of the Contras.

Cross-border attacks against Contra positions on foreign soil were not unheard of, but they were costly actions. Each time the Sandinistas violated the border, they risked escalating tensions with their neighbors and a wider regional war. In one instance—not unlike several others—Honduras mounted an air strike against Nicaraguan government forces after they crossed the border. In December 1986, approximately 250 Nicaraguan soldiers overran a Honduran border checkpoint near the town of Maquingales after an incursion by Contra forces. Honduran General Humberto Regalado Hernandez reacted to the border violation by stating, "I know the Nicaraguans are having trouble with the Contras in the border region, but this does not give them the right to violate our territory."[8] On December 8, the Honduran Air Force attacked Sandinista positions inside Nicaragua, and General Regalado remarked that if border violations continued, he would recommend a full-scale invasion to President Suazo.[9] Therefore, although the border was not an impenetrable barrier, the Nicaraguan armed forces could not conduct counterinsurgency operations at will on foreign soil.

Although toppling the Sandinista regime seemed unlikely, the resistance took a toll on Nicaragua's resources and economy. The Contras, with robust support from the United States, Honduras, Costa Rica, and other allies in the region, gained in strength and were able to mount more significant assaults on Sandinista positions, although they were never able to threaten Managua directly. For the next several years, the central government spent a large share of its budget on soldiers and armaments obtained from the Soviet Union, Cuba, and Eastern Bloc nations. Such extensive military spending and damage done by the war left the Nicaraguan economy in shambles. Between 1980 and 1990, real GDP per capita in Nicaragua fell to

7. William Drozdiak, "Ortega Vows to Press Honduras and Costa Rica on Sanctuaries," *Washington Post*, July 29, 1986, A8.

8. Bernard Trainor, "Honduras Warns Nicaragua on Crossing Border," *New York Times*, December 26, 1986, A14.

9. Ibid.

half of what it had been under Somoza.[10] Nonetheless, the conflict can be described as a war of attrition with few decisive battles. Fighting was confined to rural areas and peripheral towns. Despite extensive funding and support by the United States, the Contras could not defeat the Sandinistas in head-to-head combat and were forced to retreat to their base camps in Honduras and Costa Rica when government forces went on the offensive. According to reports, by 1986, despite several years of fighting, most Contra forces had pulled back to their positions in neighboring countries.[11] Thus, without their sanctuaries across Nicaragua's borders, the Contras could not have persisted for as long as they did.

Beginning of the Peace Process

The peace negotiations in Nicaragua consisted of two phases. The first, known as the Contadora process, began in January 1983 and ended in failure in 1986. Peace negotiations resumed in 1987 at the prodding of Costa Rican President Oscar Arias Sánchez; this phase, known as the Esquipulas talks, culminated in an end to the conflict and democratic elections in Nicaragua in 1990. Both phases of negotiations consisted of a series of offers and counteroffers that were alternatively promulgated and rejected by the major players in the conflict—particularly the Sandinistas, the Contras, Honduras, Costa Rica, and the United States. Thus, peace negotiations lumbered along for years before a final settlement acceptable to all parties was reached. The willingness to negotiate early on demonstrates that the conflict was not intractable. Yet it is important to note that for several years—at least until the Sapoá agreement in 1988—peace talks did not include the Contras. Rather, *governments* in the region debated the terms of a peace deal, fully understanding that the support of external actors was vital to the continued viability of the opposition (see Aguilar Urbina 1994; Hartzell 2002; Roberts 1990; Schultz and Schultz 1994). It was only after external actors, particularly Honduras, agreed to prohibit rebel bases on their territories that the Contras and the Nicaraguan government could finally commit to a peace and disarmament plan.

Wary of growing U.S. influence in Latin America and the threat of a regional war, Mexico, Venezuela, Colombia, and Panama pressured El Salvador,

10. Based on data from the Penn World Tables, http://pwt.econ.upenn.edu/ (accessed May 16, 2006).
11. James LeMoyne, "Most Contras Reported to Pull Out of Nicaragua," *New York Times*, January 30, 1986, A10. For a similar account, see Bernard Trainor, "Anti-Contra Drive: Ill-fated Shift in Rebel Tactics," *New York Times*, March 21, 1988, A8.

Guatemala, Nicaragua, Honduras, and Costa Rica to the bargaining table in January 1983 in order to resolve the several conflicts underway. Thus began the Contadora negotiations. That summer, a broad document of objectives was drafted that outlined twenty-one points, including a halt to the Central American arms race, the prohibition of military interference by actors outside of the region, democratization, and, importantly, the cessation of support for insurgent groups in neighboring countries (Bagley 1986; Roberts 1990). The United States gave rhetorical support to the Contadora plan, as it did not want to be perceived as blocking regional peace initiatives; however, hardliners in the Reagan administration who were committed to "rollback" the Sandinista regime in Nicaragua were skeptical of an agreement that would legitimize Sandinista rule and limit U.S. influence in Central America.

The United States used its influence among the members of the "Tegucigalpa group" (Honduras, Costa Rica, and El Salvador) to shape the terms of the Contadora peace plan. With regard to the Nicaraguan conflict, Honduras and Costa Rica in particular had considerable bargaining leverage during the talks as the Contras operated from their territory; without their cooperation, peace talks were doomed to fail. Thus, at the behest of the United States, the Tegucigalpa group worked to devise a final treaty that they believed would be too demanding for the Sandinistas to accept. In so doing, they hoped that a rejection of the plan would cast the Sandinistas in a negative light among international audiences (Bagley 1986; Roberts 1990).

The final draft of the treaty stipulated that Nicaragua would expel all Soviet military advisors, halt all arms imports, reduce the size of its army, end support to guerillas in El Salvador, hold multiparty elections, and permit external monitors to verify compliance (Bagley 1986). These demands were believed to be too great for the Sandinista government to accept. Yet on September 21, 1984, Nicaragua unexpectedly announced that it would accept the terms. Most important, Nicaragua would hold elections in November of that year. In return, the United States would stop supporting the Contras and providing military assistance to Central American allies, and neighboring countries would forbid rebel use of their territory.[12] The Sandinistas believed that without external support—armaments from the United States and bases in neighboring states—the Contras would collapse as a fighting force. With their plan having backfired, the United States and the Tegucigalpa group quickly changed their position and declared that the agreement was simply a set of talking points rather than a final document

12. Stephen Kinzer, "Nicaragua Says US No Longer Backs Peace Plan," *New York Times*, September 25, 1984, A12.

and demanded further revisions. They also expressed doubts that the November elections—which the FSLN won—would be free and fair, despite
the Sandinista invitation of international monitors. In short, they reneged
on the bargain. Thus, Honduras and Costa Rica, falling in line with the Reagan administration's demands, were able to scuttle a peace treaty in 1984
(Bagley 1986).

The Contadora members began to rewrite the treaty in earnest. In September of 1985, with much more input from the Tegucigalpa group, they proposed a new document. This version, like its predecessor, called for arms
reductions and democratic elections in Nicaragua; however, it did not prohibit Contra activities in Honduras and Costa Rica. Without such assurances,
Nicaragua was unwilling to sign the revised treaty. It would not meet the
demands of the opposition or international enemies if it had no credible assurances that the Contras would disarm. The third and final draft of the Contadora treaty, proposed in June 1986, failed to gain support in Nicaragua,
again over the issue of foreign support for the Contras. As before, Nicaragua
rejected the document, arguing that it would not offer concessions on Soviet
support and democratization without sufficient guarantees that foreign support for the Contras would end (Bagley 1986; Child 1992). Soon thereafter,
Honduras and Costa Rica announced that they would boycott the Contadora
talks altogether, arguing that Nicaragua was obstructing the peace process.[13]
The Contadora process had ended in failure.

The Reagan administration used the Sandinistas' rejection of the deal as
a pretext for overcoming growing Congressional objections to CIA operations in Central America and won support for the appropriation of $100
million in military and logistical aid to the Contras.[14] At this high-point in
their strength, the Contras occupied some twenty villages within Honduran territory, although they were unable to hold any significant areas
within Nicaragua itself (Schultz and Schultz 1994, chap. 5). The Contras'
fighting force reached roughly 15,000, and more than 70,000 Nicaraguan
refugees were located in Honduras, Costa Rica, and other countries in the
Americas.

Esquipulas

A major shift in the region occurred in 1986, when Costa Rica elected
Oscar Arias Sánchez as president. Costa Rican involvement in the Contra

13. "Two Nations Boycott Contadora," *Facts on File World News Digest*, November 28, 1986,
885, E2.
14. Ricard Meislin, "Contra Aid Is Seen as Hindering Accord," *New York Times*, September
18, 1986, A19.

war was a central issue in the 1986 campaign.[15] Arias, who ran on a prodevelopment and propeace platform, played on domestic discontent about the Nicaraguan war and anxieties about U.S. meddling in Central American affairs. In his inaugural address, he stated, "We will keep Costa Rica out of the armed conflicts of Central America and we will endeavor through diplomatic and political means to prevent Central American brothers from killing each other."[16] Upon taking office, Arias called for the resumption of negotiations to end the conflicts in the region. In 1987, Central American heads of state met in Esquipulas, Guatemala, to devise a new regional peace accord. Given his instrumental role in pushing the actors to the bargaining table and crafting the agreement, the Esquipulas treaty is often referred to as the Arias plan. With a popular mandate to pursue peace, Arias was willing to confront the Contras and the United States and take the hard steps necessary to reach an agreement.

Like Contadora, Esquipulas was an agreement between *governments* in the region and excluded the Contras. The treaty was signed on August 1987 by the presidents of Nicaragua, Honduras, Costa Rica, El Salvador, and Guatemala. Esquipulas, like Contadora, was a broad plan for peace and democratization in Central America, and it called for the dismantling of external rebel bases.[17] It also called for national reconciliation commissions in each country, free elections, and an international monitoring mission under the United Nations. This international monitoring mission was a key demand of Nicaragua, which needed credible assurances and independent verification that rebels would disband their external bases according to Article 6 of the treaty. Nicaraguan President Daniel Ortega commented that it was essential to establish a "multinational force of civilian observers at the border to guarantee an easing of tension there and to end the Contra activities that are carried out from Honduran territory. . . . If the multinational force is established, we both have a guarantee."[18]

15. Michael Tutton, "Costa Rica's Balancing Act Wavers: Nicaragua's War Has Nation Nervous as It Votes Today," *Toronto Star*, February 2, 1986, B2.

16. James LeMoyne, "Costa Rican Vows to Be a Peacemaker," *New York Times*, May 9, 1986, A3.

17. Article 6 of the treaty states, "The five countries signing this document reiterate their commitment to prevent the use of their own territory by persons, organizations or groups seeking to destabilize the Governments of Central American countries and refuse to provide them with or allow them to receive military and logistical support."

18. "Nicaragua Ortega Comments on Relations with Honduras; Conditions for Withdrawal of Legal Suit," British Broadcasting Corporation, August 20, 1988, part 4.

The United States was shocked by the signing of the agreement and quickly expressed its opposition to the accord.[19] Central American support for U.S. policy in the region was slipping, and these governments were taking a more independent stand. Signaling his commitment to the plan, in January 1988 Arias—who recently had gained substantial political capital by winning the Nobel Peace Prize for his efforts at Esquipulas—ordered Contra commanders to leave Costa Rica.[20]

Thus, the Contras had lost a key political ally, and, importantly, their southern front had lost its access to safe havens across the border. The road to peace had begun. As Kenneth Roberts writes, "A regional peace settlement was precluded so long as two basic conditions existed: the veto power wielded by hardliners in the Reagan administration, and the willingness of the Tegucigalpa group to follow Washington's policy lead. However, it was the erosion of this second condition that ultimately undermined Reagan administration policy in Central America and made possible the signing of the Arias Treaty in 1987" (1990, 87). The about-face in Costa Rica initiated this erosion of support.

The signing of Esquipulas did not bring an immediate end to the conflict. Rather, the treaty was the first step in a series of negotiations, and the difficult task of implementing the treaty's provisions proceeded slowly. Again Honduras wavered in its commitment to peace in Nicaragua; it was unwilling to take firm measures against the rebels, and the use of Honduran territory allowed the Contras to survive (Hartzell 2002; Schultz and Schultz 1994). Honduran president José Azcona was in a difficult position. On one hand, the United States and hardliners in his own government, including in the military, did not want to turn their backs on the Contras. On the other hand, the war was increasingly unpopular domestically, and obstructing the peace process would jeopardize Honduras' international image and its relations with its Latin American neighbors (Garrison and Gerner 2001).

For Nicaragua, the issue of foreign sanctuaries was critical. Esquipulas required an end to extraterritorial bases, and Nicaragua demanded that this point be adhered to before further progress could be made. According to Nicaraguan Vice Minister of Foreign Affairs Victor Hugo Tinoco, "For Nicaragua, if the mercenary forces [Contras] continue to use the territory of other neighboring countries, Nicaragua will find it difficult to comply

19. Neil A. Lewis, "US Envoys Told to Convey Doubt Over Latin Plan," *New York Times*, August 18, 1987, A1.
20. James LeMoyne, "Costa Rica in Ultimatum to Contras," *New York Times*, January 14, 1988, A8.

with the agreements that it would like to comply with" (Tinoco 1988, 39). Therefore, foreign bases were a significant stumbling block that prevented the Esquipulas process from meeting its objectives.

Honduras's Decision

Although initially showing signs of indecisiveness, Honduras ultimately came to back the implementation of Esquipulas. The costs of hosting the rebels became unacceptably high. Several international and domestic events undoubtedly affected Azcona's eventual decision to lend his support to the peace deal. First, as a broad contextual factor, the atmosphere of reform in the USSR signaled a waning of Cold War geostrategic concerns. Second, in late 1986, the Iran-Contra scandal broke out, which turned Congressional and public opinion against U.S. operations in Central America. The United States was covertly selling arms to Iran, its avowed enemy, and using the proceeds to illegally fund the Contras. Third, as a result of the scandal, in 1987 Congress narrowly rejected President Reagan's request for more economic and military aid for the Contras. Given the climate of controversy in the United States and the declining strategic importance of Central America as U.S.-Soviet relations began to thaw, Azcona feared the consequences of U.S. abandonment of Honduras and the Contras. As Garrison and Gerner write:

> The future of the Contras provided a constant threat to the stability of the Honduran state. If the United States, following the suspension of aid, chose to wipe its hands of the Contra problem, then the Honduran government would be left to clean up the mess alone. The presence of twelve thousand guerillas and one hundred thousand family members and supporters would require resources that Honduras did not have. Furthermore, the country faced the strong possibility that the guerillas would degenerate into roving bands of drug smugglers, gunrunners, hired assassins, and even criminal bandits. (2001, 4–5)

Even key Honduran military advisors feared a war against the Contras if the United States withdrew its support and the rebels had to be removed by force (Schultz and Schultz 1994, 228–29). Although Honduras wanted to keep pressure on the Sandinista regime, it was not willing to bear the costs of hosting the rebels without continued American support to guarantee its security, fund the rebels, and provide foreign aid (Child 1992, chap. 5).

Domestically, popular pressure on Azcona to evict the Contras mounted, further raising the costs of housing Honduras's "guests." The issue came to a head on April 5, 1988, when Honduran and U.S. agents seized Juan Ramón Matta, a notorious drug trafficker, and extradited him to the United States (Schultz and Schultz 1994). Matta was popular among many poor Hondurans, despite his connections to organized crime, for his contributions to charitable causes; to others, the maneuver had violated the Honduran Constitution, which prohibits the extradition of Honduran citizens.[21] Protests in Tegucigalpa over the affair became increasingly violent as anti-U.S. sentiment flared. Over 1,000 people marched on the U.S. embassy, where they set part of the compound on fire, smashed windows, overturned cars, and burned the American flag. Protests and riots continued for several days. The Matta affair was simply a spark in the tinderbox; the real frustration was over the perception that Honduras had become a U.S. stooge. One opposition leader commented that Honduras had become "like the circus dog that jumps through the hoops when its master tells it to. . . . There has been a complete submission to the United States, and people are tired of it."[22] Even after the protests over the Matta affair subsided, opposition to the war and to the United States continued. In July 1988, four U.S. service personnel were attacked, and in December the Peace Corps headquarters was bombed. Calls came from across the political spectrum to break free of U.S. influence and move against the Contras.[23] The border regions in particular cried out for relief from the unwelcome presence of Nicaraguan refugees and insurgents.[24] Azcona could no longer afford to maintain the status quo and began to assert some independence from the United States by backing the Esquipulas plan.

Continued Obstacles to Peace

Contra commanders were clearly aware of these pressures. Given that the climate in Costa Rica and Honduras was shifting, they were forced to the bargaining table with Nicaragua. In March 1988, the Sandinistas and Contras held their first formal talks in Sapoá, Nicaragua. The parties agreed to a sixty-day ceasefire and the continuation of talks on a perma-

21. Larry Rohter, "Seized Honduran: Drug Baron or Robin Hood?" *New York Times*, April 16, 1988, A4; Mike Tangeman, "Third World Report: Anti-US Tide Draws Backlash from Rightwing Activists," *The Guardian*, June 3, 1988.

22. Quoted in Larry Rohter, "Honduran Anger at U.S. Is Product Of Washington Policy, Officials Say," *New York Times*, April 13, 1988, A10.

23. Joseph Treaster, "Honduran Cooperation with Washington in Support of Contras Is Cooling," *New York Times*, March 27, 1988, Late City Final Edition, section 1, part 1, 18.

24. Wilson Ring, "Nightmare of Contra Killing Ground: The Impact of Nicaraguan Contra War on Lastrojes, Honduras," *The Guardian*, November 25, 1986; Peter Ford, "Contras in Honduras: Two Vantage Points," *Christian Science Monitor*, December 15, 1986, 1.

nent peace. The Sapoá agreement also called for a general amnesty, the repatriation of Nicaraguan exiles, and the protection of the Contras' political rights. The Reagan administration was dismayed that the Contras had entered negotiations with the Sandinistas without its blessing, but for their part, the Contras feared that they were being abandoned by regional allies and had no other choice but to strike a deal.[25] Therefore, external pressure on the combatants was a critical element in the decision to begin talks. Only a few months later, however, the ceasefire broke down when fighting erupted in the border region near Quilalí. Tellingly, during the battles that ensued, one Nicaraguan lieutenant noted that the rebels largely remained in their Honduran hideouts and periodically crossed the border to conduct raids: "One group of 40 or 60 Contras will cross into Honduras to pick up supplies, and another group will come into Nicaragua as replacements."[26]

With the ceasefire having failed, Ortega appealed directly to Honduras to evict the Contras, thereby allowing the peace process to move forward. The rebels' continued access to Honduras was seen as the key obstacle to implementing the ceasefire. On August 24, 1988, Ortega sent a personal letter to President Azcona. It is worth quoting this letter at length. In it, Ortega wrote,

> Relations between Nicaragua and Honduras have been seriously affected by the presence and activities of Contra mercenary forces in Honduran territory. . . . These circumstances, President Azcona, make it necessary to implement strong measures against these mercenary forces consonant with the commitments outlined in treaties currently in effect between the two countries and with general and generally-practiced international law. Those actions would be aimed, first, at disarming the mercenary forces and moving them away from the border. . . . Time is so crucial, President Azcona, that we can say regional peace and our people's tranquility is in your hands. . . .
>
> We also reiterate our proposal to establish, with UN guidance, a system for international observers . . . at the border between the two countries to prevent situations such as the one we are currently facing.[27]

25. Dale Nelson, "Reagan Urges Caution on Nicaragua Cease-Fire Accord," Associated Press, March 25, 1988.

26. Stephen Kinzer, "Nicaraguan Truce Beginning to Fray," *New York Times*, June 28, 1988, A1.

27. "Nicaragua's Ortega Calls on Honduras to Implement 'Strong Measures' Against Contras," British Broadcasting Corporation, August 29, 1989, part 4.

Thus, Ortega viewed the presence of Contra forces in Honduras as the basis for the rebels' viability and an impediment to further negotiations.[28] Importantly, this letter reiterated the demand for international observers to monitor the implementation of a peace agreement.

The 1988 presidential election in the United States brought fresh uncertainties in Central America. Neither Honduras nor the Contras could be certain that the Bush administration would continue to be as steadfastly anti-Sandinista as Reagan. The president-elect had yet to form his Latin America team. Thus, the implementation of the Esquipulas agreement became more urgent as the possibility of abandonment by the United States became a real threat. Central American leaders moved in earnest to bring an end to the conflict and met in Costa del Sol, El Salvador, on February 12–14, 1989, to come up with the Tesoro Beach Agreement. In exchange for the closing of rebel bases in Honduras within ninety days, Nicaragua agreed to hold elections in February 1990 and to allow international monitors to oversee all stages of the elections.

Upon hearing the news of the agreement, the Bush administration pressured Honduras not to act on its provisions; Undersecretary of State Robert Kimmitt was sent to Tegucigalpa in March to persuade Azcona not to disband rebel bases until after the scheduled elections. The United States felt that if Contra bases were disbanded before the elections, it would lose bargaining leverage should the outcome of the vote not be to its liking (Schultz and Schultz 1994, 252–56). In response, Honduras again dragged its feet as it announced that it would not evict Contra bases by force according to the ninety-day deadline; instead, it advocated the "principle of simultaneity," by which disarmament and elections would be implemented together.[29] Heartened by the announcement, Contra leaders lobbied governments in the region as well as the Bush administration to maintain its external bases.[30] Rebel commanders clearly wanted to keep the military option open. In part, they feared that if they were forced out of their safe-havens in Honduras and the Sandinistas won (or stole) the upcoming elections, they would be vulnerable to attack.

28. Ortega reiterated this demand in an August 29, 1988, speech. See "Nicaragua Ortega Announces Further Extension of Cease-fire," British Broadcasting Corporation, August 31, 1988, part 4.
29. Mark Uhlig, "Honduras, Shifting to US Stand, Won't Evict Contras from Bases," *New York Times*, March 23, 1988, A1.
30. Lee Hockstader, "Contras Lobby in Central America for Right to Keep Military Bases," *Washington Post*, July 28, 1989, A29.

The Tela Declaration

Nicaragua moved quickly to signal its commitment to holding elections and securing peace. Sandinista leaders met with domestic (non-Contra) opposition groups to hammer out the terms of the February elections, which it was committed to hold. On August 4, a forty-point accord was struck with opposition leaders that included the repeal of national security legislation restricting opposition activities, guidelines for the campaign, and specific election procedures. This agreement satisfied the main demands of the Central American governments. In response to this positive step by the Sandinistas, on August 7 Central American leaders, including President Azcona, signed the Tela Declaration, which reiterated the governments' commitment to disband rebel bases on their territories and, importantly, called on the United Nations to verify base closures, demobilization, and repatriation. Underscoring the significance of this agreement, President Ortega remarked that Nicaragua had been brought to the "gates of peace" but that it would not "let down its guard until the Contras are disbanded."[31] Three months later, the United Nations Observer Group in Central America (ONUCA) was created by the Security Council to oversee rebel disarmament; by December, UN officials were stationed in Honduras (not Nicaragua). The invitation of this monitoring mission to oversee the disarmament and repatriation process in Honduras was the decisive step toward peace and satisfied a key demand of the Sandinista government (Child 1992; Tinoco 1988, 74).

The invitation of UN peacekeepers accomplished two important tasks. First, it sent a strong signal that Honduras was now firmly committed to the peace process. Rebel hosts must themselves offer credible commitments that they will abide by demobilization agreements, and the invitation of the UN was a costly signal to that effect. If the UN found that Honduras did not follow through on its disarmament promise, there would be substantial international and domestic audience costs for its insincerity. Second, the invitation of international monitors assuaged the Sandinistas' security fears. The Sandinistas were unable to verify Contra demobilization in Honduras by themselves and were reluctant, given past failures, to accept promises by Honduras that demobilization was indeed taking place. Nicaragua was more willing to believe information supplied by a neutral observation

---

31. Juan Maltes, "Central American Accord Greeted with Anger, Joy, Caution," Associated Press, August 8, 1989.

team. With Honduras now cooperating, Nicaragua would be willing to abide by its part of the deal.

The Contras were furious that they were not consulted in the drafting of the Tela Declaration and refused to cooperate with the demobilization plan.[32] Although they were to give up their weapons in advance of the elections, deadlines came and went without compliance by the insurgents. Although Contra activities had been restricted, Honduras argued that they lacked the means to disarm the rebels—several thousand strong—by force. Notwithstanding this failure, on February 25, 1990, Nicaragua held internationally monitored elections in which Violeta Chamorro, the main opposition leader, won a victory over Sandinista candidate Daniel Ortega. The result came as a surprise to those who feared that the elections would be marred by fraud. Pressure for rebel demobilization mounted after the Sandinistas were defeated at the polls; by now, even President Bush asked Contra leaders to stand down.

The End of the Contra War

On March 15, 1990, the UN demanded that rebels in Honduras be demobilized and repatriated immediately.[33] Honduras was also eager to get rid of foreign fighters on its territory; however, whereas they lacked the will to disarm the Contras before, now they needed assistance to actually carry out repatriation. The Contras dragged their feet, claiming that they could not be certain that the Sandinistas would actually cede power by the scheduled April 25 transfer of government. These fears were exacerbated by Chamorro's decision to retain General Humberto Ortega, the former defense minister, as army chief under the new government and to allow Sandinistas to head the National Police force as gestures of national reconciliation (Hartzell 2002, 368).

The UN, in consultation with Central American governments, decided to take more aggressive measures to gain Contra compliance with the demobilization plan (Child 1992). On March 27, the Security Council authorized an armed mission to Nicaragua to assist in the demobilization and repatriation of the insurgents. This step provided the help that Honduras needed to go forward with repatriation. Venezuela sent the largest

---

32. Lindsey Gruson, "The Peace Plan Wears Thin in Nicaragua," *New York Times*, November 5, 1989, late edition, section 4, 1.

33. United Nations, "Central America: ONUCA Background," http://www.un.org/Depts/DPKO/Missions/onucabackgr.html (accessed January 16, 2006).

contingent to Honduras, including a paratrooper battalion. Pressured to leave Honduras, and no longer viable as a fighting force, the Contras could only negotiate the terms of their demobilization. Contra leaders met with the government-elect at Toncontín airport in Honduras, where the rebels agreed to disarm before Chamorro's inauguration in exchange for cash and land concessions.

Disarmament proceeded slowly, and the rebels had not fully disbanded by the time of the inauguration, but they were not actively fighting either. Understanding that change was on the horizon, the Contras gave up their armed struggle. The May 30 Managua Protocol on Disarmament between the Contras and the Nicaraguan government—now under Chamorro—was the final agreement between the state and the rebels. A few days later, in front of a gathering of Contra fighters, Chamorro declared an end to the war.[34] By July, the vast majority of the Contras had returned to Nicaragua and turned in their weapons.

Not all demobilized Contras were satisfied with the deal. Many complained that the land that was promised as part of the demobilization pact was not handed over to them or was inadequate. Some ex-fighters, known as the re-Contras, again took up arms against the state. Former Contra leaders, including Commander Rubén (Oscar Manuel Sobalvarro García) and Commander Dimas (Tomás Laguna Rayo), led the charge and were able to rally a few hundred troops (Library of Congress Federal Research Division 1993). Again, much of the fighting took place in the border region near Quilalí, but the re-Contras were unable to make significant military advances. The insecurity created by the re-Contras was intensified in late 1991 by the formation of re-Compas, former Sandinista soldiers who also demanded agricultural plots. By 1992, however, the government had regained control over the situation by establishing military dominance over Nicaraguan territory and was able to buy off many insurgents with land and cash. Unlike the Contra rebels, the re-Contras and re-Compas did not have the support of external hosts, and therefore they could not mount a successful military challenge to the state. Thus, this new uprising was short-lived and ended in defeat.

Lessons Learned

To conclude, governments in the region, particularly Costa Rica and Honduras, played key roles in the Nicaraguan peace process. Due to obstacles

---

34. Michael Molinski, "Chamorro Declares End to War," United Press International, June 9, 1990, international section.

raised by the Tegucigalpa group, the Contadora plan fell by the wayside. Peace negotiations could not move forward without the cooperation of rebel hosts. Under the presidency of Oscar Arias, who revived the peace process under the Esquipulas framework, Costa Rica moved first to expel Contra fighters from its territory. Gaining the cooperation of Honduras proved to be a more difficult matter, however. Under pressure from the United States, and wanting to pursue its own agenda against its Sandinista rivals in Nicaragua, Honduras was reluctant to forbid rebel access to its territory. Nevertheless, under growing domestic opposition to the war and fears that the mood in the United States was shifting, Honduran President Azcona finally decided supporting the insurgency was no longer in his country's best interests. The costs of continued hosting had become too high, and conciliatory gestures by the Sandinistas assuaged the sense of hostility between the two nations.

Importantly, it was only after their Honduran hosts signed the Esquipulas agreement that the Contras agreed to talk to the Nicaraguan government. Therefore, rebel hosts can play an important role in pressuring combatants to the bargaining table. Honduras's invitation of a UN peace-keeping mission through the Tela Declaration was the final step that secured the peace. In allowing ONUCA the authority to monitor Contra demobilization, Honduras demonstrated that the rebels were no longer welcome. It used a costly mechanism to signal its commitment to peace, and it provided for the credible transmission of information about disarmament on its territory. Nicaragua was willing to believe these assurances that rebel demobilization was forthcoming. Although the Contras were initially reluctant to comply and the actual process of demobilization was fraught with obstacles, they had no choice but to forgo military operations given their inability to fight the Nicaraguan government on its own turf. Instead, they opted for a peace deal with the government. The shift in Honduras helps to explain the timing of the peace in Nicaragua.

5 The Rwandan Civil War

Because they involved actors throughout the Great Lakes region of Africa, the civil conflicts in Rwanda exemplify the transnational aspects of war. Tutsis and Hutus are scattered across various states in central Africa, refugee flows contributed to the spread of conflict, and rebels and governments frequently battled one another across national boundaries. The postgenocide government of Rwanda presents an extreme case of a state that was willing to invade a neighboring country's territory—that of Zaire—in order to remove the ruling regime and eliminate transnational rebel groups. Although the government bore considerable costs in taking military action against Hutu rebels across the border, the rebels—some responsible for the 1994 genocide—presented a serious threat to Rwandan Tutsis, providing a compelling reason for the intrusion. Although Rwanda was successful in ousting the Mobutu regime in Zaire, which harbored Hutu rebels, it was neither able to remove the Kabila government, which had turned on its former Rwandan allies, nor completely defeat TNRs in the Democratic Republic of the Congo (DRC). Therefore, despite these sovereignty violations, the Rwandan government faced considerable difficulties defeating insurgents on foreign soil, even as it was quite effective in maintaining internal control. A peace agreement with the Congo and the invitation of a UN force were required to debilitate the Hutu militias. The DRC's cooperation in counterinsurgency efforts following an agreement signed in Pretoria, South Africa, dealt a critical blow to rebels hiding in the Congo's Eastern Provinces. Although as of this writing it may be too early to declare the rebels completely defeated, all signs indicate that they are defunct as a fighting force for now.

Background to the Conflicts in Central Africa

Under Belgian rule, the Tutsi minority—deemed to be more "fit" to govern according to the racial pseudoscience of the time—was favored over the Hutu majority in their access to civil service positions and influence in the colonial government. On the eve of independence, however, the Belgian administration began to shift policies toward majority rule, and ethnic parties emerged, with Hutus and Tutsis demanding a greater say in government. Clashes between these groups reached a boiling point in 1959, when ethnic riots broke out that killed several thousand Tutsis and forced many thousands more to flee to neighboring countries. After independence in 1962, Hutus assumed control of the government under President Grégoire Kayibanda, who brutally repressed the Tutsi minority. Kayibanda accused Tutsis of being agents of the Tutsi-dominated government in neighboring Burundi; in response to discriminatory policies, many fled the country. Kayibanda ruled until 1973, when a military coup removed him from power and installed Juvenal Habyarimana, also a Hutu, as president. Conditions for Rwandan Tutsis did not improve much under Habyarimana, and again many left for neighboring countries, particularly Zaire, Uganda, and Burundi (Mamdani 2001; Uvin 1999).

The refugees in Uganda would become particularly important because of their subsequent involvement in internal power struggles. The many Rwandan Tutsis born in Uganda after the 1959 exodus continued to face considerable official discrimination there. Several thousand Rwandan Tutsis in exile fought alongside Yoweri Museveni and the Ugandan National Resistance Army (NRA), contributing to the overthrow of Milton Obote in 1985 and to Museveni's rise to power in 1986. As a consequence, many Rwandans acquired positions within Museveni's government. In the mid-1980s, with a friendly regime in power in Uganda, Rwandan Tutsis in that country formed the Rwandan Patriotic Front (RPF) to demand greater rights and concessions from Habyarimana's government (Mamdani 2001).

The RPF crossed the border from Uganda and began its attacks against Rwanda in 1990, but was initially unable to make major advances. Early on in the conflict, RPF commander and close associate of Museveni, Fred Rwigema, was killed in combat and was replaced with Paul Kagame. Under Kagame's leadership, in 1991 a successful attack on the border town of Ruhengeri demonstrated the strength of the RPF, whose ranks began to swell with new recruits. On the battlefield, the tide began to turn in the RPF's favor. With the Habyarimana regime now under serious threat, the French provided significant military assistance to the Rwandan Armed

Forces (FAR) in order to prop up the government. This assistance prevented the capital, Kigali, from falling into the hands of the rebels. Unable to advance any further, the RPF agreed to a ceasefire and formal talks with the government in Arusha, Tanzania. In 1993, the government and the RPF signed a power-sharing agreement to put an end to the conflict and hold multiparty elections. Reflecting the RPF's military supremacy, the Arusha Accords gave Tutsis a disproportionate share of political power, including forty percent of the armed forces, despite the fact that Tutsis were less than twenty percent of the population. The power-sharing deal alienated hardline elements in Habyarimana's government, who were unwilling to relinquish power and who were skeptical of the RPF's motives (Mamdani 2001; Melvern 2004).

In a tragic turn of events, on April 6, 1994, Habyarimana was killed when his airplane was shot down; although official government reports blamed the rebels, RPF leader Paul Kagame denied the accusations. Hutu extremists in the government, who had been fomenting anti-Tutsi sentiment and were training armed militias, seized this opportunity to undermine the Arusha Accords. Using their access to the media, these extremists fomented fears among the civilian population that the RPF would soon invade the country once again (Philip Gourevitch 1998; Mamdani 2001; Uvin 1999). During the next three months, the FAR, along with machete-wielding popular militias—known as the Interahamwe—went on a genocidal campaign to kill Tutsis and moderate Hutus. United Nations peacekeepers on the ground, in a dramatic failure of international resolve, did little to quell the violence. The Rwandan genocide left an estimated 800,000 people dead; as UN Secretary-General Kofi Annan would comment ten years later, "an entire country was shattered."[1]

Alarmed at the slaughter, the RPF again went on the offensive. While the Interahamwe and other militias were conducting massacres, the FAR was crumbling against RPF advances. By July, the RPF had captured the capital, Kigali, and put an end to the genocide. Afraid of retaliation by the new government, thousands of Hutus fled Rwanda on a daily basis in one of the largest mass exoduses of the twentieth century. Hutu leaders encouraged this exodus and planned to launch an insurgency from across the border. Along with civilian refugees, thousands of members of the FAR and Interahamwe left the country, with the largest share going to Zaire (Mamdani

---

1. United Nations Press Release, "Rwanda Genocide 'Must Leave Us Always with a Sense of Bitter Regret and Abiding Sorrow,' Says Secretary General to New York Memorial Conference," http://www.un.org/News/Press/docs/2004/sgsm9223.doc.htm (accessed January 31, 2006).

2001). According to reports on the ground, these fighters kept large stock-piles of weapons, were allowed to remain in military uniform, and were welcomed by officials in Mobutu Sese Seko's government.[2]

As figure 5.1 shows, just as Tutsi refugees began to reenter Rwanda from Uganda and Burundi, Hutu refugees fled to Tanzania and Zaire en masse. By the end of 1994, over 1.2 million Rwandan refugees were in Zaire and more than 1 million were in Tanzania. Humanitarian aid agencies were stretched thin as camp conditions in Zaire quickly deteriorated, and an outbreak of cholera left tens of thousands dead.

Within these camps, members of the former Rwandan army and the In-terahamwe began to regroup. As Sarah Kenyon Lischer (2005) explains, in contrast to Tanzania, which took great effort to preserve the civilian nature of the refugee encampments and disarm combatants, Mobutu's govern-ment was neither willing nor able to neutralize Hutu militants in eastern Zaire. Mobutu's sympathies were with the former government, not the Tutsi-led RPF. Furthermore, with the refugee camps being run by the very people who perpetrated the gencocide, much of the humanitarian aid pro-vided by international donors was diverted toward the militants. Security in the Zairian camps posed a constant problem. Refugees believed to be sympathetic to the RPF were frequently lynched.[3] UN officials in Zaire warned that the militarization of the refugee camps could pose a serious threat to regional security. "We are sitting on a volcano," said Shahyar Khan, the Secretary General's representative in Rwanda. "We must separate the wolves from the sheep."[4]

However, neither Zaire nor the international community took steps to disarm the ex-FAR and the militias, who were beginning to conduct cross-border raids against the new Rwandan government and attack local Zairian Tutsi (known as the Banyamulenge). News reports documented the train-ing and supplying of roughly 40,000 fighters, including thousands near the town of Goma.[5] Hutu militants soon began to conduct strikes across the border. In 1995 and 1996, the RPF-led state responded to rebel attacks with sporadic, limited forays against the refugee camps. Because the new gov-ernment was still taking shape, however, it was not prepared to take more

2. Raymond Bonner, "Rwandan Army in Disarray at a Camp on the Border," *New York Times,* July 17, 1994, late edition, A1.
3. Associated Press, "Attacks Spread at Rwandan Refugee Camp," *New York Times,* August 27, 1994, late edition, A3.
4. Quoted in Raymond Bonner, "Rwanda Faces New War Unless International Force Is Sent, UN Aides Say," *New York Times,* November 6, 1994, late edition, A12.
5. "Rwandan Refugees: Crime and Nourishment," *Economist,* April 1, 1995, 34.

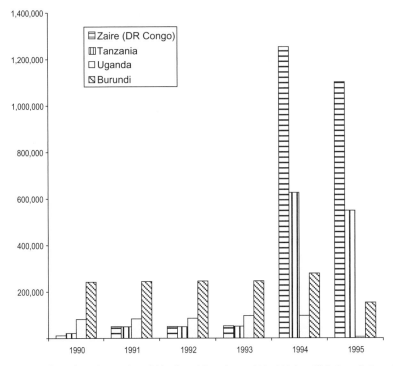

Figure 5.1. Rwandan refugees in neighboring states. *Source:* United Nations High Commissioner for Refugees.

extensive measures to root out the rebels. Thus, the former government and Interahamwe forces—perpetrators of the 1994 genocide—had become a well-armed and well-trained insurgent force.

Rwandan Intervention against Mobutu

With the failure to pacify the refugee camps and with Mobutu actively supporting the Hutu militants, violence continued in eastern Zaire (International Crisis Group 2001). A series of attacks were launched against Zairian Tutsis by ex-FAR/Interahamwe forces and local Hutus, who wished to bolster their position in North and South Kivu—provinces in eastern Zaire along the Rwandan border. Mobutu viewed this as an opportunity to move against his political rivals in the east; Zairian Tutsis were opposed to Mobutu's rule because they were denied citizenship rights by the state. Mobutu argued that Tutsis were not "indigenous" to Zaire but had migrated during colonial rule and could therefore be denied political rights

(Mamdani 2001). In late 1996, Zaire moved to displace hundreds of thousands of Tutsis living in North and South Kivu (Curtis 2005; Isima 2005). Amnesty International reported that dozens of Banyamulenge were executed, "disappeared," or arrested by Zairian security forces;[6] in addition, thousands of Tutsi refugees fled the region. Rebel forces were also escalating their attacks against Rwanda from Zairian territory.[7]

In response to these developments across the border, Rwanda decided to act. Its motives were, first, to break the back of the insurgent forces who were gaining strength and posed a serious threat to the regime; and, second, to protect Zairian Tutsis from further persecution. These objectives were intertwined. The Banyamulenge in eastern Zaire were seen as key local allies in the fight to dislodge Hutu rebels from their bases; if the Mobutu/ex-FAR ethnic cleansing campaign against the Banyamulenge were to succeed, the rebels' position would be strengthened. Rwanda intervened by arming the Banyamulenge as early as October 1996. Mobutu's armed forces clashed with local rebels supported by Rwandan troops; by November, the Zairian town of Goma had fallen into Tutsi rebel hands.[8] Thus, the presence of Rwandan Hutu rebels—supported by the Mobutu government—led to a direct confrontation between Rwanda and the Banyamulenge versus the government of Zaire. However, Rwanda recognized that it would need more than the support of local Tutsis and enlisted Laurent Kabila—a member of the Luba tribe from Katanga Province—and his Alliance of Democratic Forces for the Liberation of Congo (ADFL) to carry out the war. The Rwandan government wanted nothing less than the removal of Mobutu from power and the installation of a friendly regime that it could rely on to uproot the ex-FAR/Interahamwe forces and prevent future rebel mobilization.

The ADFL quickly consolidated support in the east. The rebel force captured much of the interior of the country and prepared for a push on the capital, Kinshasa, by May 1997. Domestic and international support for Mobutu had also crumbled. Mobutu had been a key Cold War ally of the West, but with the Soviet Union now dissolved, his international backers did not come to his defense. Moreover, due to his support of rebel movements across Africa, he had grown increasingly unpopular on the continent. Internally, decades of cronyism and underdevelopment in Zaire led

6. Amnesty International Press Release, "Zaire: Amnesty International Condemns Human Rights Violations Against Tutsi," September 20, 1996.
7. Chris Tomlinson, "Suspected Hutu Rebels Kill 28 Tutsis in Rwanda," Associated Press, June 29, 1996, International News.
8. James McKinley, "Zaire Rebels Take a Town with the Help of Rwandan Army," *New York Times*, November 3, 1996, late edition, A1.

many to openly support Kabila's advance as a welcome relief from Mobutu's rule. On May 17, 1997, only months after fighting first erupted in the Kivus, the ADFL occupied Kinshasa and renamed the country the Democratic Republic of the Congo. Mobutu fled the country and died of cancer a few months later in Morocco.

During Kabila's push toward the capital, Rwandan troops and their local allies in eastern Zaire seized on the opportunity to move against Hutu rebels in the Kivus. They worked to forcibly repatriate the refugees and clear the camps of insurgents. Most of the Rwandan Hutu refugees had been moved by Hutu leaders to the Mugunga refugee camp near Goma; the ex-FAR/Interahamwe forces were accused of using these civilian refugees as human shields. Days of relentless attacks by Rwandan forces and local militias against Mugunga succeeded in cutting off international aid to the camp and dispersing the rebels. By November 15, 1996, the major camps had been cleared and an estimated 700,000 Rwandan refugees were repatriated in one of the largest reverse-migrations in recent history.[9] A few months later, refugees at the Tingi-Tingi camp were similarly assaulted. Reports from the field alleged that in the confusion, thousands of innocent refugees had been slaughtered. In addition, the rebels were in disarray, at least temporarily.

Rwanda's action in Zaire/DRC is one of the rare examples in which a government fighting a transnational rebel group was willing to go beyond the occasional cross-border strike and undertake extensive military operations on another state's territory. International borders are not inviolable, but states face considerable costs in pursuing TNRs across the frontier. These costs include a conflict with the neighboring state, governance costs for holding neighboring territory, and international censure. In the Rwandan case, the Hutu perpetrators of the 1994 genocide presented a fundamental threat to the government and perhaps to Rwandan Tustis as a whole; therefore, the state was willing to bear considerable costs to defeat the rebels. Importantly, Rwanda sought to mitigate these costs by acting through local proxies: the Banyamulenge and the ADFL. These forces had better knowledge of the terrain and local population, and they would be instrumental in confronting Mobutu's forces and moving against Rwandan Hutus in the east. The Rwandan military role in the Congo was to be temporary. After the installation of a friendly regime, Kabila would govern the territory, freeing Rwanda of governance

9. Allan Thompson, "700,000 in Mass Exodus from Zaire," *Toronto Star*, November 16, 1996, A1.

costs. Finally, international condemnation of the sovereignty violation was muted because the international community viewed the pursuit of the perpetrators of the Rwandan genocide as legitimate and had come to view Mobutu with disdain.

Yet despite the Kabila takeover in May and the dispersal of the refugees, Rwanda's rebel problem had not been solved. Although many rebel fighters were killed, others simply dispersed into the Congo's dense forests or fled to Congo-Brazzaville, the Central African Republic, Zambia, and elsewhere (International Crisis Group 2001). Soon after the ouster of Mobutu, ex-FAR officers formed a new insurgent group, the Armée pour la Libération du Rwanda (ALiR). According to a report by the International Crisis Group, approximately 15,000 Rwandan rebels remained in the Kivus despite the removal of Mobutu and the destruction of the refugee camps (International Crisis Group 1998b). Rwanda had wagered that Kabila would use the new Congolese armed forces to oust these remaining fighters and destroy the insurgency, but this was a gamble that Kigali ultimately lost. Soon, Kabila would turn his back on his former patron and turn his support to the ALiR.

Rwanda versus Kabila

Initially Kabila included many Tutsis in his administration and in the Congolese armed forces. Rwandan advisors also played an important political role in Kinshasa. Yet he faced intense domestic criticism that he was a pawn to foreigners; in response, he moved against the Banyamulenge and Rwandan elements in the military (Curtis 2005; International Crisis Group 1998a; Scherrer 2002, chap. 10). In July 1998, over 10,000 Rwandans and Banyamulenge were expelled from the armed forces. This alarmed Rwanda, Kabila's sponsor and supporter. As the Banyamulenge again felt marginalized, within days a new rebel movement, the Rally for Congolese Democracy (RCD) emerged in the east. Rwanda backed this uprising against its former protégé because Kabila had failed to move against ALiR forces. The expulsion of Tutsis from the military confirmed Rwandan suspicion that Kabila would not be a reliable partner. Uganda also joined in to support the RCD, as the guerrillas of the Allied Democratic Forces, a Ugandan rebel outfit, held bases in the Congo as well.

Rwanda hoped that it could repeat its swift success against the Mobutu regime. It would use the RCD as cover to both unseat Kabila and move against the ALiR forces, who were gaining strength. Kabila quickly formed an alliance with the Rwandan Hutus to prevent the RCD advance (International

Crisis Group 2001, 2003). Additionally, unlike Mobutu, Kabila had important international allies who came to his defense. While the RCD, Rwanda, and Uganda were advancing west toward the capital, Angola and Zimbabwe sent forces to prop up the government. Soon at least seven foreign governments had troops in the Congo: Angola, Chad, Namibia, and Zimbabwe were backing Kabila and Rwanda, Burundi, and Uganda backed rebel forces. Africa was experiencing a continental war that would become one of the bloodiest ever fought on the continent. One report claims that some four million people died over the course of the war in the Congo as a direct result of the fighting and from preventable causes such as malnutrition and disease.[10]

This time, Rwanda's intervention in the Congo became an extremely costly endeavor, without the expected result. Rather than a quick victory, Rwanda was faced with a devastating war. Instead of rebuilding institutions at home and focusing on economic development, health, and education, government resources were stretched thin by the engagement in the Congo. The Rwandan government also became alienated on the continent. The war against Kabila and his foreign supporters distanced Rwanda from other African governments. Then Rwanda and Uganda, which had been allies, fell into disagreement about the conduct of the war and came to blows against one another for reasons that remain unclear.[11] The RCD split into two factions, one supported by Rwanda and the other by Uganda, and these factions frequently fought one another rather than the central government. With this divided opposition, the goal of unseating the government in Kinshasa became distant. In short, Rwanda's strategy against Kabila had failed.

The wider international community also condemned Rwanda for its violation of Congolese sovereignty. Security Council resolution 1234 of April 9, 1999, was the first in a series of resolutions to demand respect for "the territorial integrity, political independence, and national sovereignty" of the DRC and to call for the "withdrawal of all foreign forces."[12] Progress in fighting ALiR forces was also mixed. Although Rwanda was able to prevent a large-scale attack by Hutu rebels on its own territory, ALiR remained quite formidable. The rebels maintained 10,000–15,000 men in North Kivu

10. "3.9 Million Dead from War in Democratic Republic of Congo: The Lancet," Agence France-Presse, January 6, 2006.

11. Anna Borzello, "Uganda Declares Rwanda an Enemy," BBC News, March 10, 2001, http://news.bbc.co.uk/1/hi/world/africa/1213659.stm (accessed February 7, 2006).

12. UN Security Council Resolution 1234, April 9, 1999, http://www.un.org/Docs/scres/1999/sc99.htm. Also see resolutions 1258, 1273, 1279, 1291, 1304, 1316, 1323, 1332, 1341, 1355, 1376, 1399, 1417, 1445, 1457, 1468, 1489, 1493, and 1501.

and across Congolese territory, and many rebel leaders were sheltered in Kinshasa (International Crisis Group 2003). Rwanda's lack of knowledge of the local population and terrain hurt its counterinsurgency efforts. As President Paul Kagame would later recount in an interview, one of the primary difficulties in defeating Hutu rebels "is a geographical question. It is a question of the terrain, the expanse of the Congo. You wouldn't easily round up such forces in that whole expanse of the Congo and forces that are being supported by Kabila."[13]

The balance sheet suggested that Rwanda could not sustain military operations on its neighbor's territory for long and that its objectives could not be met through force alone. The costs to the Rwandan government, including conflict with the DRC and other African states, international censure, and direct costs of military occupation weighed against the benefits of pursuing ALiR forces in the DRC. Although the Rwandan armed forces controlled their own territory, combating the rebels on foreign soil—particularly in the vast area of the Congo—proved to be exceptionally challenging.

The Peace Process

After a series of failed negotiations, representatives from the DRC, Rwanda, Uganda, Burundi, Zimbabwe, Angola, and Namibia met in Lusaka, Zambia, to sign a ceasefire agreement on July 10, 1999. The provisions of the Lusaka Accord included an immediate end to hostilities; the establishment of a Joint Military Commission (JMC) consisting of representatives from each state to monitor the ceasefire; the disarmament of the militias; the withdrawal of foreign troops; and a request for a UN mission to enforce compliance. The UN force was asked to investigate ceasefire violations, collect weapons, and disarm fighters, by force if necessary. In response, the UN Security Council created the UN Organization Mission in Congo (MONUC) on November 30. MONUC's mandate focused on five key elements: disarmament, demobilization, repatriation, resettlement, and reintegration (these are collectively referred to as DDRRR). However, the Security Council refused to authorize a robust Chapter 7 peace-enforcement mission which could go after armed factions by force, insisting that disarmament would be entirely voluntary (Alusala 2004).

The Lusaka ceasefire was flawed from the beginning, and little real progress toward peace was made. Several obstacles to peace became

13. "Interview with Rwanda's President Paul Kagame," Patrick Smith and William Wallis, interviewers, *Africa Confidential*, October 18, 2002 http://www.africa-confidential.com/index .aspx?pageid=17&specialreportid=6 (accessed June 19, 2006).

apparent. The RCD reluctantly signed the agreement in August, but divisions within the rebel group forestalled the implementation of Lusaka's terms.[14] Moreover, the Joint Military Commission was dysfunctional because it failed to meet regularly as planned and suffered from mutual recriminations that cooperation was not forthcoming. The JMC was, after all, comprised of representatives of the belligerent parties themselves rather than neutral observers. Finally, without Chapter 7 authorization to go after the militias by force and with delays in sending peacekeepers, MONUC was essentially toothless. Thus, flouting the Lusaka Accord, Kabila continued to supply Hutu militias, and Rwanda maintained its forces in the eastern Congo. In August 2000, the DRC declared that it would no longer honor the Lusaka Accord, but a few days later suggested that the agreement needed to be revised rather than scrapped.[15] This signaled a wavering commitment to peace. Also in 2000, a new Rwandan Hutu rebel movement emerged with the backing of Kabila calling itself the Democratic Forces for the Liberation of Rwanda (FDLR). The Lusaka Accord was becoming obsolete.

Then, unexpectedly, Laurent Kabila was shot and killed by one of his bodyguards in January 2001. After an initial period of confusion, his son Joseph Kabila assumed control of the government. Joseph Kabila was relatively unknown and, unlike his father, had not earned the enmity of the Rwandan government. The new president addressed the UN Security Council in February and pledged his commitment to peace, although he continued to insist that foreign forces be withdrawn.[16] President Paul Kagame recognized that Joseph Kabila appeared to be more cooperative. In response to the succession in the DRC, Kagame remarked, "The opportunity [for peace] is available and it's not going to be there forever."[17] The two governments began talking once again.

Amid the confusion surrounding Kabila's succession, Hutu rebels continued to plot against the Rwandan government. The ALiR had approximately 12,000 men stationed in North Kivu and around the Kahuzi Biega forest. The newly formed FDLR had between 7,000 and 8,000 fighters

14. BBC News, "Congo Rebels Reject Kabila Talks Offer," BBC Online, September 16, 1999, http://news.bbc.co.uk/1/hi/world/africa/449509.stm (accessed February 9, 2006).

15. Agence France-Presse, "DR Congo Suspends Lusaka Peace Agreement," August 24, 2000; Agence France-Presse, "Kinshasa Has Not Withdrawn from Lusaka Peace Accord: Official," August 26, 2000.

16. Christopher S. Wren, "Congo's New Leader, at the UN Pledges Talks with War Foes," *New York Times*, February 3, 2001, late edition, A7.

17. Barbara Crossette, "Rwandan Leader, in US, Urges Push for Peace in Congo," *New York Times*, February 5, 2001, late edition, A4.

spread across the east (International Crisis Group 2003). These forces continued to recruit among Rwandan refugees; yet, many of the new recruits were far too young to be implicated in the 1994 genocide. Indeed, the leaders of the FDLR deliberately tried to distance themselves from the genocide in order to boost its image. In September 2000, ALiR was formally dissolved and integrated within the FDLR command structure (International Crisis Group 2003).

In May and June 2001, with renewed vigor, the FDLR launched a series of large-scale attacks. These incursions were referred to as Operation Oracle du Seigneur (Operation Lord's Oracle) and were perhaps the best-coordinated assaults on Rwanda. Kabila was accused of continuing his father's policy of support for Hutu rebels. Yet the rebels suffered a major defeat in Operation Oracle du Seigneur, as they could not establish a presence within Rwandan territory and lost around 4,000 men (International Crisis Group 2001, 2003). The FDLR retreated to their bases in the DRC. Thus, the government in Kigali had established military superiority over Rwandan soil; and the rebels were unable to contest the state's power at home and were reliant on external bases for their viability. Nonetheless, despite the continued Rwandan army presence on Congolese soil, the FDLR was relatively safe; on unfamiliar territory, the Rwandan government could not root out the rebels. It is also worth noting that the rebels attempted to establish a presence in Burundi as well, but with the cooperation of the Burundian government, its bases there were destroyed by Burundian forces (International Crisis Group 2001, 8).[18] Therefore, the insurgency's presence in the DRC—and Kinshasa's unwillingness to act decisively against it—was critical for its survival.

The Pretoria Accord

After years of fighting, the DRC and Rwanda decided that they had had enough; the costs of conflict were high and little progress was being made. A stalemate had been reached: Rwanda and the Rally for Congolese Democracy could not topple the government in Kinshasa, and the FDLR had been unsuccessful in its military operations. Moreover, because Rwandan offensives could not fully root them out, the FDLR bases in the DRC remained intact. In addition, the conflict took a heavy toll on each country's economy,

18. Rwandan Hutu fighters repeatedly attempted to establish a presence in Burundi but were not successful in doing so. In January 2001, Rwanda and Burundi agreed on a joint security arrangement which would cooperatively track down and eliminate rebel forces. See "Burundi, Rwandan Authorities Agree to Jointly Track Down Militia Group," *Financial Times*, BBC Monitoring International Reports, January 21, 2004.

military, and international image. After the failure of Lusaka, renewed peace talks began between the governments. The demands were clear: Rwanda was to leave Congolese territory in exchange for Congo's firm commitment to evict Hutu rebels. According to President Kagame, "The disarmament and repatriation of Interahamwe based in Congo is still the most important problem."[19] South Africa took the lead in mediation efforts, and on July 30, 2002, Rwanda and the DRC signed the Pretoria Accord. Congolese President Kabila made conciliatory public statements, indicating that he was prepared to follow through with the agreement. Referring to the removal of Hutu rebels, he commented, "Where force will be needed, force will be used."[20]

Kagame clearly saw the Pretoria Accord as an important step toward defeating the rebel force and ending the conflict. Nearly eight years of Rwandan presence in the DRC had failed to rout the insurgents, and this agreement provided new hope for putting an end to the rebellion. In his public appearances surrounding the Pretoria talks, Kagame made it clear that he viewed foreign bases as the key obstacle to peace in the region. In an interview, he commented that "we must, first of all, make sure that these people [ex-FAR and Interahamwe] do not get support from anywhere and, if we do that, based on the political will, it is possible to deal with the problem."[21] He added that "these people represent a threat to our country. They pose a problem in and outside Rwanda."[22] The RCD echoed Kagame's concern over foreign fighters. Joseph Mudumbi, an RCD official in charge of foreign relations, stated, "We ask that Kinshasa proceeds with the immediate arrest of the Interahamwe leaders and ex-FAR."[23] Clearly, then, foreign bases were seen as a chief impediment to counterinsurgency efforts.

Specifically, the Pretoria Accord created a timetable for the withdrawal of Rwandan forces and the disarmament of Hutu rebels. It also set up the Third-Party Verification Mechanism (TPVM), which was made up of MONUC and South African representatives, to verify compliance. This was an important step. As opposed to the JMC, which was comprised of the belligerents themselves, the TPVM would provide neutral information

19. Herve Bar, "Kigali, DR Congo to Discuss Border Security Cordon," Agence France-Presse, July 17, 2002, International News.

20. "DR Congo and Rwanda Sign Peace Pact, Call for World's Help," Agence France-Presse, July 30, 2002, International News.

21. "Central Africa: Pretoria Pact, a 'Positive Step', says Rwandan President," *All Africa, Inc.*, July 31, 2002.

22. Ibid.

23. "DR Congo Rebels Call for Immediate Arrest of Rwandan Hutu Fighters," Agence France-Presse, July 31, 2002, International News.

regarding treaty compliance. This gave Rwanda a credible source of information about rebel demobilization, assuaging its fears about compliance with the plan. It was more willing to believe information revealed by these sources than the DRC's own promises.

Acting in accordance with its treaty obligations, on September 24 the Congolese government officially banned all FDLR activities and expelled its leaders based in Kinshasa (International Crisis Group 2003). The DRC government stated "All the activities of the political branch of the Rwandan ex-fighters operating within the FDLR on Democratic Republic of Congo soil are strictly and totally banned from henceforth . . . and the leaders here are declared persona non grata and invited to leave the territory within 72 hours."[24] International pressure on the DRC helped in obtaining such a statement, as the United States had explicitly called for the measure. Several prominent rebel leaders were arrested and sent to the International Criminal Tribunal for Rwanda to face genocide charges, signaling the DRC's commitment to implementing the plan.

The Pretoria Accord, public declarations repudiating the FDLR, the creation of the TPVM, and the arrests of rebel leaders were credible signals to Rwanda that the DRC would no longer support rebel organizations on its territory. To reciprocate the DRC's demonstration of goodwill, Rwanda recalled all of its troops from Congolese territory by October 2002. In so doing, Rwanda entrusted Congo to deal with the FDLR, which, although seriously weakened, had approximately 15,000–22,000 men and many more potential recruits in the refugee camps (International Crisis Group 2003, 8).

Evicting the Rebels

At this point, the DRC faced the difficult task of following through with the disarmament and demobilization plan. The UN Organization Mission in Congo still insisted that, lacking Chapter 7 powers, it could not move against rebel strongholds with force—it would only help demobilize and repatriate those volunteering to do so. In effect, Congolese forces had to act alone. On October 31, Congolese troops launched a major assault on an FDLR camp at Kamina. This operation was regarded as a disaster, as hundreds of rebels fled the scene without capture and several civilians were killed (International Crisis Group 2003). Only a handful of militants at Kamina were eventually repatriated. Despite being a military failure, however, the operation at Kamina

---

24. "DR Congo Bans Rebel Group upon Request by Bush," Agence France-Presse, September 25, 2002, International News.

had political significance. The action against the FDLR demonstrated Congo's sincerity in expelling foreign rebels. Its actions demonstrated its poor capacity to act rather than its lack of will.

Responding to this deficiency and to calls from parties on the ground to take more significant action, the UN Security Council decided to strengthen Kabila's hand and play a much more active role in the disarmament process. Security Council Resolution 1493 of July 28, 2003, authorized MONUC to engage in Chapter 7 peace-enforcement operations; the UN could now go after the militias with force (Boshoff 2004). The FDLR fully understood that its bases in the Congo were vulnerable. In early 2004, desperate to turn the tide of the insurgency, the rebels mounted a series of raids against Rwanda, hoping to provoke a broader domestic insurgency and to reenter the country. If the rebels were no longer welcome in the DRC, they had to find a foothold within Rwanda itself. This offensive, termed Operation La Fronde (Operation Slingshot), did not succeed in its task, and the FDLR was forced to retreat back across the border once again (International Crisis Group 2005).

Soon afterward, responding to Rwandan pressure for greater action against the rebels, the DRC attacked FDLR positions in late April, killing several dozen.[25] But the progress against the Hutu rebels was halted in May when a group of Congolese soldiers mutinied against the government and eventually captured the eastern town of Bukavu.[26] Rifts within the Congo's military, which had just been reorganized after a peace deal with the Rally for Congolese Democracy, prevented unified action and diverted attention away from policing foreign fighters. Again, the DRC's weakness was evident.

In response to this growing insecurity, MONUC's forces were raised to over 16,000. Despite Chapter 7 authorization, MONUC stalled in taking decisive action in meeting its disarmament objectives and became embroiled in a series of corruption and abuse scandals. In its impatience, in late 2004 Rwanda hinted that it might reinvade eastern Congo to attack the remaining FDLR fighters. Rwandan troops were reportedly sighted on the Congolese side of the border.[27] Relations between the neighbors were again tense as the prospect of a renewed invasion mounted. This option was obviated by more robust UN action. In early 2005, after the killing of several peacekeepers drew

25. British Broadcasting Corporation, "DR Congo Army Reportedly Kills 39 Rwandan Rebels in East," BBC Monitoring Africa, April 28, 2004.

26. BBC News, "Rebels Seize DR Congo Town," BBC Online, June 2, 2004, http://news.bbc .co.uk/2/hi/africa/3768531.stm (accessed February 11, 2006).

27. "Rwandan Rebels Say Kigali Has Sent Troops into DR Congo," Agence France-Presse, November 30, 2004.

international attention to the continuing conflict in the eastern DRC, the UN finally took the offensive against the various local and foreign militias based in the DRC and conducted several assaults on FDLR positions. In a parallel development, the African Union—wanting to take a more visible role— began to seriously consider sending an armed force to the Congo to help disarm the FDLR (International Crisis Group 2005).

FDLR commanders acknowledged that after ten years of failed attempts to mount an effective challenge against the Rwandan government and Congolese/international efforts to disarm them, they had to give up their armed struggle. Rebel leaders met with representatives from the DRC in Rome and on March 31, 2005, officially declared a "vow to abandon armed struggle and turn to a political process."[28] The FDLR also condemned the 1994 genocide and called for the repatriation of Rwandan refugees. In return for forswearing armed conflict, the FDLR insisted that it be recognized as a legitimate political party, a demand that Rwanda flatly rejected (International Crisis Group 2005). Despite the Rome declaration, progress toward peace was slow. FDLR fighters on the ground were reluctant to give up their arms and feared reprisals and criminal charges should they return. Furthermore, splits between moderate and militant members of the FDLR forestalled progress in disarmament and repatriation.[29]

In the meantime, alongside Congolese troops, MONUC's forces in the east were directly engaging rebel forces.[30] In July 2005, MONUC destroyed several FDLR camps located in South Kivu and surrounding regions.[31] Then, on August 25, the DRC, Rwanda, and Uganda issued a joint statement setting a September 30 deadline for the FDLR's disarmament; rebel leaders protested the ultimatum and insisted on negotiations with Kigali as well as security guarantees upon repatriation.[32]

The rebels were thoroughly marginalized and no longer militarily viable— their former Congolese allies, the African Union, and the UN urged their disbanding. Yet the September deadline came and went without significant

28. "Rwandan Hutu Rebel Group Condemns Genocide, Says It Will Abandon Armed Struggle," Agence France-Presse, March 31, 2005.

29. "Rwandan Rebel Commander Disavowed by Political Branch after Ousting Chief," Agence France-Presse, June 25, 2005; "Clashes Between Rwandan Rebels in the Eastern DR Congo," Agence France-Presse, July 7, 2005.

30. Marc Lacey, "After Failures, UN Peacekeepers Get Tough," *International Herald Tribune*, May 24, 2005, 2.

31. "UN Destroys Six Rwandan Rebel Camps in DR Congo," Agence France-Presse, July 15, 2005.

32. "Rwandan Hutu Rebels in Eastern Congo Given One-month Disarmament Deadline," Agence France-Presse, August 25, 2005.

action by the FDLR. Then MONUC and Congolese forces followed through on their threat to move against the rebels by force. In October, some 2,000 troops from the DRC backed by 500 UN troops and attack helicopters moved into Virunga National Park to clear out rebels hiding there.[33] In December, ten rebels were killed as the UN/DRC force captured several villages the FDLR had occupied.[34] A few days later, on December 16, rebel commander Seraphin Bizimungu gave himself up along with eighty-five fighters, declaring, "The time for war is over, the time for cohabitation and peace in the Great Lakes region has come."[35] The rebel force was eroding.

Clashes between DRC/MONUC forces and the FDLR continued in early 2006, but these demonstrated the rebels' lack of organization—they were hardly able to put up a fight. Kagame viewed the developments in the Congo and relations with Kinshasa positively. In May 2006, he remarked, "We believe that the government of [DR]Congo at the moment is not supporting the FDLR or the Interahamwe in any way. . . . Let it be clear that we don't consider [DR]Congo as supporters of militias anymore."[36] It is still too early to declare the FDLR to be completely defunct; indeed Tutsi militias led by General Laurent Nkunda were still active in the DRC in early 2008, claiming that they had to protect Tutsis from the FDLR. However, the FDLR is certainly no longer a major threat to the Rwandan government and has not mounted serious attacks for several years. With broad regional cooperation and an international peacekeeping force, the rebels have lost access to their external bases in the Congo and are now fighting for their survival rather than for any political objectives they once sought to achieve.

Lessons Learned

The conflict in Rwanda and the spillover into Zaire/Congo blurs the distinction between civil and international war. Hutu refugees who fled across the border into the Congo led the Rwandan government to act first against the Mobutu government and then against Kabila. In dealing with transnational rebels, Rwanda presents a rare case where a state was willing to penetrate a neighboring country's territory extensively in order to fight the opposition.

33. BBC News. "Rebels Targeted in DR Congo Park," BBC Online, http://news.bbc.co.uk/2/hi/africa/4393836.stm (accessed February 11, 2006).

34. "Ten Rwandan Rebels Killed in Clashes with Congolese Military," Agence France-Presse, December 12, 2005.

35. "Rwandan Rebels, Chief Return Home," Agence France-Presse, December 16, 2005.

36. "Rwandan President Says DR Congo no Longer Supporting Hutu Rebels," British Broadcasting Corporation, May 9, 2006.

Whereas it was successful in removing the Mobutu government, the conflict against Kabila proved to be more difficult for Rwanda. Moreover, in neither instance were the Hutu rebels defeated outright. The Rwandan government had established military dominance over its own territory but faced considerable obstacles in fighting rebels on foreign soil.

Because Rwanda could not eliminate the rebel threat in the DRC by itself, in 1999 it opted for peace with the Congo and for a regional agreement that promised to end rebel access to external territory. Nevertheless, Laurent Kabila proved to be unwilling to follow through with the Lusaka Accord and disarm the rebels; he could not provide credible commitments that the DRC would evict Hutu rebels. After his son succeeded him, progress on disarming the rebels was again slow. After signing the 2002 Pretoria Accord, however, the DRC took several steps to demonstrate its commitment to disarming the rebels; so much so that Rwanda agreed to withdraw its troops. The invitation of the Third Party Verification Mechanism, cooperation with MONUC, and costly offensives against Hutu rebels sent credible signals that the Congo was no longer willing to harbor militants. Early actions to disarm FDLR forces revealed the DRC's lack of capability to act but demonstrated its resolve. The transformation of MONUC into a more robust peace-enforcement mission greatly enhanced the ability to move against the FDLR, and joint DRC/MONUC operations left the insurgents marginalized. Thus, the rebel threat against the Rwandan government largely came to an end after Congo agreed to cooperate with Rwanda and work with UN forces.

Evaluating the Case Studies

Both Nicaragua and Rwanda demonstrate the importance of extraterritorial bases for the prolongation of conflict and the necessity of broad regional cooperation in bringing about an end to transnational rebellions. In line with the statistical findings presented in previous chapters, rebels were able to establish bases on external territory because of regional rivalries, poor state capacity, and the presence of large refugee populations. These bases in turn allowed conflicts to erupt and endure, adding additional confirmation to the quantitative findings. These cases also show how TNRs contribute to regional hostility as well as how rebels are used by governments as an alternative to the direct use of force.

Both cases also shed light on the special bargaining problems that transnational rebellions entail. As bargaining theory suggests, resolving commitment problems was key to conflict resolution efforts in both cases. In addition to commitment problems between rebels and governments, finding permanent, credible solutions to interstate conflicts were also essential. Bargaining processes involved multiple actors in these regions. The theory of transnational rebellion suggests that for conflicts to end, rebel host states must provide credible promises of their own to demonstrate that foreign combatants on their territory are not welcome, now or in the future. They must also monitor and verify rebel disarmament. In the Nicaraguan case, the rebels and the government came to the bargaining table only after rebel hosts pressured them to do so and provided substantial guarantees that demobilization would take place. Actors were unable to come to an agreement in the absence of promises from rebel host states that their territory would be off-limits to rebels. In Rwanda, a peace agreement with the DRC paved the way for forceful actions against Hutu rebels, which seriously debilitated their fighting capabilities. These conflicts raged on for years and eluded lasting peace, but they were resolved after significant cooperation by rebel host states.

As the theory of transnational rebellion argues, even states that are militarily superior to their rebel opponents cannot easily fend off groups organized abroad. In Nicaragua and Rwanda, governments were able to prevent rebels from establishing a lasting presence on their own soil, thus displaying their military dominance at home. However, rebels across the border were difficult to overcome. Thus, the military balance between government and rebels alone cannot explain why these conflicts endured for as long as they did or why they ended at a particular point in time. Rather, the provision of sanctuary by rebel host states determined the viability of the opposition. The removal of sanctuary and actions by host states precipitated conflict termination in both cases.

In both Nicaragua and Rwanda, the intervention of the United Nations was important for fostering peace. This complements and extends theories of third party intervention. Although Walter (2002) argues that third parties are needed to enforce the peace and prevent retribution by providing security guarantees, the evidence from Nicaragua and Rwanda suggests additional roles for those who intervene. First, the invitation for external peacekeepers to become involved provided a costly signal by rebel hosts that they were serious about rebel demobilization. Honduras and the Congo faced difficulties in credibly promising to disband rebel units on their territory; allowing access to UN missions demonstrated their resolve to do so. Second, external actors served as a reliable information transmission mechanism. Target governments were reluctant to believe host country promises that rebel demobilization and disarmament were taking place and had little ability to monitor compliance on their own; independent monitors provided a more reliable verification process that assuaged these fears. Third, peacekeepers helped improve the capacity of host states to evict foreign rebels. Particularly in the Congo case, but also in Honduras, the state faced considerable obstacles in following though with threats to disarm rebels on their soil. Whereas the need for forceful disarmament was averted in Honduras by the voluntary repatriation of Contra fighters, MONUC troops played an important role in helping the Congolese government uproot Rwandan rebels. Additionally, MONUC was tasked not with implementing a peace agreement and providing security guarantees for parties that were otherwise willing to strike a deal, but with the forceful disarmament of a rebel organization.

These case narratives also illustrate the causal processes discussed in chapter 1. Rwandan and Nicaraguan rebels were largely unable to contest the strength of their respective states on their own territory. Therefore, the rebels found host states where they could shield themselves from government attacks, thereby causing conflicts to endure for longer than they would have otherwise. In both cases, the presence of transnational rebels across the border brought rebel hosts and target countries into conflict with one another and extended the "bargain" to external actors. Although Nicaragua was not willing to challenge rebel hosts with significant force, tensions in Central America certainly escalated. Rwanda was more willing to bear the burden of intruding on Congolese territory, but also acted through local proxies to mitigate some of these costs. Nonetheless, while establishing military dominance on its own soil, Rwanda could not successfully defeat rebel forces on external territory. Finally, a peace agreement in Nicaragua and the defeat of Rwandan rebels was facilitated by state-to-state negotiations rather than rebel-government interactions alone.

Although it is difficult to make broad generalizations from two cases, the evidence presented in this chapter is suggestive of broader patterns. Cooperation between India and Bhutan has helped in combating Assamese rebels from northeast India. Sudan and Uganda have at times cooperated to prevent access to one another's rebels. The civil conflict in Zimbabwe was brought to a successful resolution after rebel host states, particularly Zambia and Mozambique, cooperated in promoting a negotiated settlement. A more thorough examination of additional cases is likely to provide further insights into conflict resolution processes when rebels are organized transnationally. Nonetheless, the case evidence from Nicaragua and Rwanda lend additional empirical support to the theory of transnational rebellion and serve to complement the quantitative results by demonstrating the dynamics underlying transnational rebellions.

Conclusion:
Improving Theory and Policy

This book improves our understanding of civil and international conflict by examining the *transnational* dimensions of political violence. Rather than considering events in isolation of one another, this work advances a theory of conflict in which domestic and international processes overlap, actors span national boundaries, and bargaining takes place at multiple levels. What remains is to consider the significance of this research for the study of international politics more generally and for real-world policy discussions. The purpose of this chapter is threefold: (1) to recap the major empirical findings of the book; (2) to discuss how these findings inform theories of conflict and the study of the state, international politics, and transnationalism; and (3) to examine the practical policy implications of this book and how the international community might develop more robust responses to transnational conflicts.

Summary of Major Findings

In broad terms, the findings here lend substantial support to the contention that civil wars should not be understood as isolated events but must be situated within a broader regional and international context. Armed conflicts between governments and their political opponents are both cause and consequence of international hostilities between states. Bad geographic "neighborhoods" and transnational social processes frequently compound the problems of state weakness, instability, and violent conflict. One can discern on a map regions where peace, democracy, human rights, and economic development prevail as well as regions where war, poverty, and authoritarianism coincide. The main empirical findings of this book, therefore, indicate that interactions within and between states are not independent of one another. Through careful data collection, large-N quantitative studies, and case narratives, I have provided strong evidence that several inter- and intrastate conflicts are driven by transnational linkages and actors bridging the internal/external divide. The main conclusions to be drawn, then, are:

1. 'Bad Neighborhoods' Make Countries More Prone to Civil War

Chapter 2 developed several propositions and quantitative tests regarding how "neighborhood effects" increase the risk of civil war onset and prolong ongoing wars. In addition to these quantitative tests, the book also examined several cases in depth, including Rwandan rebels in the Democratic Republic of the Congo, Nicaraguan rebels in Honduras, and Iranian rebels in Iraq (and vice versa), among others. Whereas the quantitative results illustrated broad patterns that can be generalized across countries, the case studies provided rich detail about particular conflicts. Considerable evidence suggests a strong relationship between the regional environment in which a state is situated and the likelihood of civil war.

What are these neighborhood effects? First, weak states in the neighborhood contribute to local civil wars. Weak neighbors cannot police their territory effectively, and, in particular, countries that are themselves undergoing violent conflict are more likely to be used as havens for transnational rebel organizations. Failed states in the neighborhood contribute to the geographic diffusion of conflict, as transnational rebel groups find sanctuaries in countries that cannot establish control over their territory. A civil war in one state has been demonstrated to be one of the most robust predictors of domestic conflict in a neighboring state (Hegre and Sambanis 2006), although diffusion effects have been poorly understood. One of the most important mechanisms by which conflicts cluster within particular regions pertains to transnational actors and social processes that link multiple conflicts together.

In addition to weak states, international rivalries exert a significant influence on civil conflict because international enemies provide support and sanctuary to rebel groups. Thus, international conflicts give rise to civil wars because states support rebel groups as an alternative means of undermining their rivals. Several Central American governments, for instance, supported the Contras instead of directly attacking Nicaragua. Quantitative results show international rivals to be a significant predictor of civil war continuation. Case narratives provide numerous examples in which international rivals have sought to put pressure on their enemies, not through the direct use of force, but by empowering TNRs.

Refugee communities in neighboring states also are shown to prolong civil wars. This finding contributes to a large body of case-study literature on the "refugee warrior" phenomenon (see, e.g., Lischer 2005; Stedman and Tanner 2003; Zolberg, Suhrke, and Aguayo 1989), which suggests that rather than being passive victims of conflict and persecution, refugees may also become active participants in armed hostilities and that refugee camps serve as safe-havens for TNRs. This is particularly true when the refugee host state cannot or will not provide security to refugee encampments to preserve their civilian status, as was the case in Zaire/DRC. Although this finding should not detract from the legitimate humanitarian concerns of the international community and aid agencies, it underscores the need for more robust efforts to prevent the militarization of refugee camps.

More directly, new data on rebel access to external bases indicates that such bases significantly increase the likelihood that a civil war will persist. Additionally, indirect neighborhood indicators, including weakness and rivalry, contribute to the emergence of these bases. Importantly, this data revealed that a majority of rebel groups, about 55 percent, used external sanctuaries to some extent. Thus, although not all rebel organizations span national boundaries, over half of them are organized transnationally.

Finally, evidence presented in this book demonstrates that ethnic groups near international boundaries are more likely to rebel than those that are not. Thus, geography is an important dimension to consider when analyzing the risk of ethnic violence (see also Toft 2003; K. S. Gleditsch 2007), and borders are an important geographic factor contributing to the opportunity to rebel. Ethnic rebels in Kosovo, Chechnya, and Kurdistan, among others, have benefited tremendously from their ability to slip across national boundaries.

2. Transnational Rebels Create and Reflect Conflict between States

The second major finding of this book is that transnational rebellion is a significant source of friction between states. The quantitative analysis in chapter 3 demonstrates that the presence of an extraterritorial rebel base in a neighboring country significantly increases the odds of military conflict between states. These results were supplemented by several case narratives. Security externalities for neighbors, counterinsurgency raids that violate the border, and retaliation for hosting rebel organizations are among the sources of conflict between states when rebels use external territory. Thus, international disputes are not simply the result of bilateral contests between states over control of resources or territory; rather, transnational actors can draw states into conflict. Many scholars have largely ignored the role of nonstate actors in provoking international conflicts, focusing instead on states as the principal actors in world politics. In some cases, rebel hosts are inadvertently drawn into international wars because they are unable to prevent both rebel access and border violations by their neighbors. Rather than a deliberate choice to go to war, these conflicts are driven by the inability of an institutionally weak government to credibly commit to evicting rebels.

Transnational rebels are a source of tension between states, but they also are frequently the consequence of interstate rivalry, as countries deliberately support their enemies' opposition movements. Therefore, multiple feedback mechanisms link civil and international conflict. International rivals support and harbor rebels, and, in turn, support for rebels exacerbates antagonism between states. In many cases, rather than using their own armed forces, states work through rebel proxies and delegate part of their foreign policy to TNR groups. This was confirmed in quantitative tests that show support for a rebel group actually decreases the rate of armed conflict between rival states as countries attack their enemies indirectly. The case narratives examine how the United States, Honduras, and Costa Rica decided to fund and shelter the Contras from Nicaragua rather than fight the Sandinista government with their own military forces. Likewise, South Africa and Mozambique used rebel support as a substitute for military confrontation, as did Iran and Iraq.

3. Resolving Transnational Rebellions Requires International Cooperation

Finally, this book provides evidence, albeit preliminary, that robust regional cooperation is crucial for resolving transnational civil wars. In addition to political bargains and negotiations between governments and the opposition, neighboring states can play a critical role in facilitating peace. Because of limitations on data, quantitative results on the termination of conflict are not presented here, although this is an important direction for future empirical work. Nonetheless, it is reasonable to believe that if relations between states and bad neighborhoods contribute to the onset and duration of civil conflict, then international cooperation and the resolution of interstate rivalries are important preconditions for peace.

The case studies provide an exploratory analysis of regional bargaining dynamics, confirming that ending transnational rebellion requires regional cooperation. Peace negotiations between the Contras and the Sandinistas were seriously hindered by the unwillingness of Honduras to make credible promises to withdraw its support of the rebels. Only after Central American governments signed a regional peace accord and invited international peacekeepers to monitor compliance did the conflict come to an end. In Central Africa, the Rwandan government was not able to defeat Hutu rebels hiding in Zaire/DRC, despite significant military operations against Mobutu, Kabila, and insurgent factions across the border. Rather, counterinsurgency efforts were successful only after governments in the region cooperated to put an end to overlapping internal and international conflicts. The invitation of a UN peacekeeping force, moreover, significantly strengthened the capacity of the Democratic Republic of the Congo to act. Likewise in Mozambique, peace negotiations between the governing FRELIMO and the RENAMO rebels went forward only after the South African regime began to loosen its hard-line stance and agreed to cooperate by reining in the rebels. These examples, and many others, suggest that bargains between states are frequently as important as bargains with opposition groups in resolving civil wars.

Improving Theories of Conflict

These findings provide new insights into several areas of scholarly research, including the study of civil and international conflict, transnationalism, and state sovereignty. First, the study of civil war can benefit from broadening our analytical toolkit and taking geography into account. Most studies of civil war have taken the nation-state for granted, as countries form the primary units of analysis. An overly state-centric view ignores substantial variation *within* countries experiencing conflict because violence is rarely (if ever) uniformly spread across a state's territory (see Buhaug and Gates 2002; Kalyvas 2006; Raleigh and Hegre 2005). Moreover, a focus on the nation-state as a distinct entity ignores actors and social processes that are not confined to a particular country. Rather than treating borders as analytical priors—as in many quantitative studies of conflict that assume observational independence—appreciating transborder spillover effects, social actors, conflict diffusion, and external intervention can improve our understanding of war and political violence.

Further research into these topics is clearly needed. This study has focused primarily on transnational rebel organizations that have access to bases in neighboring countries, but this does not exhaust all modes of transnational opposition. Rebel groups also benefit from resources provided by international diaspora communities, ethnic kin, and coreligionists, as well as by foreign governments. Obtaining resources from external actors is not without costs, however, particularly if such links come with strings attached. Therefore, exploring the choice between a primarily domestic mobilization strategy and one that relies on external support is likely to be a fruitful avenue for future research. Moreover, opposition activities are not limited to armed conflict. Research should be devoted to other forms of transnational opposition as well, including the establishment of media outlets, lobbying foreign governments, and protest activity.

A second area of scholarship that this study addresses is the often considerable overlap between civil and international wars, although most research has treated these as separate fields of inquiry (but see Gleditsch and Salehyan 2007; Gleditsch, Salehyan, and Schultz 2008). International conflict research has typically focused on states, or state dyads, as the main units of analysis, and has been slow to appreciate the role that nonstate militant groups play in fomenting conflict. Bargaining theories of war, for example, have almost exclusively looked at two-actor, state-to-state strategic interactions. Quantitative empirical studies have also focused primarily on war among pairs of countries. If we admit that states often do not have a monopoly on the use of force, and nonstate militant groups such as Al-Qaeda, the Kurdistan Workers' Party (PKK), and the Tamil Tigers are transnational in scope, then we must also abandon the assumption that states are the only relevant actors in international security affairs. Nonstate groups are part of the strategic setting. State support for insurgencies and the activities of transnational violent groups are a significant source of conflict in international politics. Moreover, we must appreciate the full range of foreign policy tools available to states. In addition to going to war with their international enemies, countries have a whole array of options, including empowering insurgent groups.

Therefore, more research should be devoted to the nexus between civil and international war. I have argued that support for insurgencies is an alternative to direct military contests, but have said little about the choice between strategies. Future research should seek to explain when states are likely to delegate conflict to rebels rather than use their own forces. In addition, other potential causal pathways bridging civil and international wars have not been fully explored here. International conflicts may arise over refugee flows, human rights violations during civil wars, and economic externalities of conflict. The externalization of conflict and the incentives of outside actors to become involved is a promising area for future work.

Third, this book highlights the importance of bargaining and peace negotiations at multiple levels. It is important to consider how bargaining unfolds between multiple state and nonstate actors. Bargaining theory has offered many important insights into conflict behavior by analyzing reasons why negotiations break down; but expanding the framework beyond two-actor negotiations and looking across the domestic/international divide promises many rewards. In particular, simultaneous, "nested" interactions between nation-states as well as between governments and rebels should inform the next wave of conflict research.

Finally, beyond its implications for conflict studies, this book contributes to debates about state-society relations, state sovereignty, and the boundaries of political action. Often states and their citizens are analyzed as if they form a closed social system within a given country. Instead, we must appreciate fundamental differences in the geographic organization of actors and how state sovereignty and territoriality affect the opportunities for, and limitations on, political behavior. State agents are largely confined to a particular jurisdiction: the political institutions, legal apparatus, and coercive capabilities of the state are largely restricted to its sovereign domain. Sovereignty is territorially defined. Borders are perhaps *the most* fundamental international institutions in the modern state-system; however, their functions are mainly to demarcate mutually exclusive zones of *governmental* control. Transnational organizations, migrant diasporas, and bonds of citizenship and identity give rise to substantial incongruence between the sovereign territory of the state and the geographic scope of the polity.

All transnational actors and exchanges present challenges for the application of the legal authority of the state. Transnational organizations draw their strength from being beyond any one state's regulatory capacity. Offshore internet gambling, for instance, circumvents established laws for many countries and is difficult to regulate. Some transnational networks are merely distinct national organizations bound by a common cause and dense communication. For example, environmental campaigners in distinct countries frequently share ideas and information and coordinate action with one another. Although such networks are an important form of transnational social organization, international migrants, diaspora communities, and cross-border ethnic groups are more than a network of separate units. They form a seamless political community; they are a common people, not just people with a common cause. Although this book focuses primarily on transnational rebel organizations, many of the theoretical insights provided here apply to other transnational actors, and additional research on this topic is needed.

Policy Implications

This book also suggests several important policy implications for states and for the international community to prevent the emergence and spread of armed conflict. Leaving aside the issue of whether or not armed conflict is sometimes justified to unseat an unpopular regime, civil wars have devastating consequences for both the country itself and for others in the international system, and policymakers have an interest in limiting their occurrence. Many policy recommendations have focused on domestic solutions to what is seen as an internal problem. Building domestic institutions and state capacity, fostering economic growth, reducing corruption, and power-sharing among ethnic groups have been offered as solutions to civil war. These initiatives are clearly important and should be encouraged. But an exclusively domestic focus will only go so far in preventing political violence.

Fostering good governance should be seen as a regional initiative—particularly in developing countries—rather than solely as a national one. Democracies stand a better chance of surviving if neighboring countries are also democratic; economic development is enhanced when neighbors are also flourishing (K. S. Gleditsch 2002a). In this regard, regional organizations can help to promote transparent, accountable governments and economic policies that benefit societies as a whole. The European Union and the Organization for Security and Cooperation in Europe have played important roles in promoting growth and democracy—as well as limiting conflict and human rights violations—among member states and those aspiring to membership, particularly in Eastern Europe. Regional organizations in developing regions such as the Association of South East Asian Nations, the African Union, and the Central American Common Market are steps in the right direction, but must be strengthened to promote long-term development and peace in conflict-ridden regions. The African Union in particular has taken an increased interest in responding to security crises on the continent, but has often suffered from a lack of adequate resources. Wealthy countries can and should help to address these shortfalls.

Policymakers should take an active role in mediating and resolving international rivalries, which are both cause and consequence of internal disputes. Decades-old disputes between India and Pakistan, Iran and Iraq, and Israel and Syria, among others, threaten regional peace and stability. Finding solutions to these international disputes can go a long way in resolving festering civil conflicts. Rwanda, for example, found that unilateral military solutions against the FDLR rebels could only go so far in containing insurgent violence; it had to sit at the bargaining table with the DRC in order find cooperative solutions to its long-standing insurgency. But also, ending civil wars can contribute to improved relations between states. The mutually reinforcing relationship between civil and international war—a key theme of this book—can be broken if the international community is prepared to take a more active role in facilitating conflict resolution and peace between and within states. Regional initiatives to end the wars in Rwanda and Nicaragua provide important lessons that others can learn from.

The international community, particularly global institutions like the United Nations, must be prepared to respond to transnational militancy but is often blind to the problem. Although the UN Security Council has a mandate to respond to threats to international peace and security, it has often failed to acknowledge the problem of external support for rebel organizations. Acts of direct military aggression—such as Iraq's invasion of Kuwait—are condemned, sanctions are implemented, and military interventions are authorized. However, indirect attacks through rebel proxies are routinely ignored by the international community. The UN Security Council must treat deliberate support for another state's rebel organization as an act of war and adopt an equivalent response. There is a double-standard imposed when one state is condemned for crossing the border to attack militants but another is not condemned for harboring TNRs. The Security Council, for instance, issued resolutions condemning Rwanda's and Uganda's invasion of the DRC, but prior to that did not respond to the DRC's aid to the insurgents, nor did the UN act to disarm refugee militants. In cases where weak states harbor transnational militant groups, the UN and other regional peacekeeping forces must be prepared to assist in building state capacity, and in particular move forces toward the international border in order to prevent rebels and state forces from launching cross-border attacks. As the saying goes, good fences make good neighbors.

Where transnational rebels are present, countries can prevent the escalation of armed conflict by sharing intelligence with one another, coordinating counterinsurgency actions, and providing border security. Political negotiations and compromises at the international level are also vital to ensuring peace and stability. In the global war against one particular transnational organization, Al-Qaeda, the United States' security cooperation with states in the Middle East, South Asia, and elsewhere is critical to preventing further attacks. Unilateral military actions are not enough, and may indeed make matters worse. Instead, cooperating with friends—and even enemies—promises greater rewards in the long-run.

Finally, maintaining the civilian status of refugee communities should be a major concern of international donors and nongovernmental organizations. Several observers have noted the failure of the international community to respond effectively to the Rwandan refugee crisis following the 1994 genocide. Failure to distinguish between bona fide refugees and perpetrators of genocide led to the diversion of humanitarian resources to combatants. In many cases, armed rebels operate in refugee camps while the host state and agencies such as the United Nations High Commissioner for Refugees are powerless to stop them. Treating refugee crises on solely humanitarian terms without appreciating security dynamics fosters further violence and greater refugee flows. Aid workers and the UNHCR are aware of this problem but frequently lack the necessary resources and support by international donors. Providing security to refugee camps takes boots on the ground, not just relief supplies. International resolve is needed to keep armed combatants from utilizing humanitarian resources and to prevent recruitment among vulnerable refugees.

Contemporary Crises

As I write, devastating conflicts are raging in Iraq, Afghanistan, and Sudan that have taken thousands of lives, displaced millions, and have cost countless resources. The conflict in Sudan's Darfur region has spilled across national boundaries into Chad and the Central African Republic as militants mingle with refugees, governments in the region accuse one another of supporting rebels, and transnational rebel groups operate in several countries across the region. The conflict in Darfur has placed severe strains on neighboring Chad in particular, where an already fragile political regime faces growing unrest and the emergence of new rebel factions. Chad and Sudan accuse one another of aiding militants. The international community has been slow to respond to this humanitarian and security disaster, which threatens to spiral further out of control. The border remains porous as peacekeeping troops are not able to control the frontier.

In Afghanistan, the Taliban was removed from power by superior U.S./NATO firepower, but along with Al-Qaeda, it has reemerged as a potent rebel force from its bases across the border in Pakistan. The Pakistani military faces serious obstacles uprooting these fighters, which operate in remote tribal regions where the central government exercises limited control and is challenged by local power holders. A rise in Islamic militancy in Pakistan threatened the stability of the Pakistani government under Pervez Musharraf, whose grip on power slowly eroded, and could undermine the recently elected civilian government. These Taliban and

Al-Qaeda strongholds in Pakistan and frequent cross-border attacks have severely strained relations between Pakistan, the United States, and Afghanistan. Although the conflict in Afghanistan continues to threaten regional peace and stability, political decision-makers have failed to find lasting solutions to their common problems. Robust cooperation and coordinated efforts to seal the border and combat militants in the region have been lacking.

In Iraq, the United States blames governments in the region for contributing to the ongoing instability and chaos there. The Iranian government—or elements within it—is accused of providing training and resources to militant groups, particularly hard-line Shia factions. Syria is suspected of allowing fighters to pass through its territory en route to Iraq. And although Iraqis themselves make up the bulk of the insurgency, foreign fighters from across the region have played a major role in the conflict. Thus, even the world's preeminent military power cannot control the transnational flow of combatants and resources to Iraq. Moreover, the instability there has contributed to the increased assertiveness of the Kurdish insurgency in Turkey, which has roughly 3,000 fighters in Iraqi Kurdistan. As was mentioned in the introduction to this book, the Turkish government has launched limited strikes against PKK bases in Iraq and threatens more extensive military action, including a full-scale invasion.

All of these crises demonstrate the failure of unilateral action in dealing with transnational threats. Despite its scorched-earth campaign in Darfur, the Sudanese government cannot put an end to the rebellion after years of fighting. Despite vastly superior military resources, the United States and its allies cannot defeat insurgencies in Iraq and Afghanistan. Yet governments still insist on a military solution and have augmented their deployment of military resources and personnel, hoping to defeat the insurgents by force. The Sudanese government has stepped up its hostile rhetoric toward states in the region rather than working towards reconciliation. The United States has been reluctant to even talk with Iran, Syria, and other states in the Middle East in order to find a regional solution to Iraq's troubles. In Afghanistan and Pakistan, the focus has similarly been on military force rather than strengthening political and economic institutions and enhancing international cooperation.

Unilateral strategies see insurgency as a primarily domestic problem. Such counterinsurgency operations focus on clearing insurgents from an area and holding onto the region with a permanent troop presence. In tandem, winning the "hearts and minds" of the public—through providing security, jobs, and social services—is seen as important to ending an insurgency. States may also partake in unilateral cross-border raids and strikes against militants, but these rarely work in the long run. Turkey repeatedly attacked PKK forces in its neighbors in the 1990s and 2000s, but these efforts have hardly paid off as the Kurdish insurgency persists. When dealing with transnational rebels, unilateral tactics have only minimal success. Domestic sanctuaries are less important when insurgent groups have access to extraterritorial bases. Rebels who receive resources, sanctuary, and support from other countries, moreover, are less dependent on the goodwill of the domestic population for their viability.

A regional strategy does not deny the importance of local policing and service provision. Rather, it adds meaningful international cooperation among states in the region to the mix of solutions to a civil conflict. The conflicts in Iraq, Afghanistan, Sudan, and elsewhere will be difficult to resolve unless states in the region agree to engage in serious dialogue and compromise with one another—including with their avowed enemies. A regional strategy focuses first on mending relations between states and ending external patronage of rebels. Even rivals may be willing to cooperate in order to prevent rebellions from escalating to international war. Promoting peace abroad contributes to peace at home and vice-versa. In addition, security cooperation to fortify borders and prevent TNRs from easily moving across boundaries must be on the agenda. Helping neighbors build institutions, infrastructure, and local policing may also be needed, and the international community can help to augment state capacity where it is lacking. A regional approach establishes clear channels of communication between neighbors to prevent misunderstandings and outlines joint strategies and zones of responsibility for conducting counterinsurgency operations on both sides of the border. Stabilizing conditions enough to enable refugee repatriation, or at the very least moving refugees away from border zones and providing them meaningful livelihoods, can help deny insurgents fresh recruits. When peace negotiations with rebels are appropriate, regional partners can assist in crafting a sustainable deal and ensuring implementation. Importantly, fostering democracy, rule of law, and economic development at home and among one's immediate neighbors is vital. The United States, for instance, cannot promote democracy and development in Afghanistan without also addressing these issues in Pakistan. In short, counterinsurgency strategies must include military, political, economic, *and diplomatic* initiatives.

If civil war is more than a domestic problem, part of the solution lies in promoting meaningful international cooperation to deal with common security threats. As former UN Secretary General Kofi Annan remarked at a 2005 conference in Munich:

> In this era of interdependence, let us banish from our minds the thought that some threats affect only some of us. We all share a responsibility for each other's security, and we must work together to build a safer world. Indeed, in strengthening the security of others, we protect the security of our own.[1]

Even though such statements are now commonplace, real action toward this worthwhile objective has been lacking. Global isolationists in powerful countries would retreat from extensive engagement in failed or failing states as if we can afford to ignore them. That these conflicts do not have far-reaching effects is a myth. Others insist that the best defense against security threats is robust military action. But states cannot deal effectively with transnational militancy by themselves. Hopefully, this book will play a role in advancing the political debate and will strengthen the hand of internationalists who seek global solutions to the world's conflicts.

1. Speech delivered on February 13, 2005, http://www.securityconference.de/konferenzen/rede.php?menu_2005=&menu_konferenzen=&sprache=en&id=156& (accessed June 29, 2006).

References

Achvarina, Vera, and Simon F. Reich. 2006. No Place to Hide: Refugees, Displaced Persons, and the Recruitment of Child Soldiers. *International Security* 31 (1): 127–64.

Adamson, Fiona. 2006. Crossing Borders: International Migration and National Security. *International Security* 31 (1): 165–99.

Aguilar Urbina, Francisco José, ed. 1994. *Desmovilización, Desmilitarización, y Democratización en Centroamérica*. San José, Costa Rica: Fundación Arias Para la Paz y el Progreso Humano.

Albert, Mathias, David Jacobson, and Yosef Lapid. 2001. *Identities, Borders, Orders: Rethinking International Relations Theory*. Minneapolis: University of Minnesota Press.

Alesina, Alberto, and Roberto Perotti. 1996. Income Distribution, Political Instability, and Investment. *European Economic Review* 40:1203–28.

Alusala, Nelson. 2004. DRC: On the Road to Disarmament. In *A Step Towards Peace: Disarmament in Africa*, edited by N. Alusala and T. Thusi. Pretoria, South Africa: African Human Security Initiative, Institute for Security Studies.

Ambrosio, Thomas. 2001. *Irredentism: Ethnic Conflict and International Politics*. Westport, CT: Praeger.

Anderson, Benedict. 1998. Long-Distance Nationalism. In *The Spectre of Comparisons: Nationalism, Southeast Asia, and the World*, edited by B. Anderson. London: Verso Press.

———. 1983. *Imagined Communities: Reflections on the Origin and Spread of Nationalism*. London: Verso Editions/NLB.

Andreas, Peter. 2003. Redrawing the Line: Borders and Security in the Twenty-First Century. *International Security* 28 (2): 78–111.

Ansell, Christopher K., and Giuseppe Di Palma. 2004. *Restructuring Territoriality: Europe and the United States Compared*. New York: Cambridge University Press.

Arquilla, John, and David F. Ronfeldt. 2001. *Networks and Netwars: the Future of Terror, Crime, and Militancy*. Santa Monica, CA: Rand Corporation.

Arreguin-Toft, Ivan. 2001. How the Weak Win Wars: A Theory of Asymmetric Conflict. *International Security* 26 (1): 93–128.

Axel, Brian Keith. 2001. *The Nation's Tortured Body: Violence, Representation, and the Formation of the Sikh Diaspora*. Durham, NC: Duke University Press.

Azam, Jean-Paul, and Anke Hoeffler. 2002. Violence Against Civilians in Civil Wars: Looting or Terror? *Journal of Peace Research* 39 (4): 461–85.

Bagley, Bruce Michael. 1986. Contadora: The Failure of Diplomacy. *Journal of Interamerican Studies and World Affairs* 28 (3): 1–32.

Balch-Lindsay, Dylan, and Andrew J. Enterline. 2000. Killing Time: The World Politics of Civil War Duration, 1820–1992. *International Studies Quarterly* 44:615–42.

Bannon, Ian, and Paul Collier, eds. 2003. *Natural Resources and Violent Conflict*. Washington, DC: World Bank.

Bapat, Navin. 2007. State Support for Insurgency and International Conflict. Manuscript. Pennsylvania State University.

——. 2006. State Bargaining with Transnational Terrorist Groups. *International Studies Quarterly* 50 (2): 213–29.

——. 2005. Insurgency and the Opening of Peace Processes. *Journal of Peace Research* 42 (6): 699–717.

Barbieri, Katherine, and Gerald Schneider. 1999. Globalization and Peace: Assessing New Directions in the Study of Trade and Conflict. *Journal of Peace Research* 36 (4): 387–404.

Bates, Robert, Avner Greif, and Smita Singh. 2002. Organizing Violence. *Journal of Conflict Resolution* 46 (5): 599–628.

Beck, Nathaniel, David Epstein, Simon Jackman, and Sharyn O'Halloran. 2001. Alternative Models of Dynamics in Binary Time-Series Cross-Section Models: The Example of State Failure. Paper presented at the Annual Meeting of the Society for Political Methodology, Emory University.

Beck, Nathaniel, Jonathan N. Katz, and Richard M. Tucker. 1998. Taking Time Seriously: Time-Series Cross-Section Analysis with a Binary Dependent Variable. *American Journal of Political Science* 42 (4): 1260–88.

Beissinger, Mark R. 2002. *Nationalist Mobilization and the Collapse of the Soviet State*. New York: Cambridge University Press.

Bell, J. Bowyer. 1971. Contemporary Revolutionary Organizations. *International Organization* 25 (3): 503–18.

Bennett, Scott, and Allan Stam. 2000. EUGene: A Conceptual Manual. *International Interactions* 26:179–204.

——. 1998. The Declining Advantages of Democracy: A Combined Model of War Outcomes and Duration. *Journal of Conflict Resolution* 42 (3): 344–66.

Berk, Richard A., Bruce Western, and Robert E. Weiss. 1995. Statistical Inference for Apparent Populations. *Sociological Methodology* 25:421–58.

Bollen, Kenneth A. 1995. Apparent and Nonapparent Significance Tests. *Sociological Methodology* 25:459–68.

Booth, John A. 1991. Socioeconomic and Political Roots of National Revolts in Central America. *Latin American Research Review* 26 (1): 33–73.

Boshoff, Henri. 2004. Overview of MONUC's Military Strategy and Concept of Operations. In *The UN Mission in the Democratic Republic of the Congo*, edited by M. Malan and J. G. Porto. Pretoria, South Africa: Institute for Security Studies.

Brand, Laurie. 2006. *Citizens Abroad: Emigration and the State in the Middle East and North Africa*. Cambridge: Cambridge University Press.

Brecher, Michael, Jonathan Wilkenfeld, and Sheila Moser. 1988. *Crises in the Twentieth Century: Volume I. Handbook of International Crises.* Oxford: Pergamon.

Bremer, Stuart A. 1992. Dangerous Dyads: Conditions Affecting the Likelihood of Interstate War, 1816–1965. *Journal of Conflict Resolution* 36 (2): 309–41.

Brogan, Patrick. 1998. *World Conflicts: A Comprehensive Guide to World Strife since 1945.* Lanham, MD: Scarecrow Press.

Brown, Timothy. 2001. *The Real Contra War: Highlander Peasant Resistance in Nicaragua.* Norman: University of Oklahoma Press.

Bueno de Mesquita, Bruce, James D. Morrow, Randolph Siverson, and Alastair Smith. 1999. An Institutional Explanation of the Democratic Peace. *American Political Science Review* 93 (4): 791–808.

Buhaug, Halvard, and Scott Gates. 2002. The Geography of Civil War. *Journal of Peace Research* 39 (4): 417–33.

Bull, Hedley. 1977. *The Anarchical Society: A Study of Order in World Politics.* New York: Columbia University Press.

Byman, Daniel. 2005. *Deadly Connections: States that Sponsor Terrorism.* Cambridge: Cambridge University Press.

Byman, Daniel, Peter Chalk, Bruce Hoffman, William Rosenau, and David Brannan. 2001. *Trends in Outside Support for Insurgent Movements.* Santa Monica, CA: RAND Corporation.

Camilleri, Joseph, and Jim Falk. 1992. *The End of Sovereignty? The Politics of a Shrinking and Fragmenting World.* Brookfield, VT: Elgar.

Carment, David, and Patrick James. 1995. Internal Constraints and Interstate Ethnic Conflict: Toward a Crisis-Based Assessment of Irredentism. *Journal of Conflict Resolution* 39 (1): 82–109.

Carment, David, and Dane Rowlands. 1998. Evaluating Third-Party Intervention in Intrastate Conflict. *Journal of Conflict Resolution.* 42 (5): 572–99.

Castles, Stephen, and Mark J. Miller. 1993. *The Age of Migration: International Population Movements in the Modern World.* New York: Guilford Press.

Cederman, Lars-Erik, and Luc Girardin. 2007. Beyond Fractionalization: Mapping Ethnicity onto Nationalist Insurgencies. *American Political Science Review* 101 (1): 173–85.

Cetinyan, Rupen. 2002. Ethnic Bargaining in the Shadow of Third-Party Intervention. *International Organization* 56 (3): 645–77.

Chakravartty, Paula. 2001. The Emigration of High-Skilled Indian Workers to the United States: Flexible Citizenship and India's Information Economy. In *The International Migration of the Highly Skilled: Demand, Supply, and Development Consequences in Sending and Receiving Countries,* edited by Wayne A. Cornelius, Thomas J. Espenshade, and Idean Salehyan. La Jolla, CA: Center for Comparative Immigration Studies, University of California, San Diego.

Chazan, Naomi, ed. 1991. *Irredentism and International Politics.* Boulder, CO: Lynne Rienner.

Child, Jack. 1992. *The Central American Peace Process, 1983–1991.* Boulder, CO: Lynne Rienner.

Chiozza, Giacomo, and Hein Goemans. 2004. International Conflict and the Tenure of Leaders: Is War Still Ex Post Inefficient? *American Journal of Political Science* 48 (3): 604–19.

Cohen, Edward. 2001. Globalization and the Boundaries of the State: A Framework for Analyzing the Changing Practice of Sovereignty. *Governance* 14 (1): 75–97.

Colaresi, Michael P., and William R. Thompson. 2002. Hot Spots or Hot Hands? Serial Crisis Behavior, Escalating Risks, and Rivalry. *Journal of Politics* 64 (4): 1175–98.

Collier, Paul, and Anke Hoeffler. 2004. Greed and Grievance in Civil War. *Oxford Economic Papers* 56 (4): 563–95.

——. 1999. Justice-Seeking and Loot-Seeking in Civil War. Unpublished World Bank working paper.

Collier, Paul, V. L. Elliot, Haavard Hegre, Anke Hoeffler, Marta Reynal-Querol, and Nicholas Sambanis. 2003. *Breaking the Conflict Trap: Civil War and Development Policy.* Washington, DC: World Bank.

Cornelius, Wayne A., Thomas J. Espenshade, and Idean Salehyan. 2001. *The International Migration of the Highly Skilled: Demand, Supply, and Development Consequences in Sending and Receiving Countries.* La Jolla, CA: Center for Comparative Immigration Studies, University of California, San Diego.

Cornelius, Wayne A., and Idean Salehyan. 2007. Does Border Enforcement Deter Unauthorized Immigration? The Case of Mexican Migration to the United States. *Regulation and Governance* 1 (2): 139–53.

Cornelius, Wayne A., Takeyuki Tsuda, Philip Martin, and James Hollifield, eds. 2004. *Controlling Immigration: A Global Perspective.* Stanford, CA: Stanford University Press.

Cowhey, Peter. 1993. Domestic Institutions and the Credibility of International Commitments: Japan and the United States. *International Organization* 42 (2): 299–326.

Crisp, Jeff. 1999. Who Has Counted the Refugees? UNHCR and the Politics of Numbers. *UNHCR, New Issues in Refugee Research.* Working Paper No. 12.

Cunningham, David. 2006. Veto Players and Civil War Duration. *American Journal of Political Science* 50 (4): 875–92.

Cunningham, David, Kristian Gleditsch, and Idean Salehyan. 2007. *Dataset: Non-State Actors in Civil Wars.*

Curtis, Marcus. 2005. Raison d'Etat Unleashed: Understanding Rwanda's Foreign Policy in the Democratic Republic of the Congo. *Strategic Insights* 4 (7).

Davenport, Christian. 2004. *Minorities at Risk Dataset Users Manual.* Center for International Development and Conflict Management, University of Maryland.

Davenport, Christian, Will Moore, and Steven Poe. 2003. Sometimes you Just Have to Leave: Domestic Threats and Refugee Movements, 1964–1989. *International Interactions* 29:27–55.

Davies, Graeme. 2002. Domestic Strife and the Initiation of International Conflicts: A Directed Dyad Analysis, 1950–1982. *Journal of Conflict Resolution* 46 (5): 672–92.

Davis, David R., and Will H. Moore. 1997. Ethnicity Matters: Transnational Ethnic Alliances and Foreign Policy Behavior. *International Studies Quarterly* 41 (1): 171–84.

Della Porta, Donatella, and Sidney G. Tarrow. 2005. *Transnational Protest and Global Activism.* Lanham, MD: Rowman and Littlefield.

DeNardo, James. 1985. *Power in Numbers: The Political Strategy of Protest and Rebellion.* Princeton, NJ: Princeton University Press.

Diehl, Paul F. 1992. What Are They Fighting For? The Importance of Issues in International Conflict Research. *Journal of Peace Research* 29:333–44.

Diehl, Paul, and Gary Goertz. 2000. *War and Peace in International Rivalry.* Ann Arbor: University of Michigan Press.

Dorff, Robert H. 2005. Failed States after 9/11: What Did We Know and What Have We Learned. *International Studies Perspectives* 6 (1): 20–34.

Doyle, Michael W. 1986. Liberalism and World Politics. *American Political Science Review* 80:1151–69.

Doyle, Michael W., and Nicholas Sambanis. 2000. International Peacebuilding: A Theoretical and Quantitative Analysis. *American Political Science Review* 94 (4): 779–801.

Elbadawi, Ibrahim, and Nicholas Sambanis. 2002. How Much War Will We See?: Explaining the Prevalence of Civil War. *Journal of Conflict Resolution* 46 (3): 307–34.

——. 2000. External Interventions and the Duration of Civil War. Unpublished World Bank working paper.

Elkins, David J. 1995. *Beyond Sovereignty: Territory and Political Economy in the Twenty-First Century*. Toronto: University of Toronto Press.

Enders, Walter, and Todd Sandler. 2006. Distribution of Transnational Terrorism among Countries by Income Class and Geography after 9/11. *International Studies Quarterly* 50 (2): 367–93.

——. 1999. Transnational Terrorism in the Post-Cold War Era. *International Studies Quarterly* 43 (1): 145–67.

Evans, Peter. 1997. The Eclipse of the State? Reflections on Stateness in an Era of Globalization. *World Politics* 50:62–87.

Faist, Thomas. 2000. Transnationalization in International Migration: Implications for the Study of Citizenship and Culture. *Ethnic and Racial Studies.* 23 (2): 189–222.

Fearon, James D. 2004. Why Do some Civil Wars Last so Much Longer than Others? *Journal of Peace Research* 41 (3): 275–301.

——. 1998. Commitment Problems and the Spread of Ethnic Conflict. In *The International Spread of Ethnic Conflict,* edited by David Lake and Donald Rothchild. Princeton, NJ: Princeton University Press.

——. 1995. Rationalist Explanations for War. *International Organization* 49 (3): 379–414.

Fearon, James D., and David D. Laitin. 2003. Ethnicity, Insurgency, and Civil War. *American Political Science Review* 97 (1): 75–90.

——. 1996. Explaining Interethnic Cooperation. *American Political Science Review* 90 (4): 715–35.

Federal Research Division, Library of Congress. 1993. *Nicaragua.* Federal Research Division, 1993 [accessed January 21 2006]. http://lcweb2.loc.gov/frd/cs/cshome.html.

Filson, Darren, and Suzanne Werner. 2002. A Bargaining Model of War and Peace: Anticipating the Onset, Duration, and Outcome of War. *American Journal of Political Science* 46 (4): 819–38.

Fitzgerald, David. 2000. *Negotiating Extraterritorial Citizenship: Mexican Migration and the Transnational Politics of Community*. La Jolla, CA: Center for Comparative Immigration Studies, University of California, San Diego.

Forman, Eric M. 1972. Civil War as a Source of International Violence. *Journal of Politics* 34 (4): 1111–34

Fortna, Page. 2004. Does Peacekeeping Keep Peace?: International Intervention and the Duration of Peace after Civil War. *International Studies Quarterly* 48 (2): 269–92.

Fox, Jonathan. 2005. Unpacking Transnational Citizenship. *Annual Review of Political Science* 8:171–201.

Francisco, Ronald. 1995. The Relationship between Coercion and Protest: An Empirical Evaluation in Three Coercive States. *Journal of Conflict Resolution* 39 (2): 263–82.

Garrison, Steve, and Deborah Gerner. 2001. A Sea of Troubles: Honduras and the Contra Demobilization. *Pew Case Studies in International Affairs.* Case 247.

Gartzke, Erik. 2007. The Capitalist Peace. *American Journal of Political Science* 51 (1): 166–91.

———. 1999. War Is in the Error Term. *International Organization* 53 (3): 567–87.

———. 1998. Kant We All Just Get Along? Opportunity, Willingness, and the Origins of the Democratic Peace. *American Journal of Political Science* 42 (1): 1–27.

Gates, Scott. 2002. Recruitment and Allegiance: The Microfoundations of Rebellion. *Journal of Conflict Resolution* 46 (1): 111–30.

Gates, Scott, and Håvard Strand. 2004. Modeling the Duration of Civil Wars Measurement and Estimation Issues. Paper presented at the 2004 meeting of the Standing Group on International Relations, the Hague, Netherlands. September 9–11, 2004.

Geller, Daniel S. 1993. Power Differentials and War in Rival Dyads. *International Studies Quarterly* 37 (2): 173–93.

Gellner, Ernst. 1983. *Nations and Nationalism.* Oxford: Oxford University Press.

Ghobarah, Hazem, Paul Huth, and Bruce M. Russett. 2003. Civil Wars Kill and Maim People Long after the Shooting Stops. *American Political Science Review* 97 (2): 189–202.

Ghosn, Faten, Glenn Palmer, and Stuart Bremer. 2004. The MID3 Data Set, 1993–2001: Procedures, Coding Rules, and Description. *Conflict Management and Peace Science* 21 (2): 133–54.

Gleditsch, Kristian Skrede. 2007. Transnational Dimensions of Civil War. *Journal of Peace Research* 44 (3): 293–309.

———. 2002a. *All International Politics Is Local: The Diffusion of Conflict, Integration, and Democratization.* Ann Arbor: University of Michigan Press.

———. 2002b. Expanded Dyadic Trade and GDP Data, 1946–92. *Journal of Conflict Resolution* 46(5): 712–24.

Gleditsch, Kristian S., and Idean Salehyan. 2007. Civil Wars and Interstate Disputes. In *Resources, Governance and Civil Conflict,* edited by Kaare Strom and Magnus Öberg. London: Routledge.

Gleditsch, Kristian S., Idean Salehyan, and Kenneth A. Schultz. 2008. Fighting at Home, Fighting Abroad: How Civil Wars Lead to International Disputes. *Journal of Conflict Resolution.* 52(4): 315–326.

Gleditsch, Kristian S., and Michael D. Ward. 2001. Measuring Space: A Minimum Distance Database. *Journal of Peace Research* 38(6): 749–68.

Gleditsch, Nils Petter, Peter Wallensteen, Mikael Eriksson, Margareta Sollenberg, and Håvard Strand. 2002. Armed Conflict, 1946–2001: A New Dataset. *Journal of Peace Research* 39 (5): 615–37.

Goddard, Stacie. 2006. Uncommon Ground: Indivisible Territory and the Politics of Legitimacy. *International Organization* 60 (1): 35–68.

Gourevitch, Peter. 1978. The Second Image Reversed: The International Sources of Domestic Politics. *International Organization* 32 (4): 881–912.

Gourevitch, Philip. 1998. *We Wish to Inform You that Tomorrow We Will be Killed with our Families: Stories from Rwanda.* New York: Farrar, Straus and Giroux.

Gowa, Joanne. 1995. Democratic States and International Disputes. *International Organization* 49 (3): 511–22.

Granovetter, Mark. 1978. Threshold Models of Collective Behavior. *American Journal of Sociology* 83 (6): 1420–43.

Guarnizo, Luis, Alejandro Portes, and William J. Haller. 2003. Assimilation and Transnationalism: Determinants of Transnational Political Action among Contemporary Migrants. *American Journal of Sociology* 108 (6): 1211–48.

Guiraudon, Virginie, and Gallya Lahav. 2000. A Reappraisal of the State Sovereignty Debate: The Case of Migration Control. *Comparative Political Studies* 33 (2): 163–95.

Gurr, Ted R. 1970. *Why Men Rebel.* Princeton, NJ: Princeton University Press.

Gurr, Ted R., and Will H. Moore. 1997. Ethnopolitical Rebellion: A Cross-sectional Analysis of the 1980s with Risk Assessments for the 1990s. *American Journal of Political Science* 41 (4): 1079–1103.

Haney, Patrick, and Walter Vanderbush. 1999. The Role of Ethnic Interest Groups in US Foreign Policy: The Case of the Cuban American National Foundation. *International Studies Quarterly.* 43 (2): 341–61.

Hardin, Russell. 1995. *One for All: The Logic of Group Conflict.* Princeton, NJ: Princeton University Press.

Hartigan, Kevin. 1992. Matching Humanitarian Norms with Cold, Hard Interests: The Making of Refugee Policies in Mexico and Honduras, 1980–1989. *International Organization* 46 (3): 709–30.

Hartzell, Caroline. 2002. Peace in Stages: The Role of an Implementation Regime in Nicaragua. In *Ending Civil Wars: The Implementation of Peace Agreements*, edited by Stephen J. Stedman, Donald Rothchild, and Elizabeth M. Cousens. Boulder, CO: Lynn Rienner.

Hartzell, Caroline, Matthew Hoddie, and Donald Rothchild. 2001. Stabilizing the Peace after Civil War: An Investigation of Some Key Variables. *International Organization* 55 (1): 183–208.

Hathaway, Oona. 2002. Do Human Rights Treaties Make a Difference? *Yale Law Journal* 111 (8): 1935–2035.

Hegre, Håvard, Tanja Ellingsen, Scott Gates, and Nils Petter Gleditsch. 2001. Toward a Democratic Civil Peace? Democracy, Political Change, and Civil War, 1816–1992. *American Political Science Review* 95:33–48.

Hegre, Håvard, and Nicholas Sambanis. 2006. Sensitivity Analysis of Empirical Results on Civil War Onset. *Journal of Conflict Resolution* 50 (4): 508–35.

Helliwell, John F. 1998. *How Much Do National Borders Matter?* Washington, DC: Brookings Institution Press.

Hendrix, Cullen. 2008. *Leviathan in the Tropics.* PhD Diss., University of California, San Diego.

Hensel, Paul. 2001. Contentious Issues and World Politics: The Management of Territorial Claims in the Americas, 1816–1992. *International Studies Quarterly* 45 (1): 81–109.

Hensel, Paul, Sarah McLaughlin Mitchell, and Thomas Sowers II. 2006. Conflict Management of Riparian Disputes. *Political Geography* 25 (4): 383–411.

Herbst, Jeffrey. 2004. African Militaries and Rebellion: The Political Economy of Threat and Combat Effectiveness. *Journal of Peace Research.* 41 (3): 357–69.

——. 2000. *States and Power in Africa: Comparative Lessons in Authority and Control.* Princeton, NJ: Princeton University Press.

——. 1989. The Creation and Maintenance of National Boundaries in Africa. *International Organization* 43 (4): 673–92.

Herz, John. 1957. Rise and Demise of the Territorial State. *World Politics* 9 (4): 473–93.

Hirschman, Albert O. 1978. Exit, Voice, and the State. *World Politics* 31 (1): 90–107.

Hirschman, Albert O. 1970. *Exit, Voice, and Loyalty: Responses to Decline in Firms, Organizations, and States*. Cambridge, MA: Harvard University Press.

Horowitz, Donald L. 1985. *Ethnic Groups in Conflict*. Berkeley: University of California Press.

Horton, Lynn. 1998. *Peasants in Arms: War and Peace in the Mountains of Nicaragua*. Athens: Ohio University Center for International Studies.

Human Rights Watch. 2007. They Came Here to Kill Us: Militia Attacks and Ethnic Targeting of Civilians in Eastern Chad. New York: Human Rights Watch. January.

Huntington, Samuel. 1973. Transnational Organizations in World Politics. *World Politics* 25 (3): 333–68.

———. 1968. *Political Order in Changing Societies*. New Haven, CT: Yale University Press.

International Crisis Group. 2005. The Congo: Solving the FDLR Problem Once and For All. In *ICG Africa Briefing, No. 25*.

———. 2003. Rwandan Hutu Rebels in the Congo: A New Approach to Disarmament and Reintegration. In *ICG Africa Report, No 63*.

———. 2001. Disarmament in the Congo: Jump-Starting DDRRR to Prevent Further War. In *ICG Africa Report, No. 38*.

———. 1998a. Congo at War: A Briefing on the Internal and External Players in the Central African Conflict. In *ICG Congo Report, No 2*.

———. 1998b. North Kivu, Into the Quagmire? An Overview of the Current Crisis in North Kivu. In *ICG Kivu Report, No. 1*.

Isima, Jeffrey O. 2005. Enhancing the Chances for Disarmament: The Ex-FAR and Interhamwe in the Democratic Republic of Congo. In *From Conflict to Community: A Combatant's Return to Citizenship*, edited by A. Fitzgerald and H. Mason. Shrivenham, UK: Global Facilitation Network for Security Sector Reform.

Jackson, Robert H. 1987. Quasi-states, Dual Regimes, and Neoclassical Theory: International Jurisprudence and the Third World. *International Organization* 41 (4): 519–49.

Jacobson, David. 1996. *Rights across Borders: Immigration and the Decline of Citizenship*. Baltimore: Johns Hopkins University Press.

Jaggers, Keith, and Ted R. Gurr. 1995. Tracking Democracy's Third Wave with the Polity III Data. *Journal of Peace Research* 32 (4): 469–82.

Jenne, Erin K. 2006. *Ethnic Bargaining: The Paradox of Minority Empowerment*. Ithaca, NY: Cornell University Press.

Jervis, Robert. 1978. Cooperation under the Security Dilemma. *World Politics* 30 (2): 167–214.

Joppke, Christian. 1999. *Immigration and the Nation-state: The United States, Germany, and Great Britain*. New York: Oxford University Press.

Kahler, Miles, and Barbara Walter, eds. 2006. *Territoriality and Conflict in an Era of Globalization*. Cambridge, UK: Cambridge University Press.

Kaldor, Mary. 1999. *New and Old Wars: Organized Violence in a Global Era*. Stanford, CA: Stanford University Press.

Kalyvas, Stathis. 2006. *The Logic of Violence in Civil War*. Cambridge, UK: Cambridge University Press.

Kalyvas, Stathis. 2001. 'New' and 'Old' Civil Wars: A Valid Distinction? *World Politics* 54 (1): 99–118.

Katzenstein, Peter J. 1996. *The Culture of National Security Norms and Identity in World Politics*. New York: Columbia University Press.

Keck, Margaret E., and Kathryn Sikkink. 1998. *Activists beyond Borders: Advocacy Networks in International Politics*. Ithaca, NY: Cornell University Press.

Keohane, Robert O. 1984. *After Hegemony: Cooperation and Discord in the World Political Economy*. Princeton, NJ: Princeton University Press.

Keohane, Robert, and Joseph Nye, eds. 1971. *Transnational Relations and World Politics*. Cambridge, MA: Harvard University Press.

Kiewiet, Roderick, and Mathew D. McCubbins. 1991. *The Logic of Delegation: Congressional Parties and the Appropriations Process*. Chicago: University of Chicago Press.

King, Charles, and Neil Melvin. 1999. Diaspora Politics: Ethnic Linkages, Foreign Policy, and Security in Eurasia. *International Security* 24 (3): 108–38.

Krasner, Stephen. 1999. *Sovereignty: Organized Hypocrisy*. Princeton, NJ: Princeton University Press.

——. 1995–1996. Compromising Westphalia. *International Security* 20 (3): 115–51.

——. 1991. Global Communications and National Power: Life on the Pareto Frontier. *World Politics* 43 (3): 336–66.

Kratochwil, Friedrich. 1986. Of Systems, Boundaries, and Territoriality: An Inquiry into the Formation of the State System. *World Politics* 39 (1): 27–52.

Kuran, Timur. 1989. Sparks and Prairie Fires: A Theory of Unanticipated Revolution. *Public Choice* 61:41–74.

Lake, David. 2003. International Relations Theory and Internal Conflict: Insights from the Interstices. *International Studies Review* 5 (4): 81–89.

——. 1996. Anarchy, Hierarchy, and the Variety of International Relations. *International Organization* 50 (1): 1–33.

Lake, David, and Robert Powell. 1999. *Strategic Choice and International Relations*. Princeton, NJ: Princeton University Press.

Lake, David, and Donald Rothchild, eds. 1998. *The International Spread of Ethnic Conflict*. Princeton, NJ: Princeton University Press.

——. 1996. Containing Fear: The Origins and Management of Ethnic Conflict. *International Security* 21:41–75.

Leites, Nathan, and Charles Wolf. 1970. *Rebellion and Authority: An Analytic Essay on Insurgent Conflicts*. Santa Monica, CA: RAND Corporation.

Levitt, Peggy, and Rafael de la Dehesa. 2003. Transnational Migration and the Redefinition of the State: Variations and Explanations. *Ethnic and Racial Studies* 26 (4): 587–611.

Library of Congress Country Studies. 1989. *Iran: A Country Study*. Washington, DC: Federal Research Division, Library of Congress.

Library of Congress Country Studies. 1990. *Iraq: A Country Study*. Washington, DC: Federal Research Division, Library of Congress.

Lichbach, Mark I. 1995. *The Rebel's Dilemma*. Ann Arbor: University of Michigan Press.

Lischer, Sarah Kenyon. 2005. *Dangerous Sanctuaries: Refugee Camps, Civil War, and the Dilemmas of Humanitarian Aid*. Ithaca, NY: Cornell University Press.

——. 2003. Collateral Damage: Humanitarian Assistance as a Cause of Conflict. *International Security* 28 (1): 79–109.

Loescher, Gil. 1993. *Beyond Charity: International Cooperation and the Global Refugee Crisis*. Oxford: Oxford University Press.

Lohmann, Susanne. 1994. The Dynamics of Informational Cascades: The Monday Demonstrations in Leipzig, East Germany, 1989–91. *World Politics* 47 (1): 42–101.

Lyon, Alynna, and Emek Ucarer. 2001. Mobilizing Ethnic Conflict: Kurdish Separatism in Germany and the PKK. *Ethnic and Racial Studies* 24 (6): 925–48.

Lyons, Terrence. 2006. Diasporas and Homeland Conflict. In *Territoriality and Conflict in an Era of Globalization*, edited by M. Kalher and B. F. Walter. Cambridge: Cambridge University Press.

MacCulloch, Robert. 2004. The Impact of Income on the Taste for Revolt. *American Journal of Political Science* 48 (4): 830–48.

Mack, Andrew. 1975. Why Big Nations Lose Small Wars: The Politics of Asymmetric Conflict. *World Politics* 27 (2): 175–200.

Mamdani, Mahmood. 2001. *When Victims Become Killers: Colonialism, Nativism, and the Genocide in Rwanda*. Princeton, NJ: Princeton University Press.

Marcelli, Enrico, and Wayne Cornelius. 2005. Immigrant Voting in Home-Country Elections: Potential Consequences of Extending the Franchise to Expatriate Mexicans Residing in the United States. *Mexican Studies/Estudios Mexicanos* 21 (2): 429–60.

Marshall, Monty, and Ted R. Gurr. 2003. *Peace and Conflict: A Global Survey of Armed Conflicts, Self-Determination Movements, and Democracy*. College Park, MD: Center for International Development and Conflict Management.

Marshall, Monty, and Keith Jaggers. 2002. Polity IV Project: Political Regime Characteristics and Transitions, 1800–2002. College Park, MD: Integrated Network for Societal Conflict Research, Center for International Development and Conflict Management. www.cidcm.umd.edu/inscr/polity.

Marx, Karl, Vladimir Lenin, and Max Eastman. 1932. *Capital, the Communist Manifesto, and Other Writings*. New York: The Modern Library.

Mason, T. David, and Dale A. Krane. 1989. The Political Economy of Death Squads: Toward a Theory of the Impact of State-Sanctioned Terror. *International Studies Quarterly* 33 (2): 175–98.

Mason, T. David, and Patrick Fett. 1996. How Civil Wars End: A Rational Choice Approach. *Journal of Conflict Resolution* 40 (4): 546–68.

Mason, T. David, Joseph Weingarten, and Patrick Fett. 1999. Win, Lose, or Draw: Predicting the Outcome of Civil Wars. *Political Research Quarterly* 52 (2): 239–68.

McAdam, Doug, Sidney Tarrow, and Charles Tilly. 2001. *Dynamics of Contention*. Cambridge: Cambridge University Press.

Meernik, James. 1996. United States Military Intervention and the Promotion of Democracy. *Journal of Peace Research* 33 (4): 391–402.

Melvern, Linda. 2004. *Conspiracy to Murder: The Rwandan Genocide and the International Community*. New York: Verso.

Midlarsky, Manus, ed. 1992. *The Internationalization of Communal Strife*. New York: Routledge.

Migdal, Joel S., ed. 2004. *Boundaries and Belonging: States and Societies in the Struggle to Shape Identities and Local Practices*. Cambridge: Cambridge University Press.

Milner, Helen V. 1997. *Interests, Institutions, and Information: Domestic Politics and International Relations*. Princeton, NJPrinceton University Press.

Miranda, Roger, and William Ratliff. 1993. *The Civil War in Nicaragua: Inside the Sandinistas*. New Brunswick, NJ: Transaction Publishers.

Mitchell, Christopher. 1970. Civil Strife and the Involvement of External Parties. *International Studies Quarterly* 14 (2): 166–94.

Moore, Barrington. 1967. *Social Origins of Dictatorship and Democracy: Lord and Peasant in the Making of the Modern World*. Boston: Beacon.

Moore, Will H. 1998. Repression and Dissent: Substitution, Context and Timing. *American Journal of Political Science* 42 (3): 851–73.

Moore, Will, and Stephen Shellman. 2004. Fear of Persecution: Forced Migration, 1952–1995. *Journal of Conflict Resolution* 40 (5): 723–45.

Morgan, T. Clifton, and Glenn Palmer. 2000. A Model of Foreign Policy Substitutability: Selecting the Right Tools for the Job(s). *Journal of Conflict Resolution* 44 (1): 11–32.

Most, Benjamin, and Harvey Starr. 1989. *Inquiry, Logic, and International Politics*. Columbia: University of South Carolina Press.

——. 1984. International Relations, Foreign Policy Substitutability, and 'Nice' Laws. *World Politics* 36 (3): 383–406.

Muller, Edward N., and Mitchell A. Seligson. 1987. Inequality and Insurgency. *American Political Science Review* 87:425–51.

Muller, Edward N., and Erich Weede. 1990. Cross-National Variation in Political Violence: A Rational Action Approach. *Journal of Conflict Resolution* 34 (4): 624–51.

Murdoch, James and Todd Sandler. 2004. Civil Wars and Economic Growth: Spatial Dispersion. *American Journal of Political Science* 48 (1): 138–51.

Murshed, S. Mansoob, and Scott Gates. 2005. Spatial-Horizontal Inequality and the Maoist Insurgency in Nepal. *Review of Development Economics* 9 (1): 121–34.

Neumayer, Eric. 2005. Bogus Refugees? The Determinants of Asylum Migration to Western Europe. *International Studies Quarterly* 49 (3): 389–410.

Ohmae, Kenichi. 1990. *The Borderless World: Power and Strategy in the Interlinked Economy*. New York: Harper Business.

Olson, Mancur. 2001. *Power and Prosperity: Outgrowing Communist and Capitalist Dictatorships*. New York: Basic Books.

Pauly, Louis W., and Simon Reich. 1997. National Structures and Multinational Corporate Behavior: Enduring Differences in the Age of Globalization. *International Organization* 51 (1): 1–30.

Posen, Barry. 1993. The Security Dilemma and Ethnic Conflict. *Survival* 35 (1): 27–47.

Powell, Robert. 1999. *In the Shadow of Power: States and Strategies in International Politics*. Princeton, NJ: Princeton University Press.

Preston, Matthew. 2005. Stalemate and the Termination of Civil War: Rhodesia Reassessed. *Journal of Peace Research* 41 (1): 65–83.

Putnam, Robert. 1988. Diplomacy and Domestic Politics: The Logic of Two-Level Games. *International Organization* 42:427–60.

Rabushka, Alvin, and Kenneth A. Shepsle. 1972. *Politics in Plural Societies: A Theory of Democratic Instability*. Columbus, OH: Merrill.

Raleigh, Clionadh, and Havard Hegre. 2005. Introducing ACLED: An Armed Conflict Location and Event Dataset. Paper presented at the conference on Disaggregating the Study of Civil War and Transnational Violence, University of California, San Diego, March 7–8, 2005.

Raustiala, Kal. 2006. The Evolution of Territoriality: International Relations and American Law. In *Territoriality and Conflict in an Era of Globalization*, edited by M. Kahler and B. F. Walter. Cambridge: Cambridge University Press.

Regan, Patrick. 2002. Third-Party Interventions and the Duration of Intrastate Conflicts. *Journal of Conflict Resolution* 46 (1): 55–73.

———. 2000. *Civil Wars and Foreign Powers: Interventions and Intrastate Conflict*. Ann Arbor: University of Michigan Press.

Reynal-Querol, Marta. 2002. Ethnicity, Political Systems, and Civil Wars. *Journal of Conflict Resolution* 46 (1): 29–54.

Rice, Susan. 2003. The New National Security Strategy: Focus on Failed States. *Brookings Institution Policy Brief, No. 116*.

Risse-Kappen, Thomas ed. 1995. *Bringing Transnational Relations Back In: Non-State Actors, Domestic Structures, and International Institutions*. New York: Cambridge University Press.

Roberts, Kenneth. 1990. Bullying and Bargaining: The United States, Nicaragua, and Conflict Resolution in Central America. *International Security* 15 (2): 67–102.

Rosato, Sebastian. 2005. The Flawed Logic of the Democratic Peace Theory. *American Political Science Review* 97 (4): 585–602.

Rosenau, James N., ed. 1964. *International Aspects of Civil Strife*. Princeton, NJ,: Princeton University Press.

Rosenblum, Marc R., and Idean Salehyan. 2004. Norms and Interests in U.S. Asylum Enforcement. *Journal of Peace Research* 41 (6): 677–97.

Ross, Michael. 2004. How do Natural Resources Influence Civil War? Evidence from Thirteen Cases. *International Organization* 58 (1): 35–67.

Rudolph, Susanne Hoeber, and James Piscatori, eds. 1997. *Transnational Religion and Fading States*. Boulder, CO: Westview Press.

Rudolph, Christopher. 2005. Sovereignty and Territorial Borders in a Global Age. *International Studies Review* 7 (1): 1–20.

Ruggie, John Gerard. 1993. Territoriality and Beyond: Problematizing Modernity in International Relations. *International Organization* 47:139–74.

Russett, Bruce M., and John Oneal. 2001. *Triangulating Peace: Democracy, Interdependence, and International Organizations*. New York: Norton.

Sahlins, Peter. 1989. *Boundaries: The Making of France and Spain in the Pyrenees*. Berkeley: University of California Press.

Saideman, Stephen. 2002. Discrimination in International Relations: Analyzing External Support for Ethnic Groups. *Journal of Peace Research* 39 (1): 27–50.

———. 2001. *The Ties That Divide: Ethnic Politics, Foreign Policy, and International Conflict*. New York: Columbia University Press.

Salehyan, Idean. 2008. No Shelter Here: Rebel Sanctuaries and International Conflict. *Journal of Politics* 70 (1): 54–66.

———. 2007a. Transnational Rebels: Neighboring States as Sanctuary for Rebel Groups. *World Politics* 52 (2): 217–42.

———. 2007b. Refugees and the Study of Civil War. *Civil Wars* 9 (2): 127–41.

Salehyan, Idean, and Kristian S. Gleditsch. 2006. Refugees and the Spread of Civil War. *International Organization* 60 (2): 335–66.

Sambanis, Nicholas. 2002. A Review of Recent Advances and Future Directions in the Literature on Civil War. *Defense and Peace Economics* 13 (3): 215–43.

———. 2001. Do Ethnic and Non-Ethnic Civil Wars Have the Same Causes? A Theoretical and Empirical Inquiry. *Journal of Conflict Resolution* 45 (3): 259–82.

Sandler, Todd. 2003. Collective Action and Transnational Terrorism. *The World Economy* 26 (6): 779–802.

Sandler, Todd, John Tschirhart, and Jon Cauley. 1983. A Theoretical Analysis of Transnational Terrorism. *American Political Science Review* 77 (1): 36–54.

Sassen, Saskia. 1996. *Losing Control? Sovereignty in an Age of Globalization.* New York: Columbia University Press

Saxenian, AnnaLee. 2001. Silicon Valley's New Immigrant Entrepreneurs. In *The International Migration of the Highly Skilled: Demand, Supply, and Development Consequences in Sending and Receiving Countries,* edited by Wayne A. Cornelius, Thomas J. Espenshade and Idean Salehyan. La Jolla, CA: Center for Comparative Immigration Studies, University of California, San Diego.

Scherrer, Christian P. 2002. *Genocide and Crisis in Central Africa: Conflict Roots, Mass Violence, and Regional War.* Westport, CT: Praeger.

Schmeidl, Susanne. 1997. Exploring the Causes of Forced Migration: A Pooled Time-Series Analysis, 1971–1990. *Social Science Quarterly* 78:284–308.

Schneider, Gerald, Katherine Barbieri, and Nils Petter Gleditsch, eds. 2003. *Globalization and Armed Conflict.* Lanham MD: Rowman and Littlefield.

Schultz, Donald E., and Deborah Sundloff Schultz. 1994. *The United States, Honduras, and the Crisis in Central America.* Boulder, CO: Westview Press.

Schultz, Kenneth A. 2001. *Democracy and Coercive Diplomacy.* Cambridge: Cambridge University Press.

Shain, Yossi. 1995. Ethnic Diasporas and US Foreign Policy. *Political Science Quarterly* 109:811–42.

———. 1989. *The Frontier of Loyalty: Political Exiles in the Age of the Nation-State.* Middletown, CT: Wesleyan University Press.

Shain, Yossi, and Aharon Barth. 2003. Diasporas and International Relations Theory. *International Organization* 57 (3): 449–79.

Sheffer, Gabriel. 2003. *Diaspora Politics: At Home Abroad.* New York: Cambridge University Press.

Shelley, Louise. 1995. Transnational Organized Crime: An Imminent Threat to the Nation-State? *Journal of International Affairs* 48 (2): 463–90.

Singer, J. David, Stuart Bremer, and John Stuckey. 1972. Capability Distribution, Uncertainty, and Major Power War. In *Peace, War, and Numbers,* edited by B. M. Russett. Beverly Hills, CA: Sage.

Skocpol, Theda. 1979. *States and Social Revolutions: A Comparative Analysis of France, Russia, and China.* New York: Cambridge University Press.

Slantchev, Branislav. 2003. The Power to Hurt: Costly Conflict with Completely Informed States. *American Political Science Review* 97 (1): 123–33.

Soysal, Yasemin. 1994. *Limits of Citizenship: Migrants and Postnational Membership in Europe.* Chicago: University of Chicago Press.

Starr, Harvey. 2006. International Borders: What They Are, What They Mean, and Why We Should Care. *SAIS Review* 26 (1): 3–10.

Starr, Harvey, and Benjamin Most. 1976. The Substance and Study of Borders in International Relations Research. *International Studies Quarterly* 20:581–620.

Stedman, Stephen. 1997. Spoiler Problems in Peace Processes. *International Security* 22 (2): 5–53.

———. 1991. *Peacemaking in Civil War: International Mediation in Zimbabwe, 1974–1980.* Boulder, CO: Lynne Rienner.

Stedman, John, and Fred Tanner. 2003. *Refugee Manipulation: War, Politics, and the Abuse of Human Suffering*. Washington, DC: Brookings Institution.

Strange, Susan. 1996. *The Retreat of the State: The Diffusion of Power in the World Economy*. Cambridge: Cambridge University Press.

Tarrow, Sidney. 2005. *The New Transnational Activism*. Cambridge: Cambridge University Press.

———. 1994. *Power in Movement: Social Movements, Collective Action, and Politics*. New York: Cambridge University Press.

Tatla, Darshan Singh. 1999. *The Sikh Diaspora: The Search for Statehood*. Seattle: University of Washington Press.

Teitelbaum, Michael. 1984. Immigration, Refugees, and Foreign Policy. *International Organization* 38 (3): 429–50.

Thompson, William R. 2001. Identifying Rivals and Rivalries in World Politics. *International Studies Quarterly* 45 (4): 557–86.

Thomson, Janice. 1995. State Sovereignty in International Relations: Bridging the Gap Between Theory and Empirical Research. *International Studies Quarterly* 39 (2): 213–33.

Thyne, Clayton. 2006. Cheap Signals with Costly Consequences. *Journal of Conflict Resolution* 50 (6): 937–61.

Tilly, Charles. 1990. *Coercion, Capital, and European States, A.D. 990–1990*. Oxford: Basil Blackwell.

———. 1978. *From Mobilization to Revolution*. Reading, MA: Addison-Wesley.

Tinoco, Victor Hugo. 1988. *Conflicto y Paz: El Proceso Negociador Centroamericano*. Mexico City: Coordinadora Regional de Investigaciones Economicas y Sociales.

Toft, Monica. 2003. *The Geography of Ethnic Violence: Identity, Interests, and the Indivisibility of Territory*. Princeton, NJ: Princeton University Press.

Torpey, John C. 2000. *The Invention of the Passport: Surveillance, Citizenship, and the State*. New York: Cambridge University Press.

Trumbore, Peter F. 2003. Victims or Aggressors? Ethno-political Rebellion and Use of Force in Militarized Interstate Disputes. *International Studies Quarterly* 47 (2): 183–201.

Uvin, Peter. 1999. Ethnicity and Power in Burundi and Rwanda: Different Paths to Mass Violence. *Comparative Politics* 31 (3): 253–71.

Vanhanen, Tatu. 1999. Domestic Ethnic Conflict and Ethnic Nepotism: A Comparative Analysis. *Journal of Peace Research* 36:55–74.

Van Hear, Nicholas. 1998. *New Diasporas: The Mass Exodus, Dispersal, and Regrouping of Migrant Communities*. Seattle: University of Washington Press.

Vasquez, John. 1995. Why Do Neighbors Fight? Proximity, Interaction, or Territoriality. *Journal of Peace Research* 32 (3): 277–93.

Wagner, R. Harrison. 2000. Bargaining and War. *American Journal of Political Science* 44 (3): 469–84.

Wahlbeck, Osten. 1999. *Kurdish Diasporas: A Comparative Study of Kurdish Refugee Communities*. New York: St. Martin's Press.

Waldinger, Roger, and David Fitzgerald. 2004. Transnationalism in Question. *American Review of Sociology* 109 (5): 1177–95.

Walker, Thomas. 2003. *Nicaragua: Living in the Shadow of the Eagle*. Boulder, CO: Westview.

Walt, Stephen. 1996. *Revolution and War*. Ithaca, NY: Cornell University Press.

Walter, Barbara F. 2006. Building Reputation: Why Governments Fight Some Separatists but not Others. *American Journal of Political Science* 50 (2): 313–30.

———. 2002. *Committing to Peace: The Successful Resolution of Civil Wars*. Princeton, NJ: Princeton University Press.

———. 1997. The Critical Barrier to Civil War Settlement. *International Organization* 51 (3): 335–64.

Waltz, Kenneth N. 1979. *Theory of International Politics*. Reading, MA: Addison-Wesley.

Weber, Max. 1958. *From Max Weber*. Edited by H. H. Gerth and C. W. Mills. New York: Galaxy.

Weiner, Myron. 1996. Bad Neighbors, Bad Neighborhoods: An Inquiry into the Causes of Refugee Flows. *International Security* 21 (1): 5–42.

———. 1992–1993. Security, Stability, and International Migration. *International Security* 17 (3): 91–126.

Weinstein, Jeremy. 2007. *Inside Rebellion: the Politics of Insurgent Violence*. New York: Cambridge University Press.

———. 2005. Resources and the Information Problem in Rebel Recruitment. *Journal of Conflict Resolution* 49 (4): 598–624.

Wendt, Alexander. 1992. Anarchy Is What States Make of It: The Social Construction of Power Politics. *International Organization* 46:391–425.

Wittman, Donald. 1979. How War Ends: A Rational Model Approach. *Journal of Conflict Resolution* 23 (4): 743–63.

Woodwell, Douglas. 2004. Unwelcome Neighbors: Shared Ethnicity and International Conflict during the Cold War. *International Studies Quarterly* 48 (1): 197–223.

Zacher, Mark. 2001. The Territorial Integrity Norm: International Boundaries and the Use of Force. *International Organization* 55 (2): 215–50.

Zartman, I. William. 1985. *Ripe for Resolution: Conflict and Intervention in Africa*. New York: Oxford University Press.

Zolberg, Aristide, Astri Suhrke, and Sergio Aguayo. 1989. *Escape from Violence: Conflict and the Refugee Crisis in the Developing World*. New York: Oxford University Press.

Index